Who are you?

101 WAYS OF SEEING YOURSELF

MALCOLM GODWIN is a polymath and seer. Born and raised in London, he trained as an architect and painter at Kingston School of Art. Under the name Malcolm Carder his works have appeared in The Museum of Modern Art, New York, The Walker Arts Center in Minneapolis, The Tate Gallery in London, The Glasgow Art Gallery in Scotland, the Fondation Maeght in France, and the Kunsthalle in Cologne.

In 1974 Malcolm Godwin went to India, where he lived and worked in a spiritual community for seven years. On returning to Europe he co-founded Labyrinth Publishing in Florence, Italy, and since then he has been a full-time writer and designer. He is the author, designer and illustrator of several mind-expanding books, including *Unknown Man*, *Angels: An Endangered Species*, *The Holy Grail*, and *The Lucid Dreamer*. He has also designed and created the artwork for Stephen Hawking's *The Illustrated The Brief History of Time*, and Rita Carter's *Mapping the Mind*. He and his Dutch wife Magda live in a small town on the coast of rural Dorset, England.

CARROLL & BROWN PUBLISHERS LIMITED

Who are you?

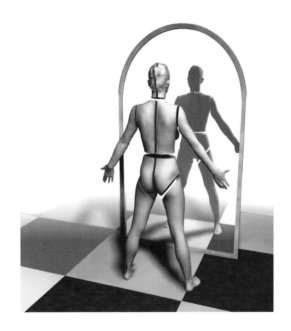

101 WAYS OF SEEING YOURSELF

Malcolm Godwin

CARROLL & BROWN PUBLISHERS LIMITED

Carroll & Brown Publishers Limited
20 Lonsdale Road
London NW6 6RD

Editor Geoffrey Chesler

Art Editor Tracy Timson

This edition published in 2001

First published in the United Kingdom in 1999
by Virgin Publishing Ltd

CONTENTS

PART I
Body types

PART II
Feeling types

PART III
Thinking types

PART IV
Spiritual types

INTRODUCTION

THIS IS A COLLECTION OF ONE HUNDRED AND ONE HUMAN TYPOLOGIES, ranging from the light-hearted to those offering a transformative insight. The assessments that accompany them are designed to be approached in a number of ways and on different levels.

Most of us tend to assume that everyone else responds to the world in much the same way as we do, and we are often taken aback when they don't. The descriptions of the many widely contrasting physical, emotional and intellectual types found in this book reveal how dramatically dissimilar people prove to be. This colourful spectrum of types enables you to understand yourself more clearly, and to anticipate how you – or someone with completely different traits – might act, and why.

It should be stressed that *some* typologies are only useful for *some* readers, and only for *some* of the time. We are not fixed in space or time, and we are constantly changing. This is just one of the reasons that no single system is able to capture our unique individuality. What is not immediately obvious is that each system gives potentially valuable insights only when it is treated lightly. The moment you begin to think that a category fits you like a glove, your hand will be cast in iron. It appears that the more conscious you become, the less likely you are to fit the descriptions of any particular type.

> *The more intelligent a person is, the more originality is found in others. Ordinary people see no difference between men.*
>
> Blaise Pascal

One of the most popular attractions of old-time fairgrounds used to be the "Hall of Mirrors". In these sideshows you would pass lines of distorting mirrors that warped your image, making you emaciated or pin-headed, contorted or tall. In much the same surreal manner we daily enter a hall of mirrors, confirming our sense of identity through the mirrors others hold up for us. Most of the time we rely on just such external reflections to tell us who we are within.

As children we began to build up a self-image through how others saw us, developing unique strategies to gain approval, acceptance and love. But our looking-glass parents, teachers, and peers all had their own warped viewpoints created by their own upbringing. They could not simply reflect who was in front of them, only what their own conditioning allowed them to. So what happened to us as children when those mirror surfaces we looked into were themselves flawed? We tried to adjust our behaviour to conform to a distorted image, and our inherent natures predisposed us to adopt our own unique brand of armour and strategy.

While such armour might be useful in childhood, for an adult it doesn't fit any more. It has survived long after the original mirrors – the teachers, parents or peers – have passed into memory. The original behavioural patterns have become habitual and unconscious, deeply embedded in who we believe we are. The absurdity of the situation is that we are now identified with a false sense of self, through a faulty mirror that actually no longer exists.

This book allows you to take an entirely new look at yourself in a hundred and one "mirror-typologies". In these diverse mirrors you can catch glimpses of the patterns that make up your personality. You will be able to reflect on how you really feel and what your body might be telling you about the way your outdated armour has influenced its shape. The sheer number of mirrors enables you gradually to reconstruct an inner picture of who you have become. Now whether they faithfully reflect the "real being" is uncertain. But that doesn't matter, for they serve another purpose – and that is to make you aware of the "unreal" you. At the same time they can show whether you, as an individual, are expanding into wholeness, integrity, and health, or becoming fragmented, contracting and falling into ill health.

The book's four sections describe body, feeling, thinking and spiritual types. In completing the assessments you may find that you score highly as one particular type in a significant number of very different tests. The beauty of having so many ways of looking at yourself is that you can begin to identify recurring traits that appear in widely different guises and dissimilar typologies. The underlying principle is that the more types you examine, the more facets of the whole individual will emerge, giving you a fuller and more accurate self-portrait.

How can you gain by these discoveries? First, you will realize that you are not alone. If you discover certain characteristics with which you instantly identify, you can be sure there is a tribe of others out there who are just like you. To many of us this revelation, in itself, is an immense relief. We suddenly find that we are able to accept what we'd always considered our worst characteristics. We also discover that we are far less responsible for our supposed "weaknesses" than we'd ever dreamed. The skeletons in our secret personality cupboard often turn out to be accidents of birth, situations outside our control, or even the result of the hard-wiring of our brains. If, from exploring all the widely different types found within these pages, you are able to accept yourself as you are, warts and all, then this book is worth the trees that were cut down to produce it.

The typological assessments can be approached on different levels. One is to treat the book simply as a game to be enjoyed. Complete the assessments by yourself or, better, in the company of others. You will soon be able to recognize patterns of behaviour among your family and friends, and possibly even to predict how the boss will panic and go into his melancholic shell under stress. You will be able to anticipate the most likely strategies to be used by your parents, lovers and children, and generally to enrich your understanding of how people interact and behave. You will also gain a more realistic knowledge of your own abilities, strengths and weaknesses.

Joyous distrust is a sign of health. Everything absolute belongs to pathology.

Nietzsche

The second approach is to observe the essential differences in the ways each of us responds to the world and how society tends to value certain types of people above others. If your type was not valued in your childhood environment, your sense of self-esteem will almost certainly have been damaged. But when you see the immensely rich variety of human types, each uniquely valuable in its own way, you will realize that you don't have to be a clone of some more socially acceptable model. In fact, the very discovery that you share similar characteristics with a large body of like-minded types is a deeply empowering insight. As soon as you know that you belong to a tribe of similar souls who are also perfect in their imperfections, you can relax and accept yourself just as you are.

You are unique. Just like everybody else.

Anon

The third approach is to use the typologies in order to understand the underlying reasons for your behaviour, and why you have come to identify with it. Most of our traits have been acquired – moulded by people and events in the past – and the majority are fixed in habitual modes that have become so familiar that we are totally unaware of them. As you explore the various typologies they can act as mirrors, truthfully reflecting these often robotic modes. Once you are conscious and aware of conforming to a fixed type, however, your behaviour will change by itself. The more conscious you become the less fixed you will be.

The unexamined life is not worth living.

Socrates

In the fourth approach you discover there is a radical difference between who you *are*, who you *think* you are, and who you have *become*. A mystic like Kabir would say that you have simply forgotten who you are. He would ask why you are constantly trying to reaffirm who you are not. For, according to the sages, we are all identifying with a false sense of self – our ego, or personality – and are blind to who we really are. A personality is just a mask that has been created through acting out certain strategic behaviours. By identifying with it so completely we forget that it is a mask and not the entity who wears it. The last part of the book examines religious and spiritual types, and gives a few reminders as to who that real person might be.

I sell mirrors in the city of the blind.

Kabir

Whichever approaches you choose, don't take any of them too seriously. For the typologies you will encounter on this journey of self-discovery are only road signs, not the destination. Treat them, if you will, as a celebration of the diversity of human nature. If they can direct you in your quest by pointing to the real or the false, then we can count the enterprise a success.

PART I

Body types

THE FIRST SECTION is devoted to what nature has dealt you, either through accident or design. Many feel that the time and the place of your birth, the pattern at that moment in the heavens, the shape of your body, your hands, your head, are part of a basic blueprint that you have to work with in life.

As you proceed through the different assessments you will discover how your physical, emotional, mental and spiritual characteristics entwine. For just as our body types influence our emotions, our minds and our attitudes, so the reverse is true – our ideas, ideals and unconscious strategies also mould our bodies. But remember, when exploring the various typologies in the four parts of this book, that the distinctions between body, emotion, thinking and spirituality merge and meld. Each part of the book is a gathering of similar typologies under one roof in order to highlight certain aspects of your individuality, which, in reality, remains a seamless whole.

THE HUMAN FAMILY

CAUCASIAN   BLACK AFRICAN   MONGOLIAN   OCEANIC

Throughout the rest of the book the small figures above will appear at the top of each test to indicate to which race or gender the assessment applies.

THE TRADITIONAL SYSTEM of racial typology on the opposite page is still widely recognized today. While the human family is in a continual state of genetic flux, and historical scientific theories about race have long been discredited, the perception of racial differences still can play a powerful role in an individual's sense of identity.

Race is one of the great dividers of peoples, especially when individuals are in a minority and thus don't match the norms of the dominant social group. In this way many fundamental life strategies can be forced on us by our own physical appearance. So, before embarking on your quest to know who you might be, first consider your own racial heritage, paying attention to how it might differ from those of other races.

Different geographic, climatic and material conditions have shaped the peoples of this world. A heavily built, sturdy Inuit from the Arctic would face a real physical handicap in the heat and sun of central Africa, just as a tall, lean Ibo tribesman would suffer badly from northern cold. Yet the people of earth are increasingly nomadic, and racial types move freely from one geographic location to another. Consider how these migrations might have shaped your own sense of self, especially if you have been brought up within a minority group.

ASSESSMENT

How much do you think your racial make-up has contributed to your mental, spiritual and psychological view of the world? Would you say that it has:

1. *allowed you to fit easily into your social group?*
2. *alienated you from your peers?*
3. *given you a social advantage?*
4. *given you a social disadvantage?*
5. *made you feel proud to be part of your race?*
6. *made you feel ashamed to be part of your race?*
7. *helped you to become outgoing?*
8. *forced you to look inward?*
9. *allowed you to excel in a chosen occupation?*
10. *deprived you of an opportunity to excel?*
11. *allowed you to merge easily into society?*
12. *made you aware that you differ from the norm?*
13. *made you feel joyful, thankful and accepted?*
14. *made you feel wretched, unworthy and rejected?*
15. *allowed you to fit in wherever you go?*
16. *forced you to join like-minded exiles?*
17. *made you feel superior in a different country?*
18. *made you feel inferior in a different country?*
19. *made you feel attractive to other races?*
20. *made you feel unattractive to other races?*
21. *made little difference to how you are?*
22. *made all the difference to how you are?*
23. *made you glad you were born as you are?*
24. *made you wish you were of some other race?*

Key: The questions are designed to test whether you are comfortable with yourself as you are, or whether you have some doubts as to your intrinsic worth. If you answer "yes" to 9 or more odd numbered question it suggests you are confident and find your race no obstacle. If you answer "yes" to 9 or more even numbered question it suggests you feel unaccepted and even unacceptable to others within your society.

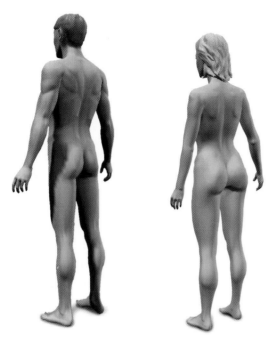

CAUCASIAN ~ *European, Indian.*

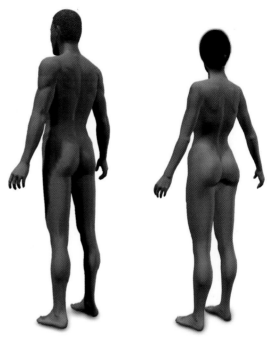

BLACK AFRICAN

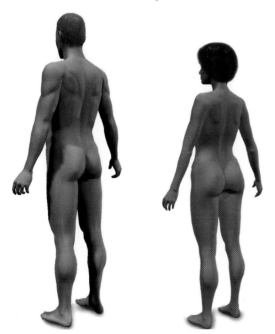

OCEANIC ~ *Melanesian, Micronesian, Polynesian,*
Australian Aboriginal.

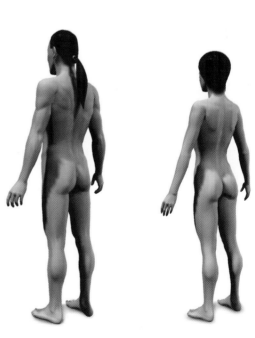

MONGOLIAN ~ *Asian, Native American.*

BODY TYPE

THERE HAVE BEEN MANY ATTEMPTS throughout history to classify human body types. In the 1940s Harvard psychologist William Sheldon[1] formulated a system based on three distinct "ingredients" which he believed were to be found in every human body.

Sheldon detected three body types as the most extreme morphological departures from the average. Each seemed to be made of an intrinsically different "substance" from the other two. He named these types endomorph, mesomorph and ectomorph, after the *endodermal*, *mesodermal* and *ectodermal* layers found within embryonic development. He suggested that these three discrete constituents were the building blocks of the body. Each of us is built in varying proportions of all three. When one component becomes dominant it creates the extremes we see below, on the left for males and on the right for females. However, most of us have a roughly even mix.

These types are easily recognized in myth and legend. The fat, jolly innkeeper, the muscular hero and the tall, lean wizard are time-honoured archetypes, as are the plump, rosy-cheeked baker's wife, the athletic heroine and the thin, wicked aunt.

ASSESSMENT

*The three body types shown below are the most extreme variants for both men and women. Read the descriptions of each and choose the two that are **least** like you.*
The remaining type is most likely to be your own.

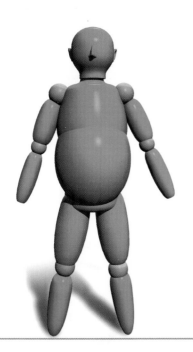  

● ENDOMORPH

Soft roundness over all the body and skin. Organs and digestive functions tend to dominate the body economy. Stores easily gained fat around the abdomen. Endomorphs have the smallest surface area relative to their mass, giving the least sensory exposure to external stimuli, and the smallest central nervous system, signifying less overall sensitivity. Their legs are often shorter than the torso and they have a heavy bone structure. Oriented towards imbibing the outside world.

- soft body, smooth skin
- underdeveloped muscles
- rounded shape
- overdeveloped digestive system
- difficulty in losing weight

● MESOMORPH

Hard, heavy rectangularity with a greater thickness of skin. The muscles, bones and connective tissues tend to dominate the body economy. Usually of medium height with developed shoulders. Although the surface area relative to mass gives an average sensory exposure, thicker skin and connective tissue allows a greater tolerance to extreme conditions, but insensitivity can be a trait. Oriented towards action.

- hard, muscular body
- overly mature appearance
- rectangular shape
- thick skin
- upright posture

● ECTOMORPH

Linearity, fragility and sensitivity in the body. Tall and thin with long legs in proportion to torso. The central nervous system tends to dominate the body economy. A larger surface area relative to mass gives the greatest sensory exposure to external stimuli. Ectomorphs have the largest brains and central nervous systems, making them sensitive and nervous. Oriented towards introversion.

- thin and often tall, flat chest
- delicate and lightly muscled build
- youthful appearance
- stoop-shouldered
- large cranium in proportion to body

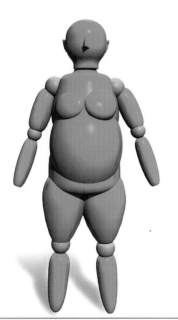

BODY~MIND TYPE

THERE HAS BEEN A PERSISTENT tradition that the physical shape of a man or woman corresponds to his, or her, personality. Sheldon[2] suggested that the three body types (see the previous assessment) were directly associated with particular characteristics of the personality.

His method to designate a person's body-mind type was based on a numerical system. The number 1 was assigned to the least degree a component was exhibited, and 7 to a maximum manifestation, with 4 being halfway. Each individual could then be described by three numerals, denoting the proportion for each component. Thus, reading left to right as endomorph, mesomorph and ectomorph, 117 would describe a physical type in which the dominant strain would be ectomorphy with a minimum score for the other two. A number 444 would describe an individual at the mid-point of all scales.

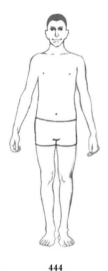

444

Let me have men about me that are fat;
Sleek-headed men and such as sleep o'nights;
Yond' Cassius has a lean and hungry look;
He thinks too much: such men are dangerous.
Julius Caesar, William Shakespeare

ASSESSMENT

Read the descriptions and choose the type that corresponds most to you. Then construct your designated number. For example, are you essentially an endomorph with a tendency towards mesomorphy but no ectomorphic traits (531), a dominant ectomorph (117), or a mesomorph who has equal amounts of the other two (252)?

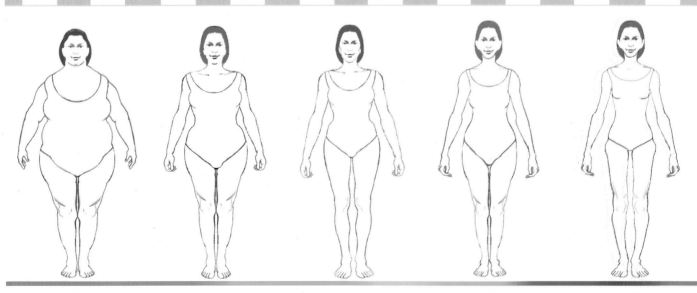

711   441   171   144   117

ENDOMORPH

Amiable and easy-going expression.

Earthy, unhurried, deliberate, predictable, amiable, warm, generous, heavy, gluttonous, relaxed, habitual, realist, practical and with a tenacious grip on the phenomenal world.
This is a person centred in the gut with a primary desire to assimilate the phenomenal and merge with it. As endomorphs live to eat, there is an inbuilt tendency to grow heavy if there is insufficient exercise. A need for confirmation of the tangible and the physical world is combined with an excellent spatial awareness and orientation.

Love of food ▪ tolerant ▪ evenness of emotions
love of comfort ▪ sociable ▪ good humoured
relaxed ▪ need for affection ▪ slow to anger

MESOMORPH

Appears open, powerful and guileless.

The mesomorph craves vigorous action and a desire to control both the environment and others. They make great leaders and conquerors and love the challenge of overcoming obstacles, especially through physical hardship. Muscular and energetic, even as infants, self-assertive, dynamic, and at times aggressive, mesomorphs often lack introspective insight, preferring to think in well-ordered and time-honoured ways. They rarely change their ideas. They eat in order to move and take delight in athletics and most other sports.

adventurous ▪ desire for power and dominance
courageous ▪ indifference to others' demands
assertive ▪ bold ▪ zest for physical activity
competitive

ECTOMORPH

Appears lean and hungry-looking.

Often over-sensitive (perhaps from the relative predominance of exposed surface skin to body mass).
High nervous energy, finds it difficult to relax, acutely attentive, cerebral, intense, inhibited about the body and personal feelings. Sleeps lightly, sees physical action as secondary to an awareness of internal tension and sensitivity. Finds it difficult to harmonize body and mind and tends to be split. An ectomorph eats in order to live.

self-conscious ▪ preference for privacy
introverted ▪ inhibited ▪ socially anxious
artistic ▪ mentally intense ▪ emotionally restrained

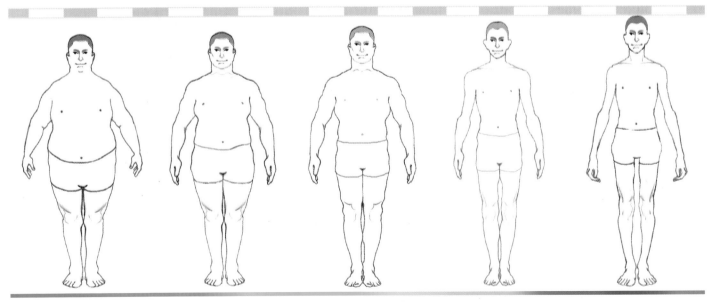

711   441   171   144   117

G~FACTOR TYPE

GYNANDROMORPHY IS A TERM COINED by a group of Italian clinical anthropologists to signify bisexuality. Every human body begins life essentially as a female, and the dominant sex becomes apparent as the embryo develops. So we all have both male and female sexualities within us. Ordinarily one set of sexual characterstics is dominant and functional, but in most bodies there appear to be traces of what might be termed secondary traits of the other sex.[3]

A man with a high "G-index" has distinctive feminine traits, while a female with a high "G-index" will be conspicuously masculine.

Many people with high G-indexes often feel confused by their bisexuality, which can exclude them from their more conventional peer group activity. Yet it would appear that a very low G-index – in which a man is all man, a woman all woman – is just as rare as a high one.

Although the media brainwash us to accept the all-male and all-female models as being the norm, it appears that these archetypes are far less common than supposed.

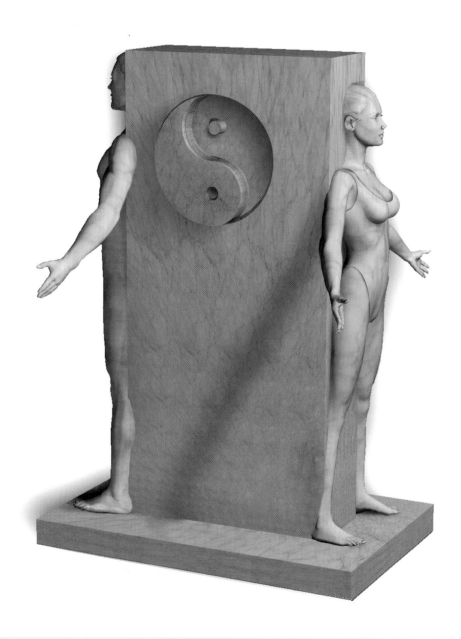

ASSESSMENT

This assessment is one of the most delicate to make since our society remains traditional in its view of an ideal man or woman. Also, many of the descriptions could equally be of people who are either under- or overweight. However, there are usually clear indications of bisexuality if you are honest in your observations. Often, the very reasons certain people are attractive or have charm and charisma are due to a unique blend of male and female characteristics. This is especially so in behavioural traits in which a man might be nurturing and gentle and a woman strong and athletic.

A low index suggests that you have virtually no characteristics usually attributed to the opposite sex while a high index denotes a strong element of the opposite gender.

Score yourself between 1 (low G-index) and 7 (high G-index).

If you feel that this inherited factor has created a psychological problem for you, keep the score as a reference and mark it on the unstable axis of the mandala in Assessment 35 at the end of this section.

HIGH G-INDEX IN A FEMALE

Masculine facial features – harder, thicker and angular.

Rectangular shoulders and strong arms, relatively long compared with the legs.
Bones are large and developed.
Narrow hips. The ribcage is wider, and the buttocks and lower abdomen are muscular. Low waist.
Abundance of secondary hair, less pubic hair.
Hardness and thickening of the subcutaneous quality of the whole body.
Little breast formation.
Muscularity of thighs and lower leg.
Square- or wedge-shaped body.

HIGH G-INDEX IN A MALE

Feminine facial features – softer, rounder, smaller.

Long eyelashes are a conspicuous feature.
Slightly rounded shoulders, relative weakness of arms. The bones are often small, the arms underdeveloped compared with the legs.
Wide hips. The ribcage is narrower. There is a fullness and rounding of the buttocks and lower abdomen. High waist.
Sparsity of secondary hair, fuller pubic hair.
Softness of the subcutaneous quality of the whole body. Presence of breast formation.
Prominence of outer curve of thighs and inner curve of lower leg.
Hourglass- or pear-shaped body.

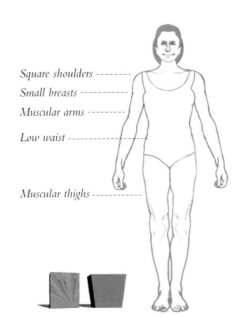

Square shoulders ----------
Small breasts ----------
Muscular arms ----------
Low waist ----------

Muscular thighs ----------

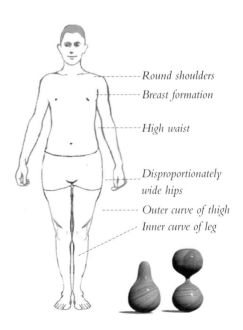

---------- *Round shoulders*
---------- *Breast formation*
---------- *High waist*
---------- *Disproportionately wide hips*
---------- *Outer curve of thigh*
---------- *Inner curve of leg*

ARE YOU DRAGON OR TIGER?

EVERYTHING EXISTENT, according to the beliefs and philosophies of the East, is attributed to two opposing yet complementary principles – Yin and Yang. Yin, or "the Dark side of the hill" is seen as the natural balance to Yang, "the Bright side of the hill."

Traditionally the Chinese Taoist sees Yin as symbolizing the passive, receptive, female aspect, while Yang represents the active, projective, male principle. A balance between the two principles is seen as a paramount condition for the harmonious functioning of all aspects of life. The traditional diagram of the Supreme Principle, the *T'ai Chi T'u*, shows two identical shapes within a circle, the dark area being Yin and the white being Yang. The small counter-circles indicate that nothing is ever one or the other. This diagram suggests the absolute point of balance between the two principles. This point is never actually reached, for a dynamic and existential balance is constantly shifting. Yet one aspect can become excessive and create an imbalance, inviting many physical and psychological disturbances.

ASSESSMENT

Opposite you will find complementary pairs of words in the left-hand box headed "qualities". From each pair, mark the word you prefer. If you score more in the left-hand column you have an essentially Yin approach to life; the right-hand column shows your inclination to Yang. It would seem obvious that, Yin being the feminine principle and Yang the masculine, women should mostly choose the left-hand column and men the right. But this is not the case, so do not be surprised at unexpected results.

With these five assessments you have begun to gain insights into your overall physical type and general attitudes.

Try to keep an overview in your mind of your changing identity in the light of these first assessments.

The traditional values for the Yin principle, symbolized by the White Tiger, and the Yang principle, symbolized by the Green Dragon, are listed in the right-hand column below.

QUALITIES	
Yin	**Yang**
○ Feminine	○ Masculine
○ Yielding	○ Dominating
○ Receptive	○ Penetrating
○ Passive	○ Active
○ Dispersing	○ Concentrating
○ Introspective	○ Extrovert
○ Defensive	○ Aggressive
○ Mystical	○ Material
○ Contemplative	○ Outgoing
○ Serious	○ Cheerful
○ Flexible	○ Inflexible
○ Negative	○ Positive
○ Submissive	○ Resilient
○ Short	○ Tall
○ Life-nurturing	○ Life-negating
○ Soft	○ Hard
○ Dark	○ Light
○ Calm	○ Moving
○ Plump	○ Slight
○ Conserving	○ Pioneering

TRADITIONAL VALUES	
Yin	**Yang**
Night	Day
Winter	Summer
Plant	Animal
Moon	Sun
Wet	Dry
Low	High
Valley	Mountain
Earth	Sky
Slow	Fast
Hollow	Solid
Spirits	Fish
Sugar	Meat
Fruit	Cheese
Milk	Salt
Spices	Eggs
Small intestine	Heart
Gall bladder	Liver
Urinary bladder	Kidney
Stomach	Spleen
Large intestine	Lungs

ARE YOU A HEALTHY WEIGHT FOR YOUR HEIGHT?

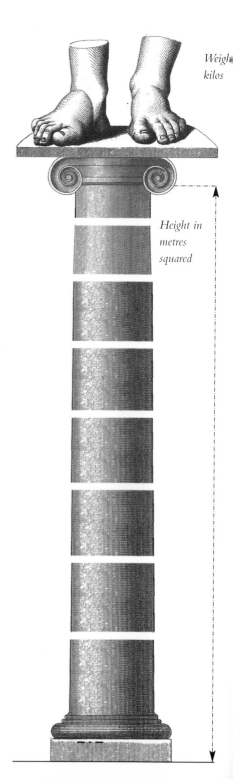

Weight kilos

Height in metres squared

THE BODY MASS INDEX (BMI) was devised as a rough guide to the levels of body weight that are considered medically healthy. It is an excellent relative indicator of overall health for the majority of the population, being designed specifically for the average person. It is not recommended for those in specialized physical occupations such as body builders or competitive athletes, or for sedentary elderly people and growing children. But if you use your body in a normal everyday way, the BMI is an excellent gauge to your general health.

The tables on the opposite page indicate how healthy your BMI figure is.

Of course this evaluation is not just about your physical state of health. It is also a guide to how you might feel about yourself. Generally Western society and the media appear to reward the lightweight and punish the heavy. The booming weight-watchers industry often appears less concerned with health than with how your body looks to your peer group. Use these tables also to reconsider what is a natural weight for you, irrespective of the social pressure to weigh always less than you do.

ASSESSMENT

The formula on the right gives a simple method to calculate your best weight. Remember, however, that your weight is governed, in part, by which body type you are. A natural endomorph or an athletic mesomorph could have a higher BMI than a natural ectomorph.

Of course, the subjective test is whether you are happy with the weight you are. There are some cultures that equate weight with wealth, so an individual in these would have no problem carrying around what in the West would be thought of as excessive baggage.

Use the following formula:

BMI = weight in kilogrammes divided by height in metres squared.
Example: A 1.9m tall person weighing 82 kg will have a BMI of 22.71 kg.
    $BMI = 82 \div 1.9^2 (3.61)$
    $BMI = 22.71$

To convert pounds to kilogrammes, divide by 2.2 and to convert inches to metres, multiply by 0.025.

MEN	RISK FACTOR	WOMEN
below 20.7	Underweight, at risk.	below 19.1
20.7 to 27.8	Normal, very low risk.	19.1 to 27.3
27.8 to 32.2	Overweight, moderate risk.	27.3 to 31.1
32.2 or over	Morbid obesity, 45.4 or over, very high risk.	31.1 or over

HEIGHT-WEIGHT TABLE USED IN HEALTHCLUBS[4]

Height	Healthy wt. kg BMI 19 - 25	Moderately overwt. kg BMI 25 - 29	Severely overwt. kg BMI 32 or over
1.47	41 - 53	54 - 62	63 or over
1.49	42 - 55	56 - 64	65 or over
1.52	44 - 57	58 - 66	67 or over
1.54	46 - 59	60 - 68	69 or over
1.57	47 - 61	62 - 71	72 or over
1.60	48 - 63	64 - 73	74 or over
1.63	50 - 65	66 - 76	77 or over
1.65	51 - 67	68 - 79	80 or over
1.67	53 - 69	70 - 80	81 or over
1.70	54 - 71	72 - 83	84 or over
1.72	56 - 73	74 - 85	86 or over
1.75	58 - 76	77 - 88	89 or over
1.78	59 - 78	79 - 90	91 or over
1.80	61 - 80	81 - 93	94 or over
1.83	63 - 82	83 - 95	96 or over
1.85	65 - 85	86 - 98	99 or over
1.88	67 - 87	88 - 101	102 or over
1.90	69 - 90	91 - 104	105 or over
1.93	70 - 92	93 - 107	108 or over

HOW DO YOU APPEAR TO OTHERS?

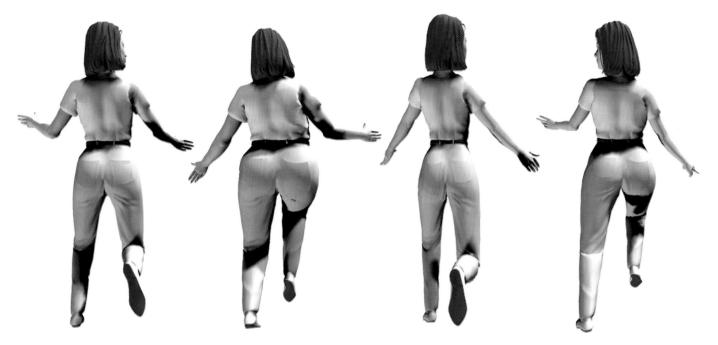

FIGURE A: *as you really are.*

A healthy and attractive weight for your height.

FIGURE B: *as you think you are.*

Often far fatter in your mind than you really are.

FIGURE C: *as you think men prefer you.*

The acceptable norm for feeling an attractive woman.

FIGURE D: *as men would prefer you.*

A little plumper than you actually are.

WE ALL HAVE IDEAS OF HOW WE APPEAR to other people. They are seldom objective. Most often we misinterpret what we see in others' eyes. Recent results from research in the United States shows that women and men react quite differently to their perceptions of how other people see them. It appears that most women disapprove of their bodies, believing themselves to be heavier (Fig. B, above) than they really are (Fig. A) and heavier than their ideal (Fig. C). They think men like them to be thinner than men actually do (Fig. D). Fifty percent of young Western women with normal body weights rate themselves fat. [5]

This pattern is almost the opposite of that found in men. Most males think themselves (Fig. B, opposite above) closer to an ideal body weight than they really are (Fig. A). They also think that women prefer them as they are, while in reality women like men to be slimmer than the male ideal (Fig. C), and thinner than what men think women like best (Fig. D). The feature women find the least attractive in a man is a beer belly. If a man is taller than average he has a potential advantage over his shorter peers. His IQ is considered to be slightly higher, and for each inch in height he is likely to earn twelve percent a year more. [6]

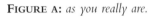

FIGURE A: *as you really are.*

You feel little discrepancy between how you are and your idea of an ideal body weight.

FIGURE B: *as you think you are.*

And what you feel is an attractive weight.

FIGURE C: *as you think women prefer you.*

With the heroic mould of wide shoulders and relatively narrow waist.

FIGURE D: *as women would prefer you.*

They like men lighter than your ideal and lighter than you think their ideal is.

As a woman if you have large breasts (37"/94cm or larger) you give a first impression of being relatively unintelligent, easy-going, and sexually available.[7] If you have small breasts (34"/86.3cm or smaller) you give the impression of being relatively intelligent, ambitious and modest. If you are taller than average you are likely to have a higher estimation of yourself than those who are shorter than average. Even though you have already read this introduction, answer the assessment on the right as honestly as you can to see whether you fit a pattern of conforming to the ideas of the majority of men and women in what you feel others might think of you.

ASSESSMENT

1. *Do you consider yourself overweight?*
2. *Do you feel you would be more attractive to the opposite sex if you were thinner?*
3. *Do you feel close to your ideal weight?*

FIT OR MIS-FIT?

IF WE ARE TO BELIEVE THE FINDINGS OF Western research then few of us feel we are attractive, or even approach the physical ideals of the time. Yet what actually dictates who is thought beautiful? Is there some universal criterion spanning all races and cultures that we feel we fall short of, or is it simply the programming of our particular culture and epoch?

There is much evidence, from the latest research[8] and using computer-generated images like those opposite, to support the theory that the faces deemed the most beautiful are also the most normally conventional, symmetrical and average. Faces appear to carry subtle clues as to the genetic fitness of their owners. There is scientific evidence that symmetry is even a genetic sign of health. Those women who scored highly in tests of attractiveness were apparently also those whose full lips and wide eyes suggested high levels of the hormone oestrogen, a desirable breeding characteristic in a potential mate.

Attractive males, on the other hand, did not score highly for features displaying high testosterone levels, like the square jaw and strong cheekbones of the classic he-man. Rather women chose the most average male faces as the most handsome. Other factors which influenced women's choice included humour, warmth, confidence – and income.

It would appear that to be accepted within a peer group it pays to be average and conventional looking. If you are physically unconventional, either racially or in any other way outside the social norm, the chances are that you will be found less attractive. This can start the self-perpetuating cycle for all those who deem themselves misfits. Take heart, however, for people who are normally thought to be physically unattractive are actually considered *more* attractive if they are seen to be happy, accepting of themselves, confident and amusing. The moral is to accept yourself as you are – you'll be more attractive for it!

ASSESSMENT

In each test below rate yourself on a scale of 7:

Your physical attractiveness
1. Noticeably ugly, others pity you.
2. Rather unattractive, sometimes made fun of by your peers.
3. Below average, seldom if ever even noticed.
4. Average.
5. Above average, noticed.
6. Very attractive, often the subject of attention.
7. Stunning, drop-dead gorgeous, the subject of adoration.

Your self acceptance and sense of worth
1. Suicidal, hating yourself.
2. Depressingly unworthy, useless, hopeless.
3. Non-accepting, unworthy, dull.
4. Like most people – good days and bad.
5. Mostly accepting, a sense of inner and outer worthiness.
6. Accepting and loving toward yourself.
7. Joyful acceptance in all moods, a sense of being worthwhile.

Happiness and delight
1. Suicidally unhappy.
2. Depressed, miserable, sad.
3. Seldom anything but dull, indifferent and gloomy.
4. Average – happy some days, unhappy others.
5. Seldom depressed, mostly cheerful and happy.
6. Always feeling happy, full of life and contentment.
7. Blissful, ecstatic, delighted, full of happy wonder.

Are your three results mutually dependent, or is there no link between your acceptance of yourself, your happiness and your outward appearance? If you score the same number in all three categories you are influenced by how others perceive you. If your ratings are different by one or more positions in each category you are more likely to have voluntarily stepped outside the norm, rather than being a misfit through fate.

The width of the eye is 3/10 the width of the face at eye level.

The width of the iris is 1/14 the distance between cheekbones. The length of the visible portion of the eyeball is 1/14 the length of her face.

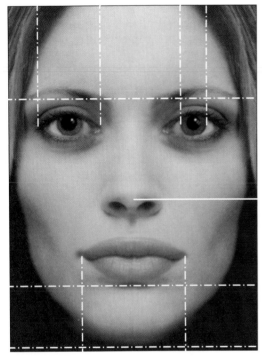

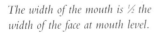

The distance from the base of the eyebrow to the centre of the pupil is 1/10 the length of the face.

The total area of the nose is less than 1/20 the total area of the face.

The length of the chin is 1/5 the overall length of the face.

The width of the mouth is 1/2 the width of the face at mouth level.

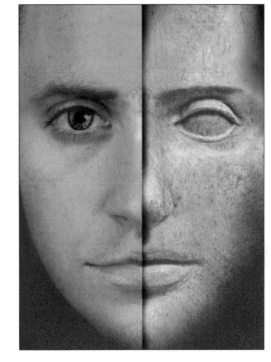

The forehead should be not less than 1/3 the length of the face.

There is a firm jaw line with a chin greater than 1/5 the length of the face.

A series of tests created by Michael Cunningham, a psychologist at the University of Louisville, was used to measure beauty. He asked white male college students to rate the attractiveness of photographs of women. More than half the images shown were of Miss Universe finalists, white, black and Asian. The physical measurements of the faces considered attractive emerged with remarkable precision and consistency. The computer reconstruction above shows the ideal beauty according to a white American male.

This computer-generated face shows some of the features of a good-looking man with a neutral expression juxtaposed with those of an ideal Greek sculpture. Such a man should be of above average height, have prominent cheekbones, a high forehead and a firm jaw. Psychologists Terry and Judy Davis tested college students who rated facial features in order of attractiveness. The list is in order of decreasing significance: mouth, eyes, overall facial structure, hair, nose.

THE DIVIDED SELF

THE CONTROVERSIAL PSYCHIATRIST Wilhelm Reich[9] proposed that our attitudes, fears, and anger become frozen within the muscles of our bodies. He coined the term "character armour" to describe the particular shape that each of us builds within our postures and musculature, reflecting the deeper strategies we use to protect ourselves in threatening situations, especially in childhood.

These distortions appear as over- or underdeveloped parts of the body, causing it to look as if it had been split. Most of us do not exhibit extreme examples of these body splits but show slight leanings one way or the other.

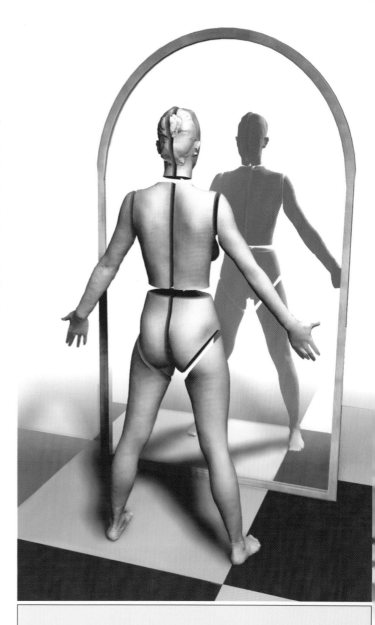

OVERDEVELOPED TOP

A "doer" with powerful ambitions, extrovert, outwardly expressive with an overriding need for action.

UNDERDEVELOPED BOTTOM

Dependency, loss of integrity and emotional stability. Lack of self-support. Actions instigated by the upper body become disconnected from the core of the being.

UNDERDEVELOPED TOP

Hyper-tense, anxiety-prone. Self-expression so lacking that pent-up feelings cannot be acted out.

OVERDEVELOPED BOTTOM

Emotional, rooted, grounded and stabilized. A strong supportive foundation which is nurturing, introspective and emotionally stable.

ASSESSMENT

Stand naked before a full-length mirror, paying close attention to the five divisions shown on the opposite page. Become aware of any imbalances of your own body.

Any parts of your body that may seem underdeveloped can also be seen as areas where potential has not yet been fulfilled.

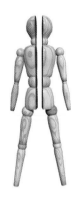

RIGHT/LEFT SPLIT

A *Is your left-hand side stronger/more developed?*

B *Is your right-hand side stronger/more developed?*

The left hemisphere of the brain (analytic, logical, rational) controls the right-hand side of the body. The right hemisphere (spatial, irrational, poetic, artistic) controls the left-hand side of the body. If the left-hand side of the body is dominant you are likely to protect your vulnerable more "feminine" self. If the right-hand side is stronger you could have developed a more masculine, assertive response to the world. Being accident-prone or having pain localized on one side indicates a one-sided orientation.

HEAD/BODY SPLIT

A *Do you live in your head?*

B *Do you forget you have a body?*

The head is the most social of our bodily aspects. In comparison, the body parts below the neck are more private or vulnerable to social taboos. As the head functions as the centre of intellect and personality, the body is seen as more instinctive and emotional. In extreme cases this creates the splits of mind/body, reason/intuition, intellect/emotion. If your head is large in proportion to your body you seem to approach the world through the intellect. A larger body suggests a more emotional response from gut feelings.

TOP/BOTTOM SPLIT

A *Do you feel rooted and like privacy?*

B *Are you outgoing and active?*

If the upper part of your body is larger and more developed than the lower, you are likely to be social, ambitious for power and influence, assertive and outwardly communicative. Expression, action and aspirations are the wings of the upper body. When the lower half of the body is more developed it suggests you are securing a strong emotional foundation. Your private roots are more stable than the self-expressing and public image. Introspection, stability, privacy and groundedness are the major attributes.

FRONT/BACK SPLIT

A *Is your back hard or tight and your front soft?*

B *Is your front hard and your back vulnerable?*

The front of the body reflects the social, conscious self – what we usually identify as the "me". The back reflects the unconscious elements of self. This is where we often store attitudes and feelings we prefer hidden, or forgotten. Many of our most powerful emotions of anger, fear and anxiety are stored in the back, resulting in tensions frozen into the muscles, which often create imbalances between soft, appeasing social fronts and powerful aggressive and tight backs. Back pains often indicate the imbalance.

TORSO/LIMBS SPLIT

A *Do you feel your "being" is in your torso?*

B *Do you feel yourself real only when in action?*

In most people the sense of their core of "being" appears to focus on the torso. The limbs are seen as the "doing" parts of our body – our contacts with the world. A split appears when there is any extreme in proportions – weak limbs, over-powerful torsos, or vice versa. An overdeveloped torso suggests powerful feelings and a strong sense of being, yet there is difficulty in expressing these. Those who have underdeveloped torsos but powerful arms and legs are often so busy in outgoing pursuits they have little time to contact themselves.

YOUR DEFENSIVE STRATEGY

BIOENERGETICS IS A FORM OF PSYCHOTHERAPY devised by Alexander Lowen,[10] a former pupil of Wilhelm Reich. He developed a classification of five personality types based on how the individual creates his or her defensive body armour as protection from psychological pain and suffering. The physical armour is apparent in the habitual, and often chronic, muscular shapes and tensions within the body. The energy cost of maintaining these defences is crippling, and the therapeutic purpose of exposing these largely unconscious patterns is to release the pure delight and pleasure that freely flowing energy can bring.

In the *Marriage of Heaven and Hell* the English mystic William Blake wrote that "Energy is eternal delight". He would surely have approved of a method that released the energy tied up in habitual body postures, enabling people to experience the fullness of the life-force.

Few of us conform exactly to the outlines of Lowen's five character types. Probably one or two physical structures predominate in each individual. Remember these are negative structures that tend to dull our sense of vitality and pleasure. Once they are seen, however, we can begin to understand and accept how they have arisen and then gently to dissociate ourselves from them.

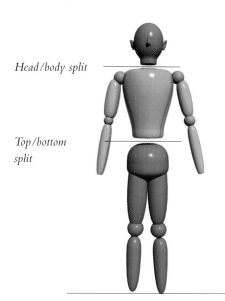

Head/body split

Top/bottom split

THE SCHIZOID

The Schizoid type is characterized by muscular patterns that "hold the body together" against the terror of falling apart. There is a loss of connection between the head and the body, revealed by an elongated neck or by the head tilting away from the central axis of the body. There can be a split between the upper and lower halves of the body, manifested by a drawn-in waist or disproportionate halves.
The body manifests a basic disassociation and split within the individual, who is out of touch with both body and environment. The fear of falling apart if one lets go for an instant is countered by keeping oneself together through constant tension in all the muscles and the joints.

ASSESSMENT

The assessment on the previous page will have determined whether you have a basic division in the body. We now turn to how these splits, and the tensions arising from them, may have created habitual personality traits. Consider each of the five defensive strategies opposite and identify any traits you might have acquired in your lifetime. Most of us have at least one of these in some form, ranging from mild to severe. If you detect a pattern revealed on the previous page as well, try to establish the time at which these defensive habits first started to appear. As you travel back in time you may have revealing flashes of memories or dreams that can start the process of releasing the tensions.

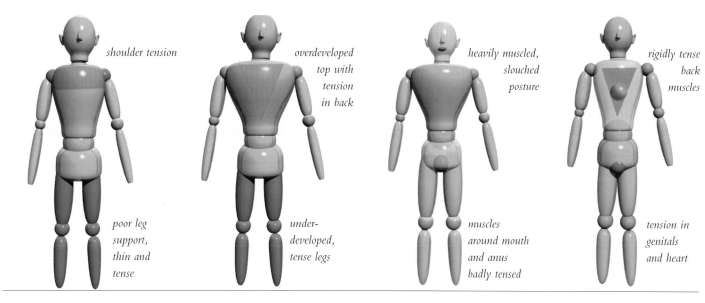

shoulder tension

poor leg support, thin and tense

overdeveloped top with tension in back

underdeveloped, tense legs

heavily muscled, slouched posture

muscles around mouth and anus badly tensed

rigidly tense back muscles

tension in genitals and heart

THE ORAL

The Oral type is characterized by tensions across the shoulder girdle and in the legs. There is likely to be a general slackness of muscle tone and this underdeveloped quality is mostly shown by thinness and lack of support in the legs.

This body type shows a strong tendency in the muscular armour to "hold on" as if they are about to be abandoned. The dread of being left behind and the suffering of loneliness and isolation causes the Oral person to cling insatiably to "significant relationships".

This whole over-dependent strategy arises from lack of support and nurturing during early life, with the consequent fear of being abandoned.

THE NARCISSIST

The Narcissistic type exhibits over-development of the upper body with a relative weakness of the lower. The character is held up by tensions in the legs and back, displaying a sense of superiority as if a cut above everyone else. This posture is also a guard against the dread of failure if he or she gives in.

The general state arises from an over-intimate parent of the opposite sex, who made the child feel special yet claimed an incestuous relationship that was not actually carried out. The child denies emotions and feelings in order to keep at bay what it intuits as a dangerous liaison. The sense of being over-special, however, remains.

THE MASOCHIST

The Masochist is heavily muscled, with the major tension being in the flexors, resulting in an unerect body posture. There is tension in the muscles controlling the outlets – the mouth and the sphincter.

This character is frequently associated with early toilet training, having the self-fulfilling fear of letting out coupled with the overwhelming need to hold in.

This is caused by an environment in which the child was forced to be submissive to the parent or to authority.

The Masochist holds in all the feelings through tension around the normal outlets for anger and frustration – the mouth and anus.

THE RIGID STRUCTURE

The Rigid type is characterized by a straight, erect, parade-ground stance, in which the rigidity of the back muscles is due to the attitude of holding back.

This is seen by the therapist as caused by early experiences of humiliation by the parent of the opposite sex to whom the child was sexually attracted.

He or she holds back to prevent further heartbreak, confusion and turmoil.

There is an overwhelming need to be in control at all times of both emotions and genitals, while fighting the longing for contact and physical acceptance.

WHAT YOUR FACE TELLS OTHERS

PHYSIOGNOMY IS THE STUDY OF FACES. Along with phrenology, or the study of bumps on the head, it enjoyed great popularity in the Victorian era. Now largely discredited by scientists, it none the less offers potentially useful typological insights.

In China this is an ancient and honoured study, called *Siang Mien,* and has been taken to extreme lengths with practitioners reading a person's character and behaviour from the smallest of facial details.

There are various classifications. The most popular system, found in many women's beauty and hair magazines, consists of five types, while the traditional Chinese system uses seven (see assessment 13).

The contours and shape of the face are considered a map of the temperament. The major traditional qualities of the six types of faces are listed below.

FACIAL CONTOURS

Square ~ *energetic, firm, stable, inflexible, stubborn, obstinate.*

Angular ~ *hard, selfish, rigid, ruthless, ambitious, greedy.*

Knotted ~ *angry, courageous, petulant, vehement.*

Pointed ~ *hypocritical, mobile, inspired, sophisticated, dishonest.*

Rounded ~ *jovial, gentle, gluttonous, indecisive, frank, slow.*

Soft ~ *passive, dull, apathetic, sensuous, gentle, lazy, lack of vital energy, slackness.*

ASSESSMENT

Measuring your face:

Ideally you should have a full frontal photograph, although a mirror can be used. You will also need some form of measuring tape or ruler.

The actual sizes are unimportant – only the relative proportions are needed. Use tracing paper over the photo, and draw the same lines across your face as pictured in the diagrams opposite. If using a mirror, use either water-based felt tip pens, eyeliner or lipstick. Close one eye and, remaining very still, mark the distances as shown for the three regions, three widths and the height of the face.

Mark the measurements in the boxes on the opposite page and check the significance of the proportions with the captions at the bottom of the page.

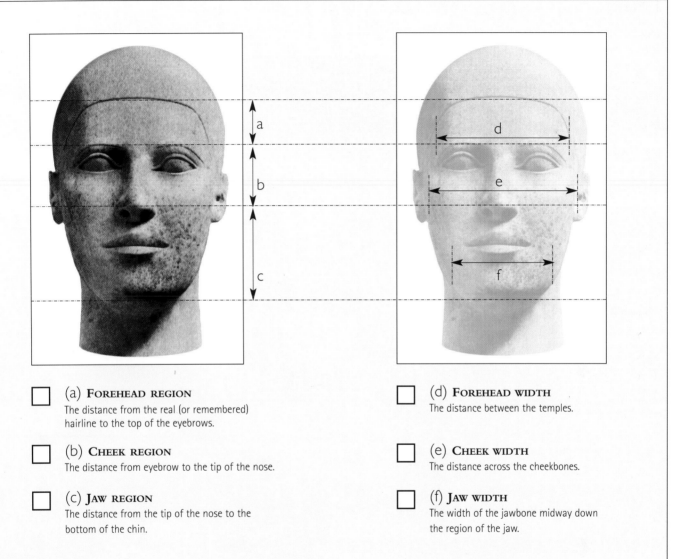

☐ (a) **FOREHEAD REGION**
The distance from the real (or remembered) hairline to the top of the eyebrows.

☐ (b) **CHEEK REGION**
The distance from eyebrow to the tip of the nose.

☐ (c) **JAW REGION**
The distance from the tip of the nose to the bottom of the chin.

☐ (d) **FOREHEAD WIDTH**
The distance between the temples.

☐ (e) **CHEEK WIDTH**
The distance across the cheekbones.

☐ (f) **JAW WIDTH**
The width of the jawbone midway down the region of the jaw.

FOREHEAD REGION

Knowledge and learning

If the greatest dimension ~ *suggests decisiveness, good memory and mental aptitudes.*

If smallest ~ *suggests poor memory, passivity and dreaming.*

CHEEK REGION

Development and will

If the greatest dimension ~ *suggests perseverance, control, discipline, strong will.*

If smallest ~ *suggests poor will, lack of discipline, no staying power.*

JAW REGION

Maturity and integrity

If the greatest dimension ~ *suggests wisdom, self-reliance, integrity, independence.*

If smallest ~ *suggests immaturity, dependence, reliance.*

THE FIVE FACES OF ADAM AND EVE

THERE ARE COUNTLESS WAYS TO READ A FACE, and we make many assumptions when we do so. Physiognomy enjoyed great success during the late eighteenth and early nineteenth centuries, when it was thought that culture and intelligence could be measured.

Intelligent faces were considered to be: large, oval, with a high, broad and prominent forehead, large eyes, small ears, a not very muscular face and a medium-sized jaw yet with a prominent chin.

Unintelligent faces were thought to be made up of a small irregular head, narrow, receding forehead, small eyes, big ears, a large and muscular face and a very pronounced jaw with a small receding chin.

Traditional methods, like the five-fold system here, have survived in the popular imagination and can still offer suprisingly accurate insights.

ASSESSMENT

Using the measurements from the previous page, choose the facial type that seems to be most like you.

TRIANGULAR

Forehead and cheeks are wide relative to the small, pointed chin.

Wild, unruly, spontaneous, instinctual, unreliable, witty, perverse, imaginative, undisciplined, adventurous, sarcastic, gifted, devious.

SQUARE

Equal widths of forehead, jaw and cheek. Combined they equal the length of the face.

Quick, energetic, stubborn, firm, critical, practical, hard-working, persevering, intolerant, materialistic, judgmental, righteous, inquisitive, solid.

CONICAL

The widths taper toward the top of the head.

Practical, down-to earth, realistic, jovial, lazy, comfort-loving, conservative, unimaginative, authoritarian, calculating, bon vivant.

OVAL

The widths of the forehead and jaw are equal. Relative to this the cheeks are wider, and the face is longer.

Mobile, impressionable, impulsive, changeable, versatile, non-persevering, credulous, prescient, intuitive.

ROUND

The widths of the forehead, jaw and cheek are the same and combined they equal the length of the face.

Active, impetuous, understanding, hasty, dominating, generous, realistic, pragmatic, sensuous, self-appreciative, passionate, self-opinionated.

THE SEVENFOLD FACES OF *SIANG MIEN*

IRON

Square ~ *the three widths are about equal, being the same dimension as the length of the face.*

Hard, tough, obdurate, leadership and political abilities, decisive, hard-headed, dedicated, stable.

FIRE

Triangle ~ *forehead wide with prominent cheekbones and pointed, triangular chin.*

Quicksilver, bright, burning, sensitive, sexual, passionate, radiant, entertaining, powerful, vivacious.

EARTH

Truncated pyramid ~ *tapering widths becoming larger at base.*

Practical, determined, stubborn, resilient, demanding, workaholic, persistent, slow, achiever.

BUCKET

Bucket-shaped ~ *each of the three widths tapers toward the base.*

Brilliant, full, inner strength, balanced, stable, generous, creative, fluctuating, ecstatic/gloomy, calm.

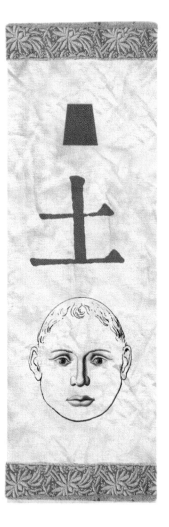

WALL

Wide rectangle ~ *the three widths are roughly equal, with the length of the face being less than its width.*

Guarded, solid, protective, present-oriented, reactionary, dreamy, uncommunicative, strong.

JADE

Diamond ~ *the width of the cheek is greater than the other two.*

Mystical, elegant, talented, durable, sharp, possessive, active, dutiful, caring, attractive.

TREE

Tall rectangle ~ *the three widths are approximately equal. The face has greater length than width.*

Courageous, assertive, nurturing, independent, mature, aggressive, abrupt, gnarled.

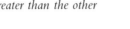

ASSESSMENT

Using the measurements from assessment 11, choose the facial type that seems to be most like you in this sevenfold system.

This facial typology is a version of *Siang Mien*, the Chinese art of reading faces.

Its adoption by Western practitioners has to be viewed in the same light as when we use any Eastern system, from Feng Shui to the benefits of rice and miso soup. Not all systems travel well from East to West, yet this seven-mode way can be very revealing for virtually all racial types.

ELEMENTAL HANDS ~ FOUR BASIC TYPES

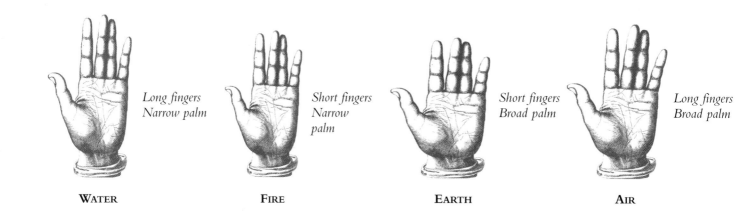

Long fingers
Narrow palm

WATER

Short fingers
Narrow palm

FIRE

Short fingers
Broad palm

EARTH

Long fingers
Broad palm

AIR

PALMISTRY AS THE STUDY OF READING CHARACTER was well known in the ancient cultures of Egypt and the Middle East. It was described over 3,600 years ago in the Indian literature of the Vedic period, and in Greece Aristotle wrote of it a thousand years later. While condemned as witchcraft in seventeenth-century England, curiously it was recognized as a scientific discipline in two German universities of the time.

In this century the psychologist, C.G. Jung was convinced the study of the hand was "of essential importance for psychologists, doctors, and educationalists", and in an introduction to Julius Spier's[8] work on the hands of children he applauded its valuable contribution to personality research.

Spier himself had collected thousands of palm prints of children and found that "they accurately predicted the true dispositions of the subjects and their likely health and psychological development".

The fourfold typology of the hand on this page is the simplest, and many consider the best. Palmists like Carl Carus described the types as Elemental, Motoric, Sensitive and Psychic. Others use Square, Round, Spatulate and Psychic. These have all been incorporated in what many regard as the most satisfactory classification of all – that of the four elements of Earth, Air, Fire and Water.

ASSESSMENT

Compare your hands with the four diagrams opposite. It is helpful to trace the outline of your hand onto a piece of paper so you can see the relative lengths of the fingers and the shape of the palm. Two of the hands have broad palms and two narrow ones; two have short fingers and two have long fingers. See which of the four elements most corresponds to your own hand, then check if they match your temperament.

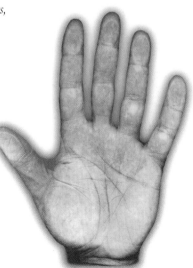

WATER

Narrow palm with long fingers, with delicate shape and fine mesh of lines.

Phlegmatic. Extremely sensitive to others and the environment. Coupled with the ectomorphic type. Feminine temperament. Sensitive, psychic, subject to the ever-changing moods of the water element. Shallow/deep, moving/still, receptive; tends to reflect the immediate environment. Astrological links with Cancer, Scorpio, Pisces.

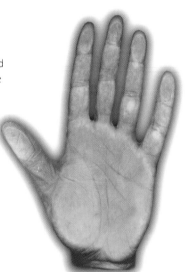

FIRE

Narrow palm with short fingers, prominent lines.

Choleric. Masculine temperament. Coupled with the mesomorphic and endomorphic types. Passionate, emotional, warm, intuitive, active, extrovert, lack of emotional balance, creative, changeable, passionate, like fire – quickly moving with sudden likes and dislikes, hot temperament. Astrological links with Aries, Leo, Sagittarius.

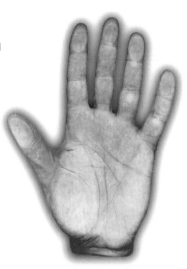

EARTH

Wide palm with short fingers, strong shape with often simple lines.

Melancholic. Often coupled with the mesomorphic and endomorphic types. Masculine temperament. Practical, honest, physically hard-working, stable, orderly, tenacious, unimaginative, sceptical, habitual, enjoys doing and making things and being physically productive. Astrological links with Taurus, Virgo, Capricorn.

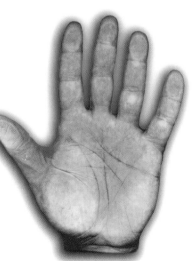

AIR

Wide palm with long fingers, strong structure with well defined lines.

Sanguine disposition. Feminine temperament coupled with all three of Sheldon's somatypes. Hopeful, confident, intellectual, powerful communicators, non-emotional, reasoning. Astrological links with Gemini, Libra, Aquarius.

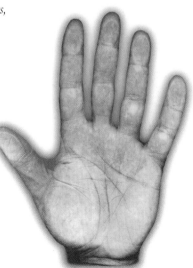

WHICH OF THE SEVEN HANDS IS YOURS?

ELEMENTARY HAND

Clumsy, large palm, short fingers.

Short-tempered, violent, simple passions, non-intellectual, instinctive, often linked with simian lines (head and heart are one line). This means even more impulsive and if angered can be destructive. A person with this hand acts before he or she thinks and does not reflect on his or her behaviour. Extrovert and egotistical.

PHILOSOPHER'S HAND

Distinctive wide and knotty joints.

Analytical, philosophical, contemplative, moderate, tolerant, in search of abstract and absolute truth. Is most likely to be concerned with ethical enterprises that require intellectual effort. Discriminating, with a strong sense of justice. Tends to be dismissive of those who are more imaginative and less intellectual.

CONICAL HAND

Fingers tapering from a broad palm, often a large hand.

Sensual, love of beauty above usefulness, prefers pleasure to hard work and dreaming to reasoning. Is often found within the arts as a patron and collector. Imaginative and creative yet seldom actually does anything with his, or her, talent.

THE SEVENFOLD CLASSIFICATION of the shape of the hand devised by the nineteenth-century French palmist Kasimir D'Arpentigny[9] is favoured by many modern practitioners. As with other typological systems found within this book, it has both strengths and weaknesses. Most of us show mixtures of tendencies and belong to two or more types.

However, each system offers certain insights and, rather like a jigsaw puzzle, a more rounded image of your character slowly begins to emerge with each new reading.

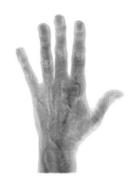

PSYCHIC HAND

Narrow palm with long, delicate and tapering fingers.

Idealistic, impractical, tends to live in dreamy inner worlds rather than respond to the actual situation. Highly sensitive, having a greater skin surface to mass, but tends to withdraw from contact rather than seek it. Can become obsessive, and often neurotic.

SPATULATE HAND

Slightly crooked with blunt, rounded finger tips.

Excitable, energetic, enthusiastic, restless, discontented, erratic and changeable. Always active and doing things, eccentric, sportive. Typical hand of explorers and travellers.

SQUARE HAND

Fingers are square and proportionate to the wide palm.

Logical, very practical and pragmatic, orderly, habitual, hard-working and tenacious, stable. Can be unimaginative, over-sceptical and not very original.

MIXED HAND

Combinations of the other six hand and finger types.

A hand that displays widely differing finger types, as above, reflects a personality that is often at odds with itself – the first finger doesn't know what the second is up to.

WHICH OF THE FOUR FINGERS IS YOURS?

SPATULATE FINGER

Medium length and very muscular.

Displays energy and unconventional, novel approaches to problems and ideas.

PSYCHIC FINGER

Long and sensitive, often very smooth.

Displays extreme intuition and expression, linked to a strong desire to communicate.

CONICAL FINGER

Neither fat nor thin, in proportion to the palm.

Displays both elegance and energy, as well as a love for beauty and harmony.

SQUARE FINGER

Solid and firm, reflecting determination.

Displays stubbornness, love of detail in work, and an inability to escape from routine.

WHICH PLANET DO YOU BELONG TO?

THE INFLUENCE OF THE PLANETS in all forms of early typology cannot be underestimated; the eightfold system on this page is an example. The fleshy areas, or "mounts", on the palm are named after the seven "planets" of traditional astrology. These mounts can be overdeveloped and fleshy, full and healthy looking, or thin and diminished. Every palmist attributes different characteristics to them. The descriptions given here, showing their importance and the state and disposition of the lines, are only approximations but they still give ample material for a comprehensive reading.

THE MOUNTS OF THE PALM

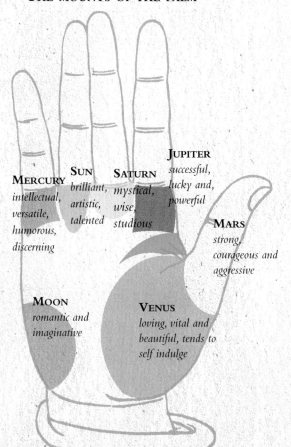

MERCURY
intellectual, versatile, humorous, discerning

SUN
brilliant, artistic, talented

SATURN
mystical, wise, studious

JUPITER
successful, lucky and, powerful

MARS
strong, courageous and aggressive

MOON
romantic and imaginative

VENUS
loving, vital and beautiful, tends to self indulge

ASSESSMENT

By now you have all the fundamental elements for a vocabulary of the hand and you should be able to read the basic shapes and lines. Each of the printed hands on these pages shows the shape, the development of the mounts and the major characteristic lines in more detail. (A diagram of the main lines can be found over the page.)
Combined with your earlier choices in the assessments of your hands, these should give you an excellent idea of both your hand type and its likely temperament.

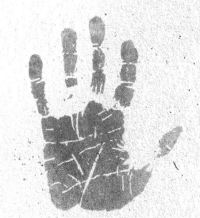

EARTH

Firm, thick hand with deeply embedded lines. Head line terminates near the Mount of Mercury; head and heart lines are close.

Slow, generous, indulgent, enthusiastic, epicurian, physical, hard-working, especially at tasks bringing the subject close to earth, like pottery. Can be stolid, insensitive, dull and unimaginative.

MERCURY

Pronounced Mount of Mercury and an extended little finger.

Quick-witted, intellectual, literate, knowledgeable, precocious, sensible, socially entertaining. Tends to stress the importance of the intellect over the emotions, and can become obsessive, anxious and critical over trivial matters.

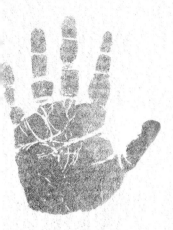

JUPITER

Heavy phalanges of the fingers near the palm, thick, soft flesh with well developed Mount of Jupiter.

Calm, equable, even temperament, generous, tolerant, optimistic, home-loving, born lucky, honourable. Tends to be dismissive of others who are less lucky than him- or herself.

MARS

Prominent Mount of Mars, short deep lines, strong thumb.

Courageous, combative, energetic, alert, strong physical endurance, sportive, vital, impetuous. Tendency to be dominant, aggressive, righteous and cruel.

SATURN

The middle finger arising from the Mount of Saturn is often noticeably longer. The life line usually connects with that mount.

Self-confident, practical, cautious, ambitious, serious, patient. Tendency to be gloomy, too serious and often solitary.

VENUS

Prominent Mount of Venus, and Line of Fate. Often a small hand with a short thumb.

Friendly, popular, active, sexually attractive, has personal magnetism, enjoys beautiful things, an attractive environment and especially the arts. Tends to follow the pleasure and beauty principle, often to the detriment of others.

SOLAR

Fourth finger arising from the Mount of Sun is often longer than the middle finger. Strong Sun line.

Ambitious, love of public recognition and acclaim, charming, possessive, a leader, enthusiastic, sociable. Tendency to need to be the focus of attention and a desire for power over others.

LUNAR

Soft palm with many fine lines. Fate line often springs from the Lunar Mount.

Extravagant, easy-going, adventurous, restless, imaginative, psychic, dreamy, likeable. Tends to be moody and changeable.

IN THE PALM OF YOUR HAND

EARLY IN THE DEVELOPMENT of the human embryo lines start to appear on the infant's hand. Palmists claim that there is a direct link between these lines and the folds of the brain and the corresponding neurological pathways that begin to form at the same stage. If so, this could mean that the lines on your hand are like a map, reflecting the ever-changing neurological routes of the mind.

Traditionally hand readers maintain that the passive hand (left for a right-handed person and right for a left-handed one) shows your potential at birth, while the dominant hand reveals what you have made of it.

Most modern palmists no longer accept this view, as it has been proved that the lines of both left and right hands are constantly changing. It is now felt that both hands are updated maps of changes in the left- and right-hand hemispheres of the brain. As the right hand is cross-wired to the left hemisphere it reflects a more analytical, logical, precise and time-sensitive picture. The left hand, connected to the right hemisphere, reveals your more emotional, creative and intuitive side.

This intellectual/emotional dualism can also be observed in the lines of the head and the heart. Most palmists agree that these two are the most important combination found in the hand.

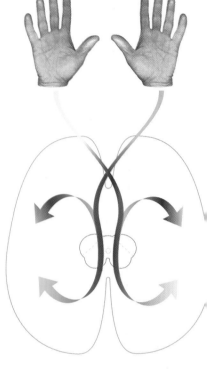

Our hands are cross-wired from left to right, linked to the opposite hemispheres of the brain.

HEART LINE

Originates on the Mount of Jupiter.

Clear and straight, this shows a steadfast love, devotion, great affection, sympathy and compassion.

Originates between the fingers of Saturn and Jupiter.

Tolerant, practical and common-sense view of love, sympathetic, sensual.

Originates on the Mount of Saturn.

Powerful sexual drive, self-satisfaction more important than the feelings of the other.

Head and Heart join as single line.

Known as the simian line, this shows a calculating, cool mentality dedicated to self; egotistical, unfeeling.

ASSESSMENT

Are you ruled by your heart or by your head?
Check the major lines in the diagram on the right and identify them in your own hands.
The traditional conflict within a personality is usually found to be between the heart and the head — between the intellect and the feelings. See which lines in the small diagrams of the Heart line (left) and the Head line (right) most closely match your own. You will then see which combinations you possess and their descriptions will reveal whether your heart tends to rule your head, or whether your head tends to rule your passions.
The beauty of palmistry is that it highlights certain trends common to us all, bringing predictable patterns and habitual traits to your attention.
Once you recognize these familiar patterns, you will be able to understand and accept them.

HEAD LINE

Originates touching the lifeline or slightly separated.

Cautious, mentally capable, spirited, independent. If touching the Lunar Mount, then strongly influenced by imagination and dreams.

Originates from the Mount of Mars within the lifeline.

Neurotic, irritable, easily influenced and worried by others, quarrelsome.

Originates on the Mount of Jupiter.

Born ruler and leader, ambitious, talented, egotistical, mentally powerful.

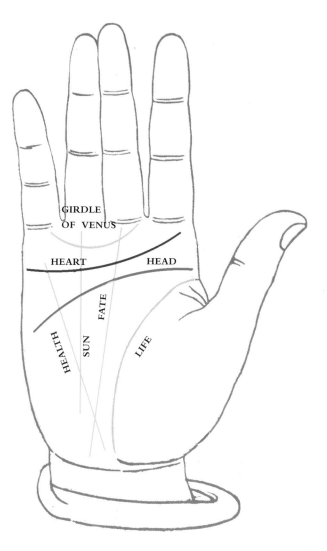

GIRDLE OF VENUS

HEART

HEAD

HEALTH

SUN

FATE

LIFE

IN YOUR ELEMENT

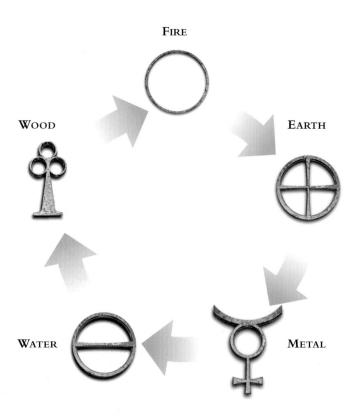

FIRE

EARTH

WOOD

WATER

METAL

ASSESSMENT

What is your essential element? Read the descriptions on the right and see which you feel most applies to you. This must be the result of an honest appraisal, relying on your intuition. Don't try to puzzle it out; just choose the one that seems to include most of your characteristics. Then check your year of birth on the following pages to see whether you have been influenced by the same element. You might find that the element of your year is on one side of the cycle on this page, suggesting either moving towards that transformation or emerging from it.

WOOD

Generous, self-confident, harmonious, compassionate, elegant, love of beauty, aesthetic, dignified.
Expansive, yet having a tendency to take more on than can be managed. A temper that is difficult to control.
Adaptable, shrewd, cunning, independent, need for freedom and movement.
Forceful, bursting with energy, with a passion for growth, expansion and awakening.

THE EASTERN THEORY OF THE FIVE ELEMENTS is fundamental to understanding the holistic approach of Oriental typologies and Eastern medicine. This theory is an expansion of the principles of Yin and Yang seen as tendencies in the movement of energy. The five Chinese elements – fire, earth, metal, water and wood – do not refer to the physical phenomena themselves, but to the types of energy they manifest. An individual's character can be described in terms of various combinations of these forces. Traditionally the five elements were seen as dancing in a creative and transforming cycle, as shown in the illustration above.[11]

FIRE

Warm, brilliant, decisive, lucid, innovative, quick, burning, changeable, adventurous, creative, joyful, intuitive.
This passionate nature often tends to self-destruct. Sharp-tongued, sometimes negative and destructive to others.
Dazzling, exciting, abundant, often enchanting and charismatic, always entertaining and magical.

EARTH

Responsible, practical, honest, slow, self-disciplined, hard-working, often to the point of being a workaholic.
Over-objectivity can lead to being unimaginative and lacking either romance or a sense of adventure.
Craggy, nurturing, peaceful, balanced, stable and solid, immovable, sustaining, rooted.

METAL

Hard, firm, clear, pure, tempered, ambitious, energetic, active, outward-going, dependable, independent, can sustain actions and effort.
Tireless and persistent, such people can become too rigid and inflexible and find it difficult to relax.
Austere, sharp, restrained, alone, a tendency to exhaust oneself and become drained and sleepy.

WATER

Receptive, flowing, communicative, passive, calm, flexible, persuasive, psychic, withdrawing, restrained.
Being too passive tends to make the subject too conciliatory and sensitive to others while failing to attend to themselves.
Knowledgeable, questioning, philosophic, wise, critical, judgmental, aspiring.

How do you relate?

THE YEAR OF YOUR BIRTH is supposedly associated with an element. Each of the five Oriental elements are said to rule two years in turn; the first year of the two is the Yang year, the second is the Yin year. The table on the right details the pairs.

You can apply the elements you have identified so far as influencing your life by referring to the illustration on the opposite page. You can then assess how your element will interact and relate with the characters of your lovers, friends, family or colleagues. The board shows those elemental, yin and yang, relationships that are compatible and those that are likely to be antagonistic and full of conflict.

Chinese fortune tellers advise us to seek out those people whose elements enhance, harmonise or balance with our own.

WOOD	FIRE	EARTH	METAL	WATER
1924(+)	1926(+)	1928(+)	1930(+)	1932(+)
1925(-)	1927(-)	1929(-)	1931(-)	1933(-)
1934(+)	1936(+)	1938(+)	1940(+)	1942(+)
1935(-)	1937(-)	1939(-)	1941(-)	1943(-)
1944(+)	1946(+)	1948(+)	1950(+)	1952(+)
1945(-)	1947(-)	1949(-)	1951(-)	1953(-)
1954(+)	1956(+)	1958(+)	1960(+)	1962(+)
1955(-)	1957(-)	1959(-)	1961(-)	1963(-)
1964(+)	1966(+)	1968(+)	1970(+)	1972(+)
1965(-)	1967(-)	1969(-)	1971(-)	1973(-)
1974(+)	1976(+)	1978(+)	1980(+)	1982(+)
1975(-)	1977(-)	1979(-)	1981(-)	1983(-)
1984(+)	1986(+)	1988(+)	1990(+)	1992(+)
1985(-)	1987(-)	1989(-)	1991(-)	1993(-)
1994(+)	1996(+)	1998(+)	2000(+)	2002(+)
1995(-)	1997(-)	1999(-)	2001(-)	2003(-)

KEY: YIN (-)   YANG (+)

ASSESSMENT

Is the element that influenced you at birth the same as your choice on the previous page?

Make sure you consult a lunar table based on the Moon's cycles and not our Western solar year (the actual dates begin on a different date in January or February so will only affect those born in those months). If you have chosen the same element as your birth year you can be assured your intuition is excellent… trust it more.

However, if you find the element you have chosen lies to either side of the actual birth sign, see whether or not it fits the clockwise path of the natural cycle found on the previous page. If it does, you are in the process of transformation; if it does not, then you should seek out situations, or people, with an abundance of the element of your birth.

HARMONY AND DISCORD ON THE ELEMENTAL YIN-YANG BOARD

ASSESSMENT

First you must discover the birth dates of those around you. Once you have established their element and whether it is Yin or Yang, you will be able to find from the board on the right if they will offer a conflicting or harmonious relationship with you.

The game pieces mark the square where two elements intersect, revealing five possible relationships, ranging from "highly compatible" to "hostile".

This particular board shows the relationship between opposites using the elements of Yin and Yang. It does not describe the meeting of two Yang or two Yin elements.

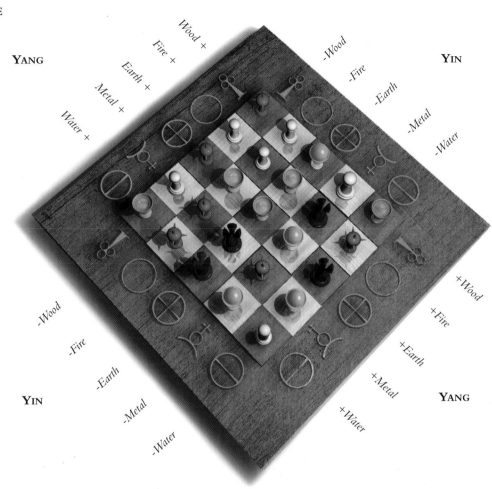

YANG

Wood +
Fire +
Earth +
Metal +
Water +

YIN

-Wood
-Fire
-Earth
-Metal
-Water

YIN

-Wood
-Fire
-Earth
-Metal
-Water

YANG

+Wood
+Fire
+Earth
+Metal
+Water

Highly compatible

Harmonious

Non-conflicting

Unsympathetic

Hostile

Find your own element and check the square which meets the corresponding element of whoever you are assessing. Whichever marker is on that square will reveal whether you are compatible or not.
For instance −(YIN) Fire meets +(YANG) Water and unsurprisingly they do not mix, while when −(YIN) Metal meets the +(YANG) Earth square they do.

WHICH TYPE ARE YOU IN CHINESE MEDICINE?

CHINESE PHILOSOPHY HOLDS that the Yin-Yang forces active in the phenomenal world also govern the cycles of change within our bodies and minds. Each of us is a cosmos in miniature and our health or illness is a manifestation of either harmony or disharmony in the flow of *Chi* energy. Modern practitioners of Oriental medicine have devised many variants on the traditional *Wu Xing* (five-phase) model which classifies phenomena in terms of five quintessential processes. This offers an almanac of human cycles of both momentary and lifelong change. Physicians and healers seek to interpret and re-balance these cycles of human behaviour. The example on this page is a distillation of the general trend in which the five phases are shown as having associations both with the five elements and with Nature's cycle of growth, maturity, stasis and renewal.

ASSESSMENT

Answering yes to any of the numbers or letters below will indicate your type. Read the descriptions on the opposite page for further confirmation.

Do you:

1. *most enjoy sitting in front of a blazing fire with a great book hearing the wind howling outside?*
2. *enjoy taking a walk along unfamiliar routes rather than well trodden paths?*
3. *enjoy finding the magical moment in otherwise normal situations?*
4. *love to see autumn leaves rather than the first crocuses in the spring snow?*
5. *love the sense of abundance in a traditional harvest scene?*
6. *place your favourite month of the year in:* a. *December, January, February*
    b. *March, April, May*
    c. *May, June, July*
    d. *July, August, September*
    e. *September, October, November*
7. *just act on the spur of the moment?*
8. *see life as full of sun and light?*
9. *enjoy bringing people or things together in unexpected ways and finding a transformation?*
10. *like a home that is comfortable even if it is a little dull and conservative?*
11. *describe yourself as harmonious?*
12. *feel disciplined and orderly?*
13. *seek some understanding and truth about the nature of experience?*
14. *find it difficult to act on impulse.*
15. *enjoy ritual and ceremony?*
16. *love innovative things or situations that are entirely new?*

Explorer *(b, 2, 7, 16)*
Magician *(c, 3, 8, 9)*
Nurturer *(d, 5, 10, 11)*
Alchemist *(e, 4, 12, 15)*
Thinker *(a, 1, 13, 14)*

THE EXPLORER

Taming the Wild

A desire to penetrate the unknown, adventurous, independent, adaptive, attracted to all walks and paths, whether geographic or in fields of endeavour. Determined action is the driving force behind such a character. Often infatuated with the "new" or revolutionary, the explorer is a pioneer of innovation and change. The archetype is wood: symbolized by the young wood of Spring, of rebirth and sudden and spectacular growth and movement.
The body organ most associated with the Explorer is the liver, instigating movement and intensity.

THE MAGICIAN

Radiant Wonder

Transformation of the mundane into the wondrous. Dazzling, afire, a catalytic energy which synthesizes, bringing together the most divergent elements. A magical and even mystical power of wonder and awareness that brings joy and a rich sense of sharing.

The archetype is Fire: symbolized by the heat of the early Summer sun, by the light and warmth and the acceleration of the life forces.

The body organ associated with the Magician is the heart, regulating the flow of blood within the organism.

THE NURTURER

Quiet on the Mountain

Nurturing, sharing, bringing together, unifying, serene, stable, harmonious, peaceful, ability to put others at ease, creating a caring environment, conservative, preserving, balancing, nourishing.

The archetype is Earth: symbolized by the abundance of the land in late Summer, the ripening and maturing.

The body organ associated with the Nurturer is the spleen, incorporating nourishment and experience into the organism.

THE ALCHEMIST

Returning to the Source

Discerning, purifying, distilling the essentials, defining, refining, concerned with aesthetics, beauty, virtue and morals. Enjoys the discipline of order, ritual and ceremony.

The archetype is Metal: symbolized by the letting go of Autumn, restraint, separation, elimination and a return to the source.

The body organ associated with the Alchemist is the lung, signifying transformation by the organism taking a deep breath and then letting it go, expelling the "impure" air.

THE THINKER

Sound of Running Water

Knowledge is the hallmark of the Philosopher, on a perpetual quest for truth and understanding. Longing to find meaning and significance in human affairs but, as if in hibernation, unable to act existentially.

The archetype is Water: symbolized by the flowing, primal chaos deep within the subterranean nature of Winter. On the surface this appears to be a time of quiescence, hibernation and sleep, and yet it contains the hidden potential of the new.

The body organ associated with the Thinker is the kidney, symbolically harbouring the seed of renewal.

CHOOSE YOUR TYPE FROM THE VEDAS

AYURVEDIC MEDICINE IS THE sacred, holistic life science of India that embraces the study of mind, body, behaviour, environment and religion. The root *Ayu* is ancient Sanskrit for "life" while *veda* implies "knowing". It has been practised in India for over 5,000 years, and was formalized as one of the four *Vedas*, or sacred Hindu texts.[12]

Modern Ayurvedic practice has absorbed disciplines from many other cultures, but at its heart is the holistic understanding that energy and matter are one, and give rise to five basic principles or elements – Ether (space), Air, Fire, Water and Earth.

These elements combine in the human body as the three *doshas: Vata, Pitta* and *Kapha. Vata* (Wind) is composed of Air and Ether. *Pitta* (Sun) comprises Fire and Earth, while *Kapha* (Moon) consists of Earth and Water.

We inherit our genetic makeup, and the original Ayurvedic sages recognized three particular types of constitution, with many subtle variations. While these constitutions remain unaltered, we change and evolve over a lifetime in response to external forces, as the essential doshas, the cosmic forces, dance through our organism. We are seldom completely at ease with ourselves or harmonious in our body-minds. Imbalances in the doshas create many of the physical and mental illnesses we suffer. The Ayurvedic system creates a balance of forces within the individual by altering diet and behaviour to counteract changes in the external environment.

Each dosha has certain characteristics. To *Vata* belong all the functions associated with air: respiration, movement of the bowels, the bladder, the testes, wind and flatulence. *Pitta* is related to the liver, the bile, the spleen, the heart and eyes. *Kapha*, like the moon, influences the ebb and flow of the body tides, the body fluids, saliva and the secretions of the brain. Thus, taste is of fundamental importance to a type whose dosha is governed by *Kapha*.

The physician's task is to maintain a balance between the three forces through the administration of food, minerals and natural remedies.

ASSESSMENT

Mark yourself on a scale between 1–7 for each question on the opposite page as follows:

1–2   Doesn't really apply to you.
3–5   Sometimes or even often applies.
6–7   Mostly or entirely applies to you.

Count up your score for each of the three doshas. This will indicate which body type you mostly belong to. If one dosha is significantly higher than the others, you can consider yourself a single dosha type (e.g. Vata 100, Pitta 40, Kapha 35). If no dosha is dominant then you are probably a two-dosha type (e.g. Vata 90, Pitta 80, Kapha 40). In rare instances you might score similarly for all three. This makes you a three-dosha type, which is considered highly unusual.

(This assessment is an abbreviated version based on a similar questionnaire devised by the Maharishi Ayur-Ved Association of America.)

THE THREE DOSHAS

AIR	ETHER	FIRE	EARTH	EARTH	WATER

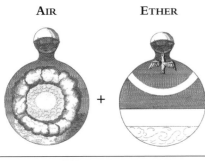 +   + 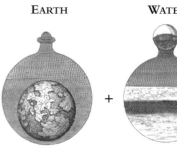 +

VATA

- I do things quickly
- Have a poor retentive memory
- I am enthusiastic
- Don't gain weight quickly
- I am a quick learner
- I have a fast, light walking style
- Difficulty making decisions
- Suffer from wind/constipation
- Often have cold extremities
- Frequently anxious and worried
- Don't like cold weather/climates
- Talkative with fast delivery
- Moody and emotional
- Difficulty in falling asleep
- Dry skin especially in winter
- Imaginative mind
- Energetic in bursts
- Easily excitable
- Irregular habits
- Learn quickly – forget quickly
- Restless sleep
- Eat on spur of moment
- Restless inner feelings
- Always doing something

Total Vata score = max 24x7=168

PITTA

- I am efficient
- Precise in actions
- Favour an ordered life
- Hot weather is often distressing
- I perspire easily
- Easily irritated
- Hair – early greying or balding
- Become angry quickly
- Good appetite
- Like regular meals
- Considered stubborn or rigid
- Regular bowel movements
- A perfectionist in details
- Easily impatient
- Enjoy ice-cold drinks and ice creams
- Feel too hot in warm rooms
- Like challenges
- Over-critical of myself and others
- Persistent in things I want
- Poor tolerance of others' opinions
- Don't like spicy, hot foods
- Am easily angered
- Have thin blonde, sandy or red hair
- Become tired in hot weather

Total Pitta score = max 24x7=168

KAPHA

- I am mostly relaxed
- People think me slow
- Gain weight quickly, lose it slowly
- Am reasonably calm and placid
- Asthmatic, and sinus congestion
- Need plenty of sleep
- I sleep very deeply
- Do not anger easily
- Slow to learn but remember well
- Tendency to put on weight
- Cool and damp climate unsettling
- Hair is dark, thick and wavy
- Smooth, soft, light-coloured skin
- A large, heavy and solid body
- Affectionate and forgiving nature
- Feel heavy and tired after eating
- Can endure physical hardship
- Slow in walking style
- Oversleep and slow to wake
- Slow and methodical in action
- Slow eater, slow digestion
- Others consider me sweet-natured
- Excess mucus and phlegm
- Not easily ruffled

Total Kapha score = max 24x7=168

22

WHAT IS YOUR DOSHA BALANCE?

BALANCING THE THREE DOSHAS within the organism is the task of the Ayurvedic physician. However, now that you have identified your own body type, you can recognize those healthy and unhealthy traits associated with it.

A dual principle known in Ayurveda as *Samanya* (similarities) and *Vishesha* (opposites) determines that the tastes and qualities of foods most like your body type increase your body's dosha characteristics, simply because like increases like. Cold, dry, light, bitter elements increase *Vata*; hot, spicy, dry, light foods increase the fiery *Pitta*; cold, oily, heavy and sweet substances increase *Kapha*. It is said that a man becomes what he eats. The Ayurvedic physician would heartily agree.

ASSESSMENT

The columns below left show the balanced and unbalanced characteristics for each type. The columns below right give simple indications of what food to avoid and what to eat to bring the most harmony to your system.

Count all the descriptions on the opposite page you feel apply to you and mark the score for each type in the appropriate box. This will give you an additional insight into your own nature.

GENERAL DOSHA CHARACTERISTICS

VATA	PITTA	KAPHA
Balanced	*Balanced*	*Balanced*
Joyful	Energetic	Relaxed, easy-going
Lively, alert	Charismatic	Strong stamina
Quick to learn	Good appetite	Steady, methodical
Self-confident	Warm, friendly	Well-built
Light, sound sleep	Curious, organized	Sound sleep
Smooth skin	Radiant skin	Regular digestion
Regular bowels	Good digestion	Abundant hair
Light movement	Enterprising	Tranquil
Unbalanced	*Unbalanced*	*Unbalanced*
Anxious, worried	Stressed	Depressed
Nervous energy	Time-conscious	Bored
Forgetful	Task-oriented	Dull and listless
Distracted	Irritable	Lethargic
Easily exhausted	Stomach problems	Overweight
Insomnia	Hair loss	Uninterested
Dry skin	Overly critical	Poor appetite
Constipated	Too excitable	Colds, sinusitus
Sluggish, stiff	Feels pressured	Excessive sleeping

APPROPRIATE FOODS FOR EACH DOSHA

VATA	PITTA	KAPHA
Favour	*Favour*	*Favour*
Warm food/drink	Cool food/drink	Warm food/drink
Sweet tastes	Sweet tastes	Pungent tastes
Sour tastes	Bitter tastes	Bitter tastes
Salty tastes	Astringent tastes	Astringent tastes
Hot, oily food	Cold, oily food	Light, dry, hot food
Small amounts	Regular meals	Light meals
Frequent amounts	Salads	Salads
Rich foods	Rich foods	Soups, appetizers
Avoid	*Avoid*	*Avoid*
Cold foods	Hot foods	Cold foods
Chilled drinks	Hot drinks	Cold drinks
Diet foods	Pungent tastes	Sweet tastes
Bitter tastes	Sour tastes	Sour tastes
Astringent tastes	Salty tastes	Salty tastes
Pungent tastes	Light, hot, dry food	Cold, oily food
Heavy meals	Infrequent meals	Heavy meals
Infrequent meals	Quick snacks	"Between" snacks
Cold, dry, light food	Irregular meals	Rich desserts

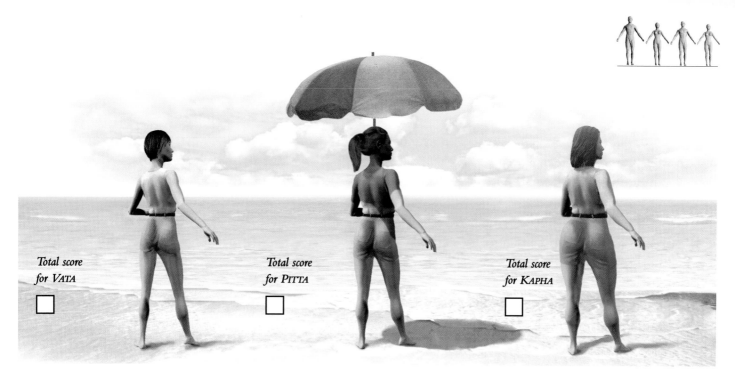

Total score for VATA ☐

Total score for PITTA ☐

Total score for KAPHA ☐

YOUR CONSTITUTIONAL MAKE-UP

VATA

You are:

thin and light	a worrier/anxious
quick in actions	easily overtaxed
an irregular eater	unpredictable
a light sleeper	a fast walker
imaginative	great at starting
excitable/moody	poor at finishing
quick to learn	sensitive to noise
quick to forget	vivacious/lively

Vata dosha *(Air-Ether) is the principle of change – governing the central nervous system, nerve pulses from the brain, breathing muscles and the digestive tract. Its major response to the world is through sound and touch. Usually thin, this type has narrow hips and shoulders and tends to appear physically irregular. It can eat anything without weight gain, but in later life this can change. When unbalanced this type displays nervous disorders, chronic exhaustion and obsessive anxiety.*

PITTA

You have:

a medium build	fair, ruddy skin
average strength	precise speech
an urgent hunger	ambition
tendency to anger	a jealous nature
an aversion to sun	combative impulse
love of challenge	a determined walk
an enterprising nature	an eye on time
a sharp mind	short temper

Pitta dosha *(Fire-Earth) is the principle of intensity, of fire, heat and passion. It is often expressed through hot-headedness and its major response to the world is through vision. It has a low tolerance for exposure to the sun. The physical type is well-proportioned, usually medium build and maintains weight easily. The hair is mostly straight, fair to red, prematurely greying or balding. When this dosha is out of balance, the type can be irritable, demanding, argumentative and abrasive.*

KAPHA

You are:

powerfully built	affectionate
strong and enduring	slow to anger
graceful and tolerant	complacent
a heavy sleeper	difficult to wake
tranquil and relaxed	slow at decisions
a slow learner	thick skinned
retentive and habitual	a slow speaker
quick to gain weight	a hoarder

Kapha dosha *(Earth-Water) is the principle of stability, relaxation and serenity. Kaphas have curvaceous bodies with wide hips and shoulders. Their skin is smooth, thick and often oily. They gain weight easily and lose it slowly. Their major response to the world is through taste and smell. Everything about Kaphas is slow. Slow to anger, slow to eat, slow to digest. They tend to store… possessions, money, food and fat. Unbalanced, this turns into greed, stubbornness and procrastination.*

23

WHAT IS YOUR HUMOUR?

HIPPOCRATES, THE GREAT GREEK PHYSICIAN, developed the idea of the four root elements – Fire, Air, Earth and Water – finding expression in the human body as the four "humours". This concept permeated Western thought and medicine well into the modern age. Human temperament corresponded to the physical type, and the four humours traditionally associated with the elements are melancholic (earth), phlegmatic (water), sanguine (air) and choleric (fire).

Choler is the Greek word for bile, and the choleric person is one who is active, energetic and a "doer". He or she is also prone to erupt into rages and tempers if the bile overflows.

The sanguine person has a fresh and often ruddy complexion, revealing a healthy flow of blood, as if driven by the wind and air.

Phlegmatics are placid, methodical, unruffled, slow moving, flowing like a wide river. But they can stagnate or burst their banks on occasion.

The melancholic is practical, earthy, but also traditionally the type who has black bile – with dark moods and withdrawing into him- or herself like earth in winter.

The diagram on the right shows that the choleric and phlegmatic types are diametrically opposed and seldom unite in one person. The same is true of the sanguine and melancholic humours. Yet a temperament is likely to share traces of its neighbours on either side. In fact few of us are one type entirely. The path to psychological integration and balance is found in those qualities in the neighbour who complements your temperament – being a passive partner to your active traits, or vice versa. The red arrows in the small diagram above suggest the likely paths to disintegration and imbalance while the blue arrows suggest the way to balance your characteristics.

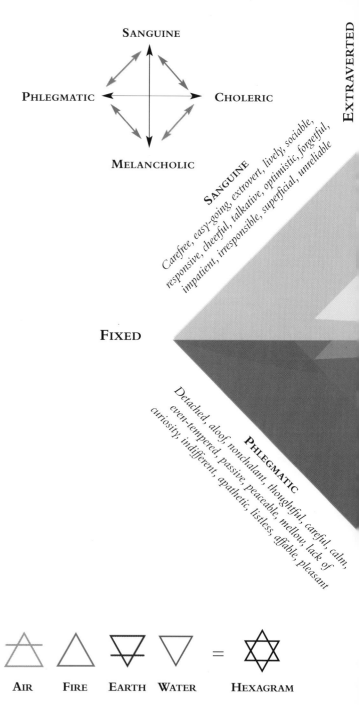

The four elements meet and merge in a six-sided figure – the hexagram. Traditionally this suggests the three-sided nature of balance and imbalance in combination.

INTROVERTED

Tends to react very quickly to situations and becomes easily over-excited, impulsive, restless, energetic, ruddy, noisy, poor retention, angry, heroic, impatient

CHOLERIC

CHANGEABLE

MELANCHOLIC

Quiet and often withdrawn, pessimistic, sad, reserved, thoughtful, brooding, inconsolable, sober, good retention especially about imagined wrongs, internal orientation

SANGUINE	CHOLERIC	MELANCHOLIC	PHLEGMATIC
carefree	impulsive	pessimistic	careful
easy-going	restless	gloomy	methodical
lively	quick temper	moody	even-tempered
vivacious	active	sober	passive
sociable	excitable	nervous	peaceable
responsive	ruddy	withdrawn	thoughtful
talkative	aggressive	quiet	calm
quick actions	a leader	reserved	controlled
workaholic	forceful	resigned	comfortable
chatterer	energetic	sad	placid
eloquent	extrovert	droopy	unhurried
superficial	boisterous	thoughtful	slow
outgoing	impatient	introspective	relentless
talkative	initiator	egotistic	measured
friendly	pioneer	demanding	untroubled
adaptable	noisy	easily hurt	inner
colourful	practical	reader	reserved
bright	dramatic	slow	dreamy
impatient	poor retention	drab	enjoys routine
irresponsible	sportive	brooding	slow learner
unreliable	competitive	intellectual	persevering
fleeting	strong stamina	good retention	obstinate
flexible	domineering	observer	shy
generous	intolerant	ungrateful	habitual
early riser	obstinate	unsatisfied	wise
butterfly-like	angry	self-sacrificer	indifferent
happy	heroic	inconsolable	dull

ASSESSMENT

To find your own humour, choose those words from the lists on the right that most describe you. Working across the columns, only choose one word for each line, and enter the final score for each column. Whichever is greatest is probably your type, almost certainly if it is greater by over half the sum of the other scores.

24

REVISIT THE CHILD

RUDOLF STEINER'S[13] ANTHROPOSOPHICAL VISION endures most in his work with young children. He maintained that the traditional Western fourfold characterization of human temperament, found in the previous assessment, offered basic insights into understanding the needs of the young, and saw the task of education as bringing the four aspects into harmony within each child.

According to Steiner, each child is a combination of four inborn temperaments. These physical and psychological blueprints determine our behaviour and responses to the world around us. Usually one "component" is dominant, and from that platform we develop our strategies to deal with the stresses and challenges of our world.

The assessment below should be compared with assessment 23 to determine how you have changed since childhood.

ASSESSMENT

Find an old photo of yourself as a child, preferably when you were between five and seven years old. Try to re-establish an identity with that picture. Remember what it was like being that age – your concerns, whether you were accepted by your peers, how you coped with emergencies, with stress and your family. Read the descriptions of the four temperaments on these pages and feel which one would have matched you best at that time.

CHOLERIC

Usually stocky, ruddy-faced, appearing larger than life and with a restless aura about them, cholerics are energetic, purposeful, forceful and self-assured. They are born leaders and feel that only they are really able to rule. They are impatient with those who disagree. They often set themselves impossible goals, will not admit they might be wrong and blame others when their wild schemes are not realized. Sitting silently is completely unnatural to them. They are great at organizing others, but have little eye for detail. They look for heroic role models and can be generous friends, but are often impulsive and insensitive to others' needs.

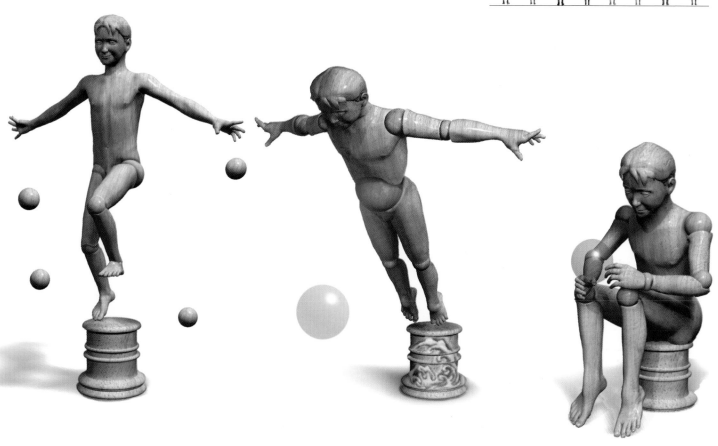

SANGUINE

Slender, lightweight, well-proportioned and mobile, the sanguine type is happy and carefree and has a quick and dancing step with an airy, buoyant quality. The sanguine is a great chatterer, although much of what is said is superficial, with the mind behind the tongue like a butterfly flitting from impression to impression. They love the new and the changing. In this they are the least habitual of the four types. They will promise anything, and promptly forget it. Living in the immediate, he or she craves instant gratification, but the experiences are seldom really digested. Impatience and irresponsibly leaving things unfinished are hallmarks of the type.

PHLEGMATIC

Heavily-built, round, portly and sometimes flabby, the phlegmatic is comfortable and unhurried, concise and logical as well as accurate and reliable in his or her dealings. They live within themselves and are calm and untroubled by what happens around them. Good-humoured, they mix well once shyness is overcome, are faithful, honest, orderly and conscientious and will always complete what has been started. They learn slowly but remember everything. They are habitual, like ritual, routine and a regulated life with set times for eating and sleeping. They can become torpid, lacking interest, but are the easiest of all types of children to raise.

MELANCHOLIC

A sense of weightiness about the body with a feeling of quiet resignation gives melancholics the appearance of not quite being of this world. They are withdrawn, introspective, with an air of sadness and gloom. Self-centred and living in the past, they chew over real and imagined wrongs. Voracious readers or absorbed in computer games, they feed their egocentric view of the world with brooding fantasies in which they avenge imagined injuries. Intellectual, with a rich imaginative life, this type is often happiest when miserable. They are prepared to sacrifice themselves for any cause that increases self-esteem.

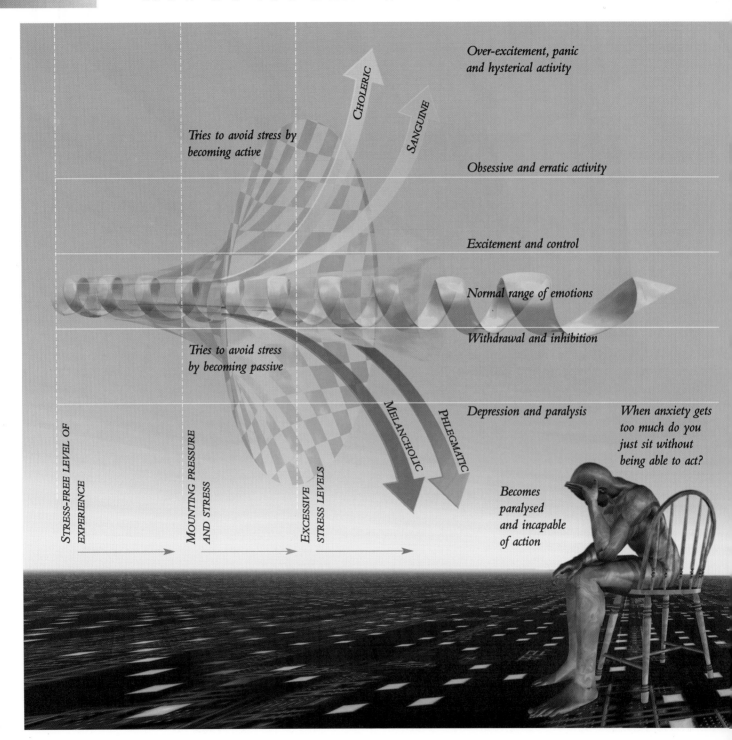

Over-excitement, panic and hysterical activity

CHOLERIC

SANGUINE

Tries to avoid stress by becoming active

Obsessive and erratic activity

Excitement and control

Normal range of emotions

Withdrawal and inhibition

Tries to avoid stress by becoming passive

MELANCHOLIC

PHLEGMATIC

Depression and paralysis

When anxiety gets too much do you just sit without being able to act?

STRESS-FREE LEVEL OF EXPERIENCE

MOUNTING PRESSURE AND STRESS

EXCESSIVE STRESS LEVELS

Becomes paralysed and incapable of action

B Y NOW YOU WILL HAVE BUILT up a reasonably clear picture of your physiological type and temperament. Each of the four humours responds differently to stress, abrupt change and anxiety. Certain types react to increasing levels of stress in remarkably distinctive fashions.

We all experience stress in some form, from spilling the morning coffee to avoiding being run over by a lorry. Some of us love the excitement and drama of an unexpected change to our routine, while others are appalled. Watch the effects of a long delay on passengers in the airport lounge, or in traffic jams on the motorway. Some rage while others become very withdrawn and dangerously quiet. The chart opposite shows the likely strategy of each character type for dealing with such stresses as sudden or impending change, danger, boredom, fear of death, fear of confrontation, pain and discomfort.

PHLEGMATIC

Slow, relaxed and methodical.
Is resistant to stress but when overloaded tries to control and becomes inert, stubborn and rigid.

MELANCHOLIC

Usually quietly gloomy, but this changes to a drawn out depression, withdrawal and frozen inactivity.

CHOLERIC

Impulsive and excitable. Early over-reaction to stress by becoming hyperactive, over-stimulated and excited.

SANGUINE

Usually lively and carefree. Resistant to mounting pressure but then suddenly over-reacts by frantic activity.

When anxiety gets too much do you have to rush off and do something?

26

WHICH IS YOUR DOMINANT BRAIN?

GEORGIADES IVANOVITCH GURDJIEFF,[14] the charismatic Armenian mystic and teacher of the first half of this century, maintained that human beings are wonderful stimulus-response mechanisms which, he said, "eat impressions and excrete behaviour".

He proposed that we are all three-brained beings, each brain forming a different centre of awareness. He taught that an individual is dominated by one of the three, which constitutes his type – in Man Number One this is the moving brain, in Number Two it is the emotional brain, while in Number Three it is the intellectual brain. Each of us has a lifelong predisposition towards either the belly, the heart or the head. Gurdjieff's aim was to bring about an integrity between the disparate urges of each of these brains, or centres of consciousness, so that the individual could begin to wake up to his or her real potential by using all three in harmony.

In the year of his death, in 1949, Gurdjieff might have seen a number of neurologists come to the remarkably similar conclusion that there are indeed three distinct brains that carry within themselves the whole history of our evolution. Prehistoric fish evolved specialized bundles of nerves along the spine which became sensitive to smell, light and sound. These clusters became what is known as the reptilian brain, corresponding to our own most ancient brain – the cerebellum. It deals with the five mechanical and instinctual responses of flight, fight, freeze, food and reproduction.

A further evolutionary refinement, ensuring far better odds of survival, was the limbic system, or emotional brain. Although unconscious, it added powerful urges to the five basic instincts, ensuring faster and more appropriate responses to the environment. This is the mammalian brain. Crowning this neurological explosion was the cortex, with frontal lobes which apparently triggered a conscious awareness of self.

The hard-wired connections between the three brains is anything but efficient. Often communication breaks down between all three. This can cause a split in which we tend to operate in only one mode – physical, emotional or mental.

The three types can be easily identified in caricature as Shakespeare's Falstaff, the instinctual man of the body, Othello, the emotional lover, and Hamlet, the divided man of the mind.

ASSESSMENT

With which do you most identify?

Type Number One
You enjoy acting impulsively, on instinct, rather than reasoning out a course of action. You trust that your whole body will instinctively act for you. You seldom bother to reflect on your actions. You take pleasure in the immediate things of life – food, drink, sex, and in the delight of energy and the action of your body.

Type Number Two
You know that you respond to people and situations in a very emotional way. You are passionate and value love above all reason. You sometimes act foolishly simply because you feel driven by an overwhelming impulse you can't explain. You become insanely jealous while you know you have no reason to.

Type Number Three
You enjoy the delights of intellectual challenge, the world of ideas and of creative dreaming. You want to increase your knowledge and seek the truth and the meaning of existence. You do not trust your emotions, preferring logic and careful reasoning.

THE EVOLUTIONARY STRUCTURE OF THE HUMAN BRAIN

THE CORTEX

This area of the brain is concerned with language, thinking, planning, organising and consciousness. It has fewer neural pathways to the other brains than from them.

THE LIMBIC SYSTEM

The emotional centre that creates feelings but is not conscious in itself. It is the most powerful generator of urges in the nervous system and has the greatest influence on our behaviour.

BRAINSTEM AND CEREBELLUM

The most ancient of the three brains is responsible for the more mechanical aspects of the body, being dedicated to movement, the physical senses and instinctual responses.

GURDJIEFF'S THREE BRAIN TYPES

MAN NUMBER THREE (HAMLET)

The Head

The Reasoning intelligence, living in the head and in an environment of ideas. Using the reasoning powers of the mind, logical and strategic, mathematical, knowledgeable, mind-created experience.

MAN NUMBER TWO (OTHELLO)

The Heart

The Feeling intelligence. Lives in the emotions, passionate, jealous, possesssed and possessive, expressive, moody and unreasonable.

MAN NUMBER ONE (FALSTAFF)

The Belly/Hand

Instinctual intelligence. Lives in the phenomenal environment, in the moment. Acts on impulse, instinctive, body-oriented, materialistic, non-reflective, lusty and bound by the earth.

27

WHO PUSHES YOUR BUTTONS?

FEW OF US WOULD CARE TO ADMIT that we are not in control of our emotions or that we are slaves to our reactions. As we have seen, the brainstem, or reptilian brain, which is part of our evolutionary inheritance, is also the oldest brain. This seat of the basic intelligence that helps us to survive is dedicated to the responses of "fight", "flight", "food" and "reproduction". Recently another category has been added – "freeze".

These fundamental instinctual responses determine our immediate reactions to unexpected stimulae and are the major survival tactics in almost all animals. As with many things we do, such strategies can become habitual and obsessive.

As children we often have to respond to threatening situations that involve a tactical choice. We can choose, for example, either to fight a gang, or to run. We can find comfort in food, in the diversion of sexual experiments, or we can freeze when the level of stress simply becomes too confusing.

Such patterns are natural, but if we constantly choose one particular response to the virtual exclusion of all others they begin to dictate our behaviour in an unhealthy way. While it is prudent to run from a gang who might hurt you, this reflex is not necessary for a situation that is only mildly threatening. When gradually *everything* is seen as a potential threat, and we are already too busy running to actually discover whether we need to or not, the reflex has taken control. Because there is a direct connection to the most ancient and unconscious part of the brain, these instinctual reactions are both difficult to detect and even more difficult to change.

Any aspect of ourselves that is essentially unconscious is also prone to become robotic. It can become mechanical and unmoved by sentiment or sensitivity – a jump in the groove of an old record, endlessly playing the same few notes until something or someone jolts it sufficiently to break the recurring cycle.

Consider the five instinctual reactions. Do you tend to use one more than any of the others, and if so, why? The idea that we might be merely an unconscious slave to something little more than a robot is enough to nudge most of us out of any rut.

ASSESSMENT

The two situations below might give you some idea of which instinctual "react-or" is strongest in your makeup. Choose one answer from each.

Your attractive companion at a party gets drunk and behaves very embarrassingly to the other guests.

Do you:
1. *Become aggressive and force him or her to leave?*
2. *Quietly withdraw?*
3. *Get bored and find the buffet?*
4. *Find you are sexually excited by the wild behaviour?*
5. *Become helplessly embarrassed and do absolutely nothing?*

You have been told you have one day left to live.

Do you:
1. *Rage against death and try to find a way to avoid it happening?*
2. *Ignore it all and carry on as if nothing is going to happen?*
3. *Throw a party and eat the finest meal you can buy?*
4. *Throw a wild party and make love to as many partners as possible?*
5. *Sit alone, paralyzed with fear?*

KEY: FIGHT 1   SEX 4
FLIGHT 2   FREEZE 5
FOOD 3

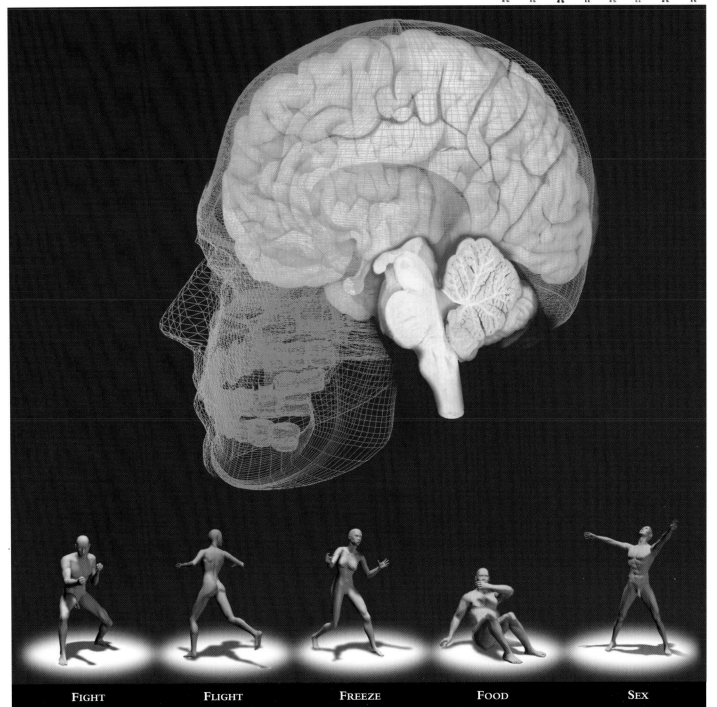

FIGHT   FLIGHT   FREEZE   FOOD   SEX

28

WHICH HEMISPHERE DO YOU LIVE IN?

THE HUMAN BRAIN IS A PARTNERSHIP of two quite distinct minds. The two hemispheres of the brain are linked by connecting fibres that allow them to carry on such a continuous dialogue that the end result appears to be the product of only one mind.[15] However, compare their distinct realms of consciousness and you will find two strangers in your skull. The most popular set of labels ascribed to the twin halves might read like this:

LEFT HEMISPHERE	RIGHT HEMISPHERE
Verbal	Non-verbal, visuo-spatial
Sequential, temporal, linear	Simultaneous, spatial, analogic
Logical, analytic	Holistic, synthetic
Rational, intellectual	Intuitive, sensuous
Western philosophy	Eastern mysticism

Such two-part divisions are largely verbal concepts and neurologists have coined the term "dichoto-mania myth" to describe the tsunami of popular literature on the subject. Yet sometimes a popular myth is more useful than the over-complex truth of the expert. Brain-imaging studies have shown that both halves of the brain are hard-wired in very different ways, ascribing specific skills to each.

The right hemisphere appears more emotional than the left, often responsible for feelings of sadness and despair. Spatial awareness and facial recognition, the ability to recognize camouflaged images in a landscape and comprehend patterns at a glance also happen on the right side.

The left brain can analyse complex patterns into their component parts, but tends not to see the wood for the trees. It is a great deducer, using symbols and language to find its way around the environment. Its ability to calculate, conceive, plan and communicate has largely contributed to making our species so remarkably successful.

The two differing aptitudes of the holistic and analytic hemispheres could be simply due to an innate physical difference. The right brain has more white matter and the left has more grey. This means that the right brain is more loosely arranged with long-ranging connectors to distant neurons, which could explain why it is good at broad brush strokes which are often vague, while the left brain is more densely woven, with closely packed neurons adapted for the intricate and sharp details.

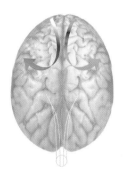

SMELL

Smell, the oldest sense, is the only one that doesn't cross over. Odours are processed on the same side as they are received.

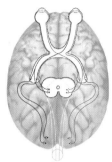

VISION

Most sensory input from one side of the body crosses over to the opposite hemisphere. The right eye is connected to the left brain and vice versa.

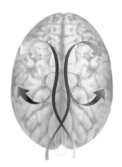

TOUCH

Almost all the neural pathways of the body cross over to the other side of the brain.

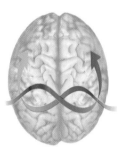

HEARING

Most auditory input is processed on the opposite side of the brain to the ear by which it entered.

ASSESSMENT

Check the number of statements in both columns that are most typical for you.
If one score is significantly higher than the other then the hemisphere above that column dominates your type of thinking. If the scores are roughly the same, neither brain-half dominates.

LEFT HEMISPHERE OF THE BRAIN

Normally I:
1. *enjoy expressing ideas in words.*
2. *prefer logical reasoning to emotional or intuitive feeling.*
3. *like to have my facts straight before making a decision.*
4. *prefer maths and science to art and poetry.*
5. *am very punctual and have an accurate sense of time.*
6. *like to understand the reasons for others' behaviour.*
7. *seldom think in visual terms.*
8. *take great pleasure solving difficult problems or puzzles.*
9. *am really good at word games and verbal play.*
10. *generally prefer non-fiction to fiction or fantasy.*
11. *am good at analysing problems and finding solutions.*
12. *do not show my feelings and can control my temper.*
13. *prefer to rely on a rational solution rather than a hunch.*
14. *am organized and have my life reasonably ordered.*
15. *am not impressed by dreams but see the reason for them.*
16. *love to plan new projects in minute detail.*
17. *have always been good with numbers.*
18. *abstract relevant information from situations easily.*
19. *enjoy working with symbols rather than physical reality.*
20. *think in clear linear sequences and logical progressions.*
21. *am not attracted to Eastern ideas or mystical philosophy.*
22. *consider myself a realist and not a dreamy idealist.*
23. *prefer explicit rather than implicit behaviour.*
24. *prefer facts to opinions based on feelings only.*
25. *like to deal with proven truths rather than vague ones.*
26. *am considered objective by my friends.*
27. *reach conclusions by marshalling all the relevant facts.*
28. *like music but am not very musical or absorbed by it.*
29. *generally do not wave my arms about when talking.*
30. *am good at communicating ideas in words.*

RIGHT HEMISPHERE OF THE BRAIN

Normally I:
1. *find it difficult to find words to describe my feelings.*
2. *reach an intuitive grasp of the situation without thinking.*
3. *rely on my gut feelings to make a decision.*
4. *prefer artistic subjects to those of science and maths.*
5. *am a dreadful timekeeper and am seldom punctual.*
6. *feel how others are yet am mystified by their motivations.*
7. *have thoughts that appear in picture form.*
8. *am terrible at solving puzzles and who cares anyway?*
9. *don't enjoy word games and find them boring.*
10. *prefer fiction, poetry and fantasy to non-fiction.*
11. *don't like analysis; prefer to deal with the whole picture.*
12. *tend to let my feelings show and let it all hang out.*
13. *rely on my instincts, intuition and definitely my hunches.*
14. *seldom bother to order things.*
15. *dream very vividly and find it difficult not to daydream.*
16. *hate to plan and prefer to do something on impulse.*
17. *am lousy at anything to do with numbers.*
18. *have to see the whole wood and not individual trees.*
19. *prefer to know things directly – not symbols about them.*
20. *think in overall pictures with no particular sequence.*
21. *am attracted to Eastern mysticism and esoteric ideas.*
22. *am not very realistic and am considered dreamy.*
23. *trust tacit and implicit rather than explicit behaviour.*
24. *trust my feelings above so-called facts.*
25. *value the elusive mystery of truth.*
26. *am thought of as subjective by my friends.*
27. *reach conclusions by waiting for that "eureka" revelation.*
28. *adore music and have some musical ability.*
29. *tend to gesticulate furiously as I talk.*
30. *cannot find the right words to explain my ideas.*

THE KEYS TO YOUR ELEMENT

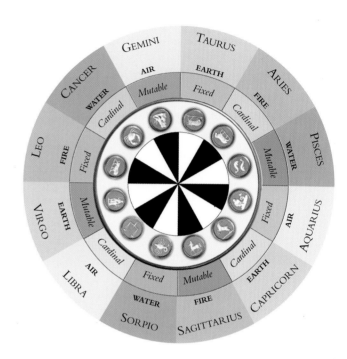

THE CIRCLE OF THE TWELVE ZODIACAL SIGNS is made up of a number of interacting principles. The two-fold principle expresses the duality of masculine and feminine – the active/passive (black and white segments in the chart on the right). The threefold principle embodies the conditions of the *Cardinal,* which acts upon, or uses things intensely; the *Fixed,* which tends to stabilise; and the *Mutable,* which is the most flexible and tends to adapt. The fourfold principle embraces the elements of *Earth, Water, Fire* and *Air.* These principles make up the twelve partitions of the zodiac.

It does not necessarily mean that an individual who obviously bears many of the characteristics of a particular element, say Earth, is actually born under that sign. However, it is likely that there will be a predominance of that element within the birth chart as a whole. [16]

EARTH ~ SENSING

Taurus, Virgo, Capricorn

Earth is sensation and at home with the body, often over-identifying with it, as if reality stops at the material, phenomenal edge of things. As an empirical thinker, all three signs are practical and realistic. Happy and affectionate, being a lover of nature and beautiful things. Can be narrow-minded, conservative and dismissive of what cannot be immediately observed or touched. Lacks the intuitive element and so often over-compensates by fascination with the esoteric, becoming fanatical about some outward religious belief system without having had the real inner experience.

WATER ~ FEELING

Cancer, Scorpio, Pisces

Water approaches life mostly at an unconscious level, responding intuitively and through feeling. There is an overwhelming sense of the importance of personal relationships. Most actions and thoughts are at an unconscious, impulsive and unpredictable level. This type is usually sensitive, compassionate and empathic. The darker side shows as emotional blackmail, possessiveness, brooding heaviness and a lack of principles.
The three signs are of the most ancient of creatures, symbolic of the instinctual nature of the element.

FIRE ~ INTUITING

Aries, Leo, Sagittarius

Fire brings the element of myth into experience. This essentially inner world is often removed from the simple reality of a situation. Fire types are vital and spontaneous and often live in a rich fantasy world more attuned to the theatre than the workplace. They need to experience life dramatically and significantly so their behaviours are exaggerated. The three types associated with fire are all colourful figures, full of mythological splendour and heroism. The type is often self-centred and self-absorbed, but is also warm, psychic and lively.

THE FOUR FUNCTIONAL TYPES

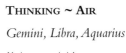

SENSING ~ EARTH

Taurus, Virgo, Capricorn

Earth celebrates the existence of the world through the senses, through material and concrete phenomena. Taurus stabilizes resources to create a sense of permanence. Virgo adapts resources to improve situations; Capricorn uses resources to accomplish aims.
All have a problem with intuition.

THINKING ~ AIR

Gemini, Libra, Aquarius

Air has a real drive to encompass all experience within a symbolic framework of controllable ideas.
Gemini adapts ideas in order to communicate; Libra uses ideas in order to judge; Aquarius stabilizes ideas to revolutionize.
All have a problem with feeling.

FEELING ~ WATER

Cancer, Scorpio, Pisces

Water flows through life on an unconscious level, responding intuitively to the surroundings. Cancer uses emotion to generate compassion; Scorpio stabilizes emotions in order to trust; Pisces adapts emotions in order to be sympathetic.
All have a problem with thinking.

INTUITING ~ FIRE

Aries, Leo, Sagittarius

Fire brings myth and drama to experience, relating them to an inner world of its own which reflects, but is often removed from, reality. Aries uses energy for outward action; Leo stabilizes energy in order to create; Sagittarius adapts energy in order to explore.
All have a problem with sensuality.

AIR ~ THINKING

Gemini, Libra, Aquarius

Air has an overwhelming drive to relate all experiences of life to a symbolic framework of ideas. This ensures a certain rational detachment from the more emotional and sensual types. As air is the element furthest removed from the instinctual nature of the animal kingdom, it represents consciousness as thinking, rather than experiencing. This is the philosopher, the scientist, the analyst—the impersonal assessor, the lover of structure and system. Air has a very real problem with feeling.

Two of the sub-types within the element of air are human, while the third is the balancing scales which reveal air as the most intellectual and civilizing element, yet at the cost of losing contact with the emotions and instinct.

ASSESSMENT

Read the descriptions of the characteristic element associated with your birth sign on the left. This is the raw stuff from which you have been formed. These four elements, linked with the functional types of sensing, feeling, intuiting and thinking, are most clearly observed in the key diagram above. By combining the descriptions you will get a complete reading of your elemental type.

30

YOU AND YOUR SHADOW

Ask someone to describe the type of person he or she really cannot abide and you will probably receive a full description of that person's own repressed characteristics – a detailed account of his, or her, *doppelgänger* or shadow side. This dark aspect is the part of your personality that you least know, simply because it is your polar opposite.

Look at the diagram on the right and you will see how those elements and associated signs opposing one another create the unconscious shadows that haunt us – the ghosts in our machine.[17]

AIR ~ THINKING

Gemini, Libra, Aquarius

POSITIVE	NEGATIVE
Air is the only element not containing animal symbolism, revealing it as being the most human. It is also the furthest removed from our instinctual nature. Air signs collect, analyse, symbolise and categorise information. A highly developed mind, a capacity for impersonal assessment, love of culture, appreciation of system structures and an adherence to principles and rules. Air is almost exclusively mental, interested in the world of ideas and thoughts.	The air type has a real problem with feeling. Feelings, of course, cannot be classified, structured or analysed to fit into any framework. Feelings become bottled up, especially as the type considers emotional display a weakness. Geminis abhor being pinned down or caged in any personal relationship. Librans refuse to commit themselves and sit on a fence. Aquarians have a real distaste for emotional expression that results in a cold and distant detachment.

WATER ~ FEELING

Cancer, Scorpio, Pisces

POSITIVE	NEGATIVE
Feeling is essential. Human relationships and the rich world of feelings are of paramount value. Water types tend to evoke emotional responses in others. They are compassionate, empathetic, and feel what others feel, assessing situations and relationships in an irrational way. They can be highly sensitive, subtle, charming, insightful and able to unite and counsel others, instinctively understanding the other person's needs.	The water type has a very real problem with rationality. Any move towards being impersonal, intellectual or experiencing life through a preconceived or planned framework of ideas is strenuously resisted. Water types like Cancer can be possessive and full of anxiety for the future. Scorpios have a tendency to indulge in emotional and brooding obsessions. Pisces become over-sentimental, unrealistically romantic, escapist, with a lack of real integrity.

EARTH ~ SENSING

Taurus, Virgo, Capricorn

POSITIVE	NEGATIVE
Earth types relate to the phenomenal world of the senses. They are most at ease with material existence. They are at home with their physical bodies and with expressing their physical drives directly. It is said they have a gift for actualising material desires. The earth type is a realist, is practical, fond of money, status and security, and for these comforts is prepared to become organised and work hard. An empirical thinker and careful statistician.	The earth type has a major problem with the world beyond the senses. In emphasising the value of sensation at the cost of intuitition, feeling has atrophied and is lacking. Earth types like Taurus can be dogmatic, narrow-minded, and overpossessive. Virgos can lose their overview in excessive details and irrelevant trivia and never see the point of their hard work. Capricorns tend to justify the means by the end or fit their behaviour to others' expectations.

FIRE ~ INTUITING

Aries, Leo, Sagittarius

POSITIVE	NEGATIVE
Fire types are the flamboyant drama-tists. They cannot help but exaggerate. They enhance their world of experience by creating a myth from it, for in truth many find the world dull and colourless. This need of some joy and drama motivates the type. Even the three signs associated with the element are mythic, heroic and full of vitality, spontaneity and play. The fire types are on a continual quest to reinvent themselves and this appears to be their path of self discovery.	Fire has a problem in coping with the material world. It often sees it as drab and threatening. Imagination is real life to fire types and there is a strong element of fantasy in their relationships. At worst this can produce physical illness or problems connected to feelings of inferiority over their sexuality. Aries can display ill-tempered egoism and irrational aggression. Leos can be self-centred or arrogant. Sagittari-ans can be unreliable and exaggerated in their promises.

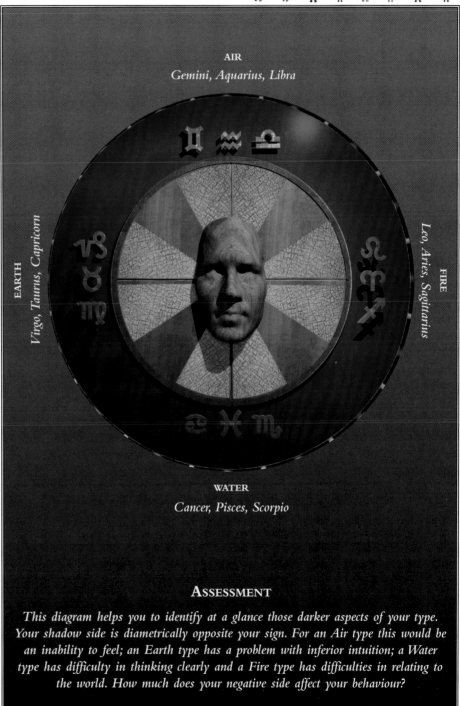

AIR
Gemini, Aquarius, Libra

EARTH
Virgo, Taurus, Capricorn

FIRE
Leo, Aries, Sagittarius

WATER
Cancer, Pisces, Scorpio

ASSESSMENT

This diagram helps you to identify at a glance those darker aspects of your type. Your shadow side is diametrically opposite your sign. For an Air type this would be an inability to feel; an Earth type has a problem with inferior intuition; a Water type has difficulty in thinking clearly and a Fire type has difficulties in relating to the world. How much does your negative side affect your behaviour?

31

YOUR ESSENCE ~ THE SUN SIGN

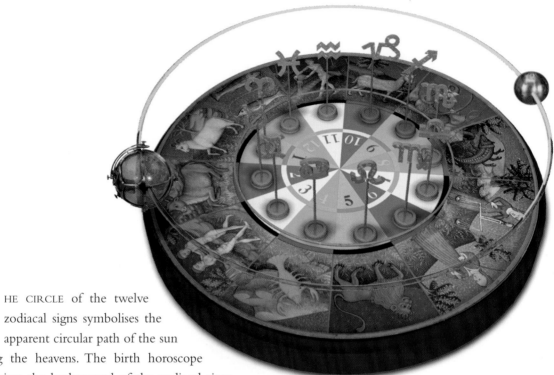

THE CIRCLE of the twelve zodiacal signs symbolises the apparent circular path of the sun traversing the heavens. The birth horoscope maps, against the background of the zodiacal signs, the positions of the sun, the moon and eight planets as they appear at the exact point in time and place of the birth of any individual.

The common, traditional descriptions of the twelve major astrological personality types have proved remarkably resistant to the passing fashions of each age. You could pick up a book on astrology written four hundred years ago and the types would still be instantly recognisable.

Whether the heavenly bodies actually do have an effect upon us remains scientifically unproven, but the descriptions of human types in terms of the twelve characteristics of the sun signs are surprisingly accurate and full of insight.

ASSESSMENT

If you are unfamiliar with astrology first check your own birth date against the twelve sun signs on the opposite page. From the brief descriptions you will see the basic strengths (+) and weaknesses (-) of each sign. Is your particular sign a good description of what you know about your own characteristics? If not, see if any other sign seems more appropriate to your type. This is most likely to occur with those signs which are immediate neighbours to your own, especially if your birth date is close to them.

ARIES
(Active, Cardinal, Fire) ~ *March 22–April 20*
+ innocent, courageous, impulsive, daring, self-starting,
enthusiastic, initiating, original, spontaneous.
– intolerant, hasty, impetuous, aggressive, tactless,
quick-tempered, dominating, stubborn.

TAURUS
(Receptive, Fixed, Earth) ~ *April 21–May 21*
+ consistent, dependable, productive, thorough, sensual,
durable, attentive, deeply loving, faithful.
– possessive, over-conservative, self-indulgent, obstinate,
materialistic, slow, lascivious, stubborn.

GEMINI
(Active, Mutable, Air) ~ *May 22–June 22*
+ curious, searching, versatile, experimental, dexterous,
unprejudiced, adventurous, expressive, quick-witted.
– restless, cunning, easily disracted, lacking concentration,
uncommitted, scattered, confused, a "butterfly".

CANCER
(Receptive, Cardinal, Water) ~ *June 23–July 23*
+ protective, sensitive, nourishing, caring, tenacious,
intuitive, excellent retention, helpful, sustaining.
– moody, easily hurt, smothering, lazy, unrealistic,
 overpowering, uncertain, overeat when stressed.

LEO
(Active, Fixed, Fire) ~ *July 24–August 23*
+confident, noble, proud, creative, dramatic, powerful,
generous, energetic, helpful, dignified, directive.
– vain, mildly cruel, pretentious, self-absorbed, bossy,
needs to be superior and important, a show-off.

VIRGO
(Receptive, Mutable, Earth) ~ *August 24–Sept 23*
+ analytic, harvesting, skillful, studious, humane,
logical, scientific, meticulous, sensual, detail-oriented.
– petty, sceptical, melancholic, sloppy, untidy,
emotionally insecure, perfectionist, prudish, lost.

LIBRA
(Active, Cardinal, Air) ~ *Sept 24–Oct 23*
+ considerate, harmonising, social, diplomatic,
cooperative, refined, aesthetic, charming, persuasive.
– in two minds, apathetic, a fence-sitter, indecisive,
fearful, needing admiration, enjoys intrigue.

SCORPIO
(Receptive, Fixed, Water) ~ *Oct 24–Nov 22*
+ healing, radical, passionate, intense, investigative,
motivated, penetrating, probing, sexual, protective.
– vengeful, suspicious, jealous, intolerant, possessive,
obsessive, overbearing, demands the impossible.

SAGITTARIUS
(Active, Mutable, Fire) ~ *Nov 23–Dec 22*
+ optimistic, adventurous, extravagant, just, honest,
happily disposed, stimulating, religious, boisterous.
– argumentative, impatient, fanatical, hot-headed,
indulgent, tendency to preach, hides sadness.

CAPRICORN
(Receptive, Cardinal, Earth) ~ *Dec 23–Jan19*
+ responsible, having integrity, authoritative, austere,
committed, scrupulous, organised, constructive.
– severe, unforgiving, fatalistic, depressive, status seeking,
righteous, egotistical, uses others, oppressive.

AQUARIUS
(Active, Fixed, Air) ~ *Jan 20–Feb 19*
+ inventive, idealistic, humane, altruistic, logical, caring,
rebellious, persistent, independent, radical, objective.
– unpredictable, impersonal, cold, unreliable, eccentric,
fixed opinions, stubbornly holds an idea, rigid.

PISCES
(Receptive, Mutable, Water) ~ *Feb 20–Mar 21*
+ mystical, poetic, vulnerable, sensitive, intuitive, kind,
compassionate, introspective, inspired, imaginative.
– confused, pessimistic, indolent, flighty, timid,
helpless, self-pitying, over-emotional, fearful.

32

YOUR HOUSE AND THE PERSONA

ACCORDING TO TRADITIONAL ASTROLOGY CHARTS, we are embodied at birth within a "focus", created by the intersection of the East-West horizon and the vertical meridian. In the northern hemisphere the Ascendant is the place on the eastern horizon where the planets rise at dawn. This is the outward, social mask we wear, the personality. The Descendant is where they set in the West.

Thus the left-hand, upper side of the diagram opposite represents the dawn of the "evolving" entity, while the right upper side symbolises the evening and the "involving" aspect. The lines that divide the chart are called "cusps" and indicate the twelve houses of the horoscope. They offer twelve existential challenges, as listed below. The positions of the houses shown in the diagram opposite are for one particular person's arrangement of the signs.

THE HOUSES

First house ~ *The quest for your true identity*
Second house ~ *Your resources, abilities and characteristics*
Third house ~ *Your relationship to the environment*
Fourth house ~ *Your grounding ~ body, sense of place, tradition*
Fifth house ~ *Your spontaneous sense of play and creativity*
Sixth house ~ *Your sense of responsibility in what you do*
Seventh house ~ *Your relationship to others*
Eighth house ~ *Letting go of your identity ~ your mystical aspect*
Ninth house ~ *Your personal vision and philosophy*
Tenth house ~ *Your vocation, career and purpose in life*
Eleventh house ~ *Your participation with others*
Twelfth house ~ *Your quest for the essential self*

THE PLANETS

Sun ~ *Yourself, essence*
Moon ~ *Emotions, moods*
Mercury ~ *Thoughts, ideas*
Venus ~ *Love, relationships*
Mars ~ *Energy, drive, sex*
Jupiter ~ *Optimism, luck*
Saturn ~ *Wisdom gained*
Uranus ~ *Individual expression*
Neptune ~ *Imagination, dreams*
Pluto ~ *Personal power*

THE ASCENDANT

*The sign rising over the eastern horizon when you were born represents your psychological mask, your persona or personality.
While the sun sign is your essential self, the ascendant is the persona you become in order to deal with the world.*

ASSESSMENT

*This assessment is for those of you who already have a birth chart. Each house stands for a particular human activity and a central quest or challenge. Consider what you know of your birth chart from this perspective. Clusterings of planets in any house on your chart would indicate the importance of that particular quest or direction.
These quests are listed on the sample chart on the opposite page with Aries as the ascendant. The relative position of the houses remains constant with number one as the position of the ascendant.
After finding in which houses the planets on your birth chart are located, consult the planet list on the left for their prime attributes.
This small astrological identity kit will generate a simple but effective image of your personality.*

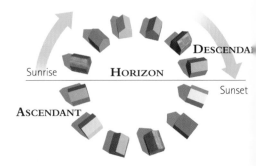

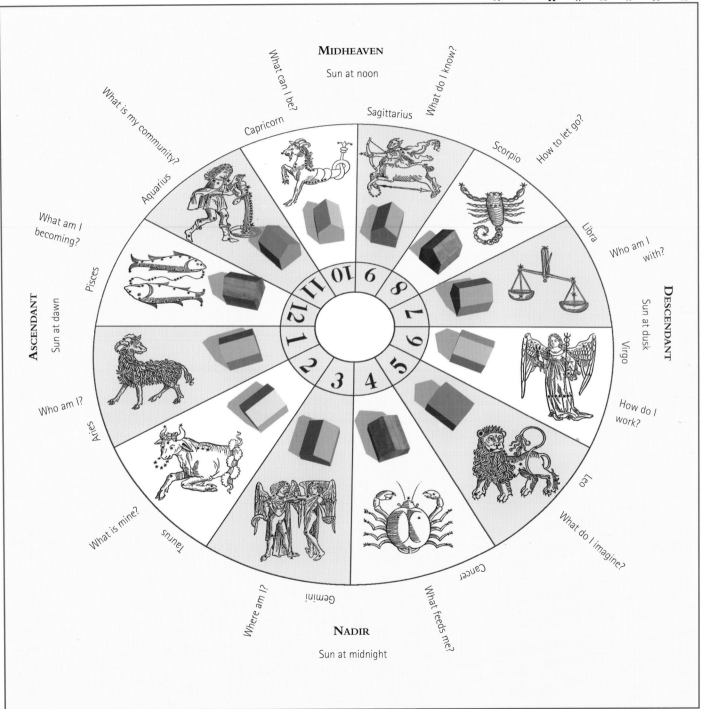

MIDHEAVEN
Sun at noon

What can I be?

What do I know?

What is my community?

Capricorn

Sagittarius

Scorpio

How to let go?

Aquarius

Libra

What am I becoming?

Who am I with?

Pisces

DESCENDANT
Sun at dusk

ASCENDANT
Sun at dawn

Virgo

How do I work?

Who am I?

Aries

Leo

What do I imagine?

What is mine?

Taurus

Cancer

Gemini

What feeds me?

Where am I?

NADIR
Sun at midnight

33

THE ANIMAL THAT HIDES IN YOUR HEART

THE FOLKLORE OF CHINESE HOROSCOPES has long endured in the East and has a unique set of types represented by animals that can surprise even the most sceptical of us.[18]

"The animal that hides in your heart" is the traditional Chinese way of describing the animal that rules the year of your birth (see chart below). The characteristics of each animal are supposed to reflect your essential being, influence your behaviour, your way of life and the patterns of your personality. This system is based on the lunar year which commences in either January or February of each solar year.

The twelve animals appear to embrace the whole spectrum of human behaviour in a very revealing way and the descriptions, based upon compilations of popular Chinese lore, legends, mythology and traditional fortune tellers, give both the positive and negative aspects of each sign.

There is also an animal sign that rules the exact hour of your birth (below right). This is said to be your travelling companion, the second self, who can both advise and thwart you. For your companion can be either hostile or friendly to the animal that rules your year, depending on its type.

ASSESSMENT

The left-hand table below gives the animal of your birth year, your essence sign, and the right-hand table gives the animal of the actual hour of your birth, your companion.
Check on the opposite page for the positive (+) and negative (-) descriptions of both typologies.
In assessment 34 you will find which pairs of animals are likely to be compatible and which pairs are most likely to produce conflict.

THE ANIMAL THAT RULES THE YEAR OF YOUR BIRTH

Rat	1900	1912	1924	1936	1948	1960	1972	1984	1996
Ox	1901	1913	1925	1937	1949	1961	1973	1985	1997
Tiger	1902	1914	1926	1938	1950	1962	1974	1986	1998
Rabbit	1903	1915	1927	1939	1951	1963	1975	1987	1999
Dragon	1904	1916	1928	1940	1952	1964	1976	1988	2000
Snake	1905	1917	1929	1941	1953	1965	1977	1989	2001
Horse	1906	1918	1930	1942	1954	1966	1978	1990	2002
Sheep	1907	1919	1931	1943	1955	1967	1979	1991	2003
Monkey	1908	1920	1932	1944	1956	1968	1980	1992	2004
Rooster	1909	1921	1933	1945	1957	1969	1981	1993	2005
Dog	1910	1922	1934	1946	1958	1970	1982	1994	2006
Boar	1911	1923	1935	1947	1959	1971	1983	1995	2007

YOUR COMPANION	Time of birth
Rat	2300-0100
Ox	0100-0300
Tiger	0300-0500
Rabbit	0500-0700
Dragon	0700-0900
Snake	0900-1100
Horse	1100-1300
Sheep	1300-1500
Monkey	1500-1700
Rooster	1700-1900
Dog	1900-2100
Boar	2100-2300

TIGER

+ enthusiastic, sincere, humorous, magnetic, affectionate, powerful, daring, optimistic.
– restless, rash, quick-tempered, reckless, demanding, stubborn.

SHEEP

+ gentle, kind-hearted, peaceful, adaptable, compassionate, lucky, creative, romantic.
– irresponsible, timid, weak-willed, sulky, self-pitying, weak.

DOG

+ faithful, dependable, tough, generous, toler-ant, unpretentious, hardworking, helpful.
– cynical, antisocial, pugnacious, black-humoured, pessimistic.

HORSE

+ quick-witted, sexy, vivacious, energetic, enterprising, loyal, agile, cheerful.
– inconsiderate, hot-headed, selfish, irate, unpredictable, childish.

RABBIT

+ diplomatic, happy, discreet, intuitive, tol-erant, honest, prudent, attentive, caring.
– superficial, pedantic, snobbish, moody, cunning, sentimental.

MONKEY

+ gregarious, amusing, shrewd, versatile, clear-sighted, observant, lively, entertaining.
– critical, vain, superior, vengeful, tricky, sly, charlatan, impatient.

BOAR

+ gallant, gentle, lively, impulsive, chivalrous, courageous, generous, gregarious, sincere.
– thick-skinned, shallow, vulnerable, materialistic.

DRAGON

+ vital, energetic, magical, fascinating, eager, a self-starter, a doer, scrupulous.
– intolerant, brash, demanding, irritable, tactless, easily bored.

RAT

+ imaginative, clever, intellectually creative, passionate, quick, charming, generous.
– avaricious, anxious, suspicious, calculating, opportunistic.

ROOSTER

+ colourful, creative, bold, sincere, entertaining, brave, positive, high stamina.
– boastful, abrasive, opinionated, given to empty bravado.

SNAKE

+ wise, calm, gentle, intuitive, charismatic, quiet, reserved, elegant, helpful, reflective.
– jealous, clinging, lazy, dishonest, miserly, suffocating, cold.

OX

+ responsible, loyal, methodical, practical, trustworthy, self-reliant, down-to-earth.
– slow, conventional, authoritarian, rude, stubborn, proud.

34

How to tell friend from foe

EACH OF THE TWELVE ANIMALS can be assigned a position on a circle. Those that form a triangle are said to have the greatest affinity, while those directly opposite are usually in conflict. This is as true for your essential being and the travelling companion, as it is for people in the outer world.

The first triangle is made up of the Rat, the Dragon and the Monkey. These are active and self-motivating signs, innovative, full of dynamic energy and future plans.

The second triangle, made up of the Ox, the Snake and the Rooster, is the triangle of constancy and determination. Intellectual and preferring decisions made by the head rather than the heart, they achieve their goals by steadfast grit and purpose.

The third triangle is formed by the Tiger, the Horse and the Dog. They form strong links with others and seek to create avenues of communication and understanding between people. Basically honest, their extrovert and energetic natures allow them to relate well with others.

The fourth triangle is formed by the Rabbit, the Sheep and the Boar. They are guided by their senses and emotions. Peaceful, loving, intuitive and compassionate, they tend to adapt to the energy and drives of the other more assertive and aggresssive signs.

Incompatible pairs, shown below, reveal whether your travelling companion is likely to give you trouble. You can gauge the form any clash might take by comparing the opposing animals and from their characteristics predict the most likely areas of conflict.

ASSESSMENT

This assessment is meant for your outer contacts as well as the inner companion of the previous page. For your friends, family and associates, check their birth dates on the previous page. Then consult the chart opposite and the animal pairs below to see if there is some truth in this ancient typology.

If you recognise traits in yourself and feel identified with the animal that has them, even if it does not fit the traditional yearly interpretation, follow your intuition. If, on reading the descriptions, you have an instant aversion to one particular animal it could well be your own inner travelling companion.

OX   **SHEEP**

DOG   **DRAGON**

ROOSTER   **RABBIT**

HORSE   **RAT**

TIGER   **MONKEY**

BOAR   **SNAKE**

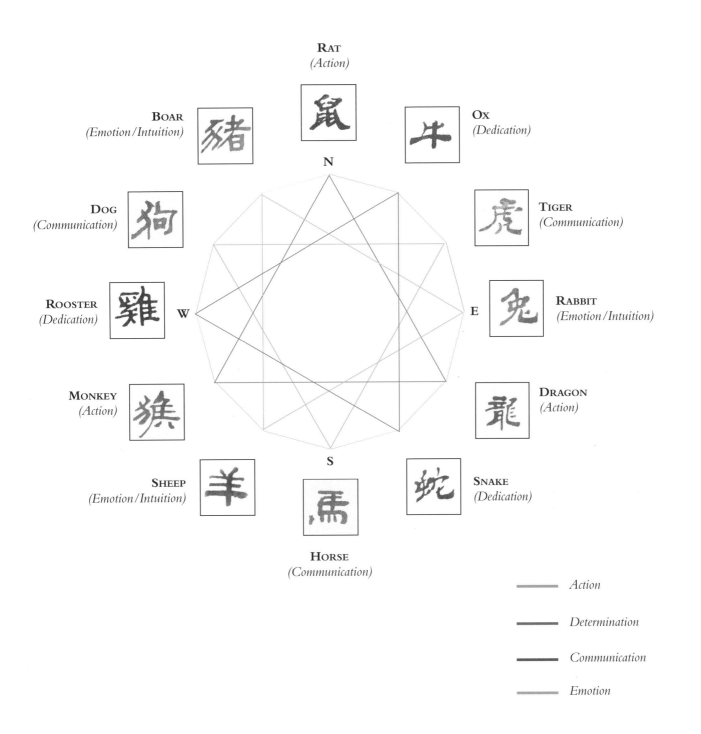

RAT
(Action)

BOAR
(Emotion/Intuition)

OX
(Dedication)

DOG
(Communication)

TIGER
(Communication)

N

ROOSTER
(Dedication)

W

E

RABBIT
(Emotion/Intuition)

MONKEY
(Action)

DRAGON
(Action)

S

SHEEP
(Emotion/Intuition)

SNAKE
(Dedication)

HORSE
(Communication)

Action

Determination

Communication

Emotion

35

BODY/MIND IDENTITY KIT

WHILE THERE IS NO single map on which to chart all your discoveries so far, the mandalas shown below are just two ways of seeing your major physical and behavioural traits at a glance. A sample profile has been created to demonstrate how to use them. [19]

The list on the opposite page shows one woman's response to each assessment. These results are then plotted on the diagrams below to reveal the overall patterns of her type. In the first mandala (below left), which demonstrates a tendency toward thinking, feeling, intuition and sensing, her behavioural patterns tend to gravitate towards the quadrant of "feeling". In the second mandala they cluster in the introverted, unbalanced sectors, leaving the rest of the chart almost empty.

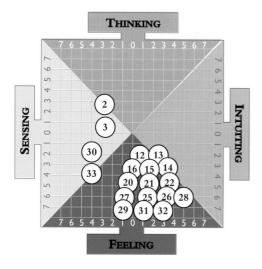

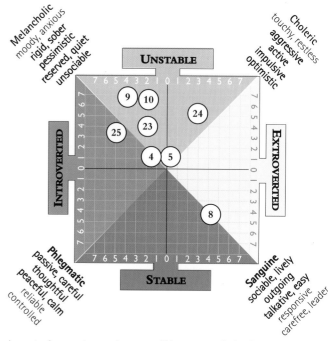

The results from the sample assessment on the opposite page are shown above. In the left-hand mandala most of the results are located in the "feeling" quadrant. The precise location of your assessments in either mandala is determined by where you feel, on a seven-point scale, the results would best fit. For example, in the mandala on the right, the result for assessment **25** was the tendency to freeze when under stress. This outcome is far from any extrovert action, suggesting a **6** on the introvert axis, but is also the typical behaviour of an introspective melancholic, suggesting a **3** on the unstable axis. You can use the descriptions of the original assessments, and also those found in the quadrants of *Sanguine, Phlegmatic, Choleric* and *Melancholic*, as your guide.

A SAMPLE FEMALE ASSESSMENT

(0) *The numbered circle indicates the assessment. The brief description is her resulting evaluation.*

(1) Caucasian, she feels comfortable with her racial characteristics.

(2) Mesomorphic, outward going.

(3) Somatype 531.

(4) G-Index ~ male tendency = 3.

(5) Yin, presence of Yang.

(6) Weight ~ average small in height.

(7) Feels that she is heavier than she really is.

(8) Attractive, accepting, mostly happy.

(9) Top/bottom split. Legs are shorter than personal ideal, and experienced as less supportive and thinner than they actually are.

(10) Oral type, armour in shoulder girdle and legs.

(11) Face ~ triangular

(12) Fire type with a powerful tendency

(13) towards feeling.

(14) Elemental fire, philosophic and

(15) solar hands. Two are heat and fire hands,

(16) one with male trait.

(17) Heart and feeling-oriented palm lines.

(18) Eastern "Element" is fire.

(19) Relates with Earth (Element of long-time partner).

(20) Chinese medicine: the Magician, which is a fire sign.

(21) Ayurvedic sign is *Vata*, which

(22) has a strong element of fire.

(23) Sanguine with Melancholic streak.

(24) Emotional ~ very dominant limbic system.

(25) Under stress becomes paralysed. Strong melancholic-sanguine dichotomy caught between action/non-action.

(26) Emotional brain is dominant.

(27) Strong feelings, sexually expressed

(28) Right-hand brain, dreamer, artist, confirms tendency for introversion

(29) Element ~ Fire

(30) Shadow ~ Earth

(31) Sun sign ~ Leo and Fire sign

(32) Ascendant ~ Leo and Fire sign

(33) Ox ~ Earth (Shadow element in Western astrology)

(34) Compatible with Rat (long-time partner)

 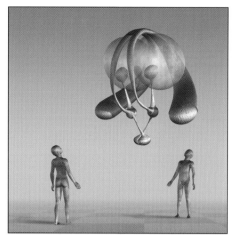 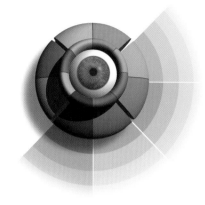

 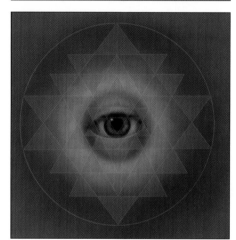 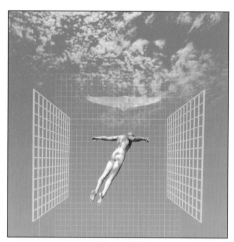

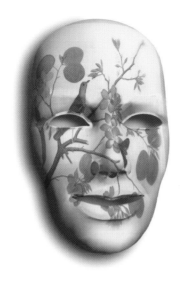

PART II

Feeling types

EMOTIONS ARE MOST difficult to assess for they do not lend themselves easily to testing. The emotional brain, or limbic system, was nature's second evolutionary stroke of genius in the grand design of the neural system, when it added the emotions to our survival-orientated brainstem. This was a quantum leap in the human ability to distinguish between the pleasant and the dangerous or unpleasant.

Curiously, the emotional brain is, in itself, unconscious, although it influences our lives far more than the more recently evolved cortex, the reasoning part of our brain. There are far more neural connections entering the cortex from the emotional brain than vice versa. This effectively means that, when it comes to a crisis, feelings tend to overpower the thinking part of the brain.

The messages from the emotional centre are exchanged with and acted upon by the body long before we are conscious of any changes that have occurred within us. This section outlines some of the dilemmas we face because of this.

36

DO YOUR EMOTIONS RULE YOU?

W E HAVE ALREADY INTRODUCED the concept of the three-tiered brain. Our emotional, or, in evolutionary terms, "mammalian", brain is the most central part of the trio, set deep within the protective shell of the outer cortex. It is more ancient than the cognitive apparatus of the cerebral cortex and so the pathways leading from it far outnumber those returning to it from its thinking, conscious partner. That would not, at least on the surface, appear to be important, as the emotional brain is believed to be completely unconscious. Only when it is activated by some stimulus do its reactions filter up towards the conscious brain. So this relatively small but largely unconscious mechanism, called the limbic system, influences and moulds our behaviour out of all proportion to its size. And in this it is far more powerful than its much larger neighbour, the cortex.

Most of our urges and appetites are either dealt with or originate in this area, which has a number of easily recognized parts, shown in the illustration opposite.[20]

Incoming stimuli are generally registered in the limbic system well before they reach the cortex by more circuitous routes. This often means that an unexpected situation is dealt with *before* the conscious cortex even recognizes the need to respond at all. The consequences of the hormonal and neurotransmitter changes instigated by the limbic area – such as a rise in heart rate or a heightening of blood pressure – happen a second before being consciously registered. Often these experiences are mistaken for emotions rather than the original, direct communication from the limbic system to the cortex. This is not only a vital strategy for survival; it also determines a great deal of our unconscious behaviour.

The traffic between the limbic sytem and the cortex does flow in both directions but, while the direct roads from the limbic system to the cortex are super highways with multiple lanes, the traffic from the cortex back to the limbic system has to be content with country lanes, and very few of them at that. This effectively means that emotions call the shots as far as our unconscious behaviour is concerned, and there is very little we can do about it except to become aware of it.

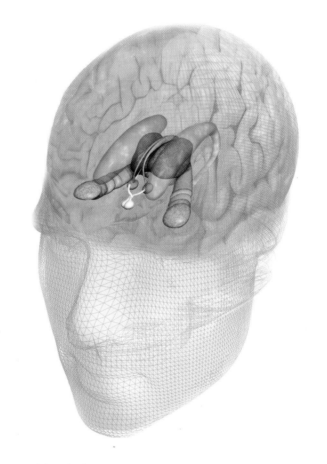

Above: *Although the limbic system, which is the seat of the emotions, is the smallest of the three parts of the brain, its influence over our behaviour is far greater than the other two.*

The Emotional Brain

(a) Thalamus
Allows sight, hearing, smell and touch to be used together. It relays incoming information to the appropriate parts of the brain for processing.

(b) Hypothalamus
Constantly adjusts the body in order to adapt to the conditions found within its immediate environment.

(c) Hippocampus
Is involved in processing long-term memory which it transfers to the cortex in due course.

(d) Amygdala
Generates and registers fear and anxiety as well as having a unique memory system of its own.

(e) Putamen
Controls familiar motor skills. If over-active it can trigger inappropriate skills at odd moments.

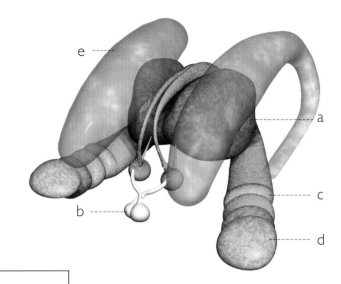

Assessment

Do you:
1. become angry for no reason?
2. control your emotions?
3. sometimes blurt out things you didn't really intend to say?
4. have a fairly even temper?
5. love watching weepy movies?
6. never have strong mood swings?
7. find other's moods affect you?
8. find sad stories a little boring?
9. easily identify the nature of all your emotions?
10. usually remain calm in unexpected or alarming situations?
11. experience vague feelings that you just can't pin down?
12. seldom get shocked by your unexpected emotions?
13. find that your emotions sometimes dominate your reasoning?
14. find it easy to control your feelings?
15. sometimes feel overwhelmed by inexpressible feelings?
16. like to analyze a work of art to see how it ticks?
17. like a painting even when others say it's poorly executed?
18. distrust some of your wilder feelings?
19. find your emotions enslave you?
20. consider that being over-emotional is a sign of weakness?

Key: If you answer "yes" to more than 7 of the odd numbered questions and "no" to more than 7 of the even numbered questions, you have a definite tendency to be ruled by your emotions. Reverse the "yes" and "no" and you have a distinct tendency to control your emotions.

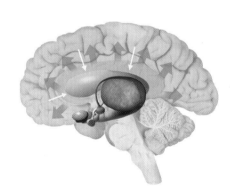

Top: *The major components of the limbic, or emotional, brain.* Above: *The pathways from the limbic system far outnumber those coming from the cortex.*

37

ARE YOU IN TOUCH WITH YOUR EMOTIONS?

SOME OF THE FOLLOWING psychological tests may at first seem to have a negative bias. Psychology is, by its very nature, concerned with dysfunction rather than health. While psycho-healers and practitioners strive for integrity, balance and harmony in their patients, they seldom define what the naturally healthy, and presumably joyful, human state might be. Happiness is therefore often defined as the absence of unhappiness. It is obviously a condition where there is neither physical nor emotional pain. Any psychologist knows it does not include fear, anxiety (a frozen fear) or stress. Its two essentially positive traits are a feeling of well-being and a sense of meaning.

This tendency to describe being well in terms of not being unwell is partly due to the fact that our emotional roots are almost all unconscious. The emotional brain requires a conscious partner to interpret what it feels. This is normally where the cortex comes in, although it appears that Nature is still working on the links between the three evolutionary brains as there are often misunderstandings and faults in the hard-wiring between them. While Nature is perfecting its artwork we remain un-blissfully unaware of what really is going on inside our heads.

However, the moment our unconscious behaviour is brought to our awareness, it immediately changes. Most of the following assessments are devised to reveal how your emotional, unconscious centre continues to dominate your actions without your waking consent. Becoming aware of its actions is the first step towards taking conscious charge of how you behave.

ASSESSMENT

Do you:
1. *feel some music brings uncontrollable tears?*
2. *feel affected by a sob story?*
3. *indulge in emotional reactions?*
4. *enjoy being sentimental?*
5. *enjoy dramatic outpourings from others?*
6. *enjoy expressing your emotions to others?*
7. *feel helpless and depressed for no reason?*
8. *cry in the cinema?*
9. *prefer emotional highs to a job well done?*
10. *often feel inflamed by irrational urges?*
11. *feel you are considered to be a space-case and yet don't really know why?*
12. *cry when something touches you deeply?*
13. *tend to be emotional rather than intellectual?*
14. *trust your feelings about someone rather than excellent references and a CV?*
15. *feel that irrational fears tend to influence your life?*
16. *feel that the heart is usually a better judge than the head?*
17. *feel that you are over-sentimental or romantic sometimes?*
18. *feel that you are easily upset even by trivial occurrences?*
19. *often feel nervous even when there is no direct threat?*
20. *hate planning ahead?*

Key: If you answer "yes" to more than 12 of these questions you are well in touch with your feelings and emotions. If your score is higher than 16, you are decidedly more emotional than most.
If you answer "no" to more than 11 of these questions you are more head-oriented. If your score is higher than 15, you probably have real difficulties being in touch with your feelings.

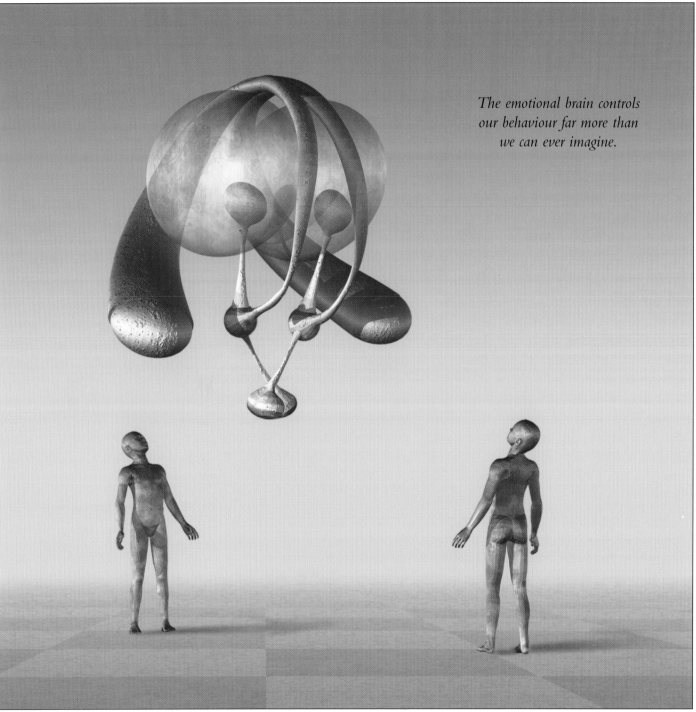

The emotional brain controls our behaviour far more than we can ever imagine.

38

ARE YOU TRAPPED OR FREE?

THE SIMPLE MECHANISM of reward and punishment employed by the limbic system seems to be expressed as feelings of expansion and contraction. In all our experiences of well-being, euphoria, ecstasy and meaningfulness, the overwhelming sense is that of an expansion of consciousness, of feeling boundless and free. In a greatly extended form this orgasmic experience is present in every religious and mystical tradition. "Expansion of consciousness" is a term used by most religions and is particularly popular today. Its polar opposite is the limited and contracted consciousness that is the lot of most of us. The pain, anguish, depression and sense of being imprisoned is only too common in modern psychological dysfunctions.

Yet we strive to embrace the limitless. Some do it through mind- or mood-altering drugs or alcohol, others through the temporary sense of freedom that romance, the acquisition of money or power seems to provide. Some even do it through their body, in risky sports like skydiving or mountain climbing.

Happiness and misery are increasingly found to be due to the effect of our own under- or over-privileged chemical plants. While much of our physical functioning is out of our immediate control, changes in conscious attention have been known to alter the chemistry of the emotional system. An increase in awareness creates a greater chance to alter the nature of our unconscious patterns of behaviour.

Within the brain different types of cell secrete some fifty separate neurotransmitters – biochemical substances that transmit nerve impulses from one cell to another. The six most important of these have been isolated as:

SERATONIN

The neurotransmitter that is enhanced by the most popular anti-depressant, the "feel-good" chemical Prozac, that has such a profound effect on mood and anxiety. It creates serenity, a sense of calm and optimism.

ACETYCHOLINE

Associated with attention, memory and learning.

NORADRENALINE

Excitatory chemical creating mental arousal and heightening of mood.

GLUTAMATE

Excitatory neurotransmitter that helps create links between neurons. It also forms the basis for long-term memory and learning.

ENCEPHALINS AND ENDORPHINS

Counteract pain and stress and give a floating sensation of inner calm.

ASSESSMENT

Make two lists, each on a separate sheet of paper. On one sheet list those experiences that create feelings of expansion in you, those that you find delight in. They could include the pleasure of the smell of new bread or gazing at a sunlit ocean. On the other list those experiences that make you feel contracted, like an acutely embarrassing situation or anxiety about your bank balance. Take at least ten minutes to compile them and see how many experiences you can come up with in that time. Then check the lists. Whichever is the longer or was most easily compiled — expansive or contractive — will give you a clear indication of the present state of your emotional brain and of your likely corresponding behaviour. The very act of making such a list will actually begin to change it. You will have brought it to consciousness.

Birds make great sky-circles
of their freedom.
How do they learn it?

They fall, and falling,
they're given wings.

Jalal ud-Din Rumi
(Sufi mystic)

39

HOW JOYFUL ARE YOU?

AS WE HAVE SEEN, modern psychologists have not been very forthcoming when asked to define a healthy psychological state. Typologies tend to define health by what it is not – for instance, happiness, which one would imagine is fairly clear cut, is described as the absence of negative emotion.

Many of the assessments based upon psychological models suffer from this lack of a positive base, giving as they do, too much emphasis to negative factors. Yet this also highlights the underlying fact that many of our unconscious strategies are basically negative. As the emotional mind is largely unconscious, by design, and as the wiring of the brain definitely favours emotions, then by implication the major part of our lives is actually unconscious. Mystics have been trying to tell us this for millennia and modern neurological research is now increasingly confirming this view.

In order to raise our consciousness at least one notch let us consider the anatomy of happiness. Neurologists tell us that happiness is a difficult-to-define cocktail of physical pleasure, absence of pain, sense of meaning and a feeling of well-being.

Much of the pleasure is caused by the reward of the neurotransmitter dopamine. One intriguing reason that scientists define happiness by an absence of negative emotion is that it can be exactly that. The action of the amygdala, which is responsible for anxiety, fear and negative feelings, is dampened, thus allowing the sense of well-being to be felt to the full.[21]

Strange to acknowledge is the fact that women, in general, are more attuned to the sad, right-hand hemisphere, while men favour the happy left. However, women have greater access to both sides and tend to use both hemispheres more than men.

ASSESSMENT

Do you:
1. *often wake up in the mornings depressed for no reason?*
2. *agree with William Blake that "Energy is Delight"?*
3. *sometimes feel life has dealt you a rotten hand?*
4. *tend to dance whenever you hear music you like?*
5. *tend to become serious when tired?*
6. *enjoy most of the things that you do?*
7. *often feel drained of energy?*
8. *laugh a lot at situations that others don't find funny?*
9. *get irritated when people insist that you enjoy yourself?*
10. *often have an excess of energy that bubbles up?*
11. *sometimes see little meaning in your life?*
12. *try to resist laughing when people are serious over trifles?*
13. *find jovial and boisterous friends too much sometimes?*
14. *suddenly start singing without thinking?*
15. *sometimes do not care what happens to you?*
16. *generally feel in good spirits and full of energy?*
17. *feel it is always someone else who gets the breaks?*
18. *just enjoy life as it comes without worrying about later?*
19. *forget when last you felt on top of the world?*
20. *feel grateful for being alive?*

Key: If you answer "yes" to 8 or more of the odd *numbered questions, your amygdala is working overtime.*
*If you answer "yes" to 8 or more of the even *numbered questions, you are probably joyful, with more than your fair share of dopamine flooding your system.*

THE CHEMICAL PATHWAYS OF HAPPINESS

Happiness does not appear to be a single state and the attempts to define it are often reduced to naming what is absent when happiness is being experienced. It would seem that the very foundation of joy requires that either pain or negative emotions are absent.

The positive components, however, are often defined as physical pleasure and an overall sense of well-being and meaningfulness. The sense of well-being is largely the result of a flood of dopamine throughout the reward system. This appears to be felt mostly in an area of the pre-frontal cortex, which brings a sense of the cohesiveness of all and everything. When this area is deprived of the necessary neurotransmitters, a person feels depressed and the world appears fragmentary and meaningless.

The true villain, however, remains the amygdala, which is always more than ready to generate negative emotions of anxiety, sorrow and fear. Working on something that holds our attention tends to soothe the amygdala, which may account for the popular homily that work is a cure for the blues.

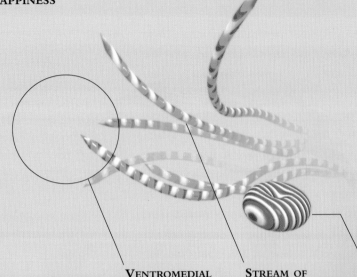

VENTROMEDIAL PRE-FRONTAL CORTEX

Not actually part of the limbic system, but closely connected and responsible for the creation of all-pervading sense of well-being. However, if over stimulated it is said to be a possible cause of mania.

STREAM OF REWARD-GIVING DOPAMINE

This neurotransmitter floods the brain reaching into the whole cortex. This effectively creates the euphoric and joyful states that in their turn suppress the action around the amygdala which is always ready to generate anxiety and gloom.

AMYGDALA

Dedicated to generating the negative emotions of anxiety and fear, this tiny centre is one of the primary survival strategists, but is often guilty of sending messages of gloom and doom at totally inappropriate times.

40

THE EBB AND FLOW OF DOPAMINE TIDES

THE NEUROTRANSMITTER DOPAMINE is increasingly seen by researchers as the major player in many of the extreme dysfunctions of the brain.[22] Too much of this chemical appears to cause hallucinations, paranoia, over-excitement, euphoria and exaggerated feelings of meaningfulness. Too little, however, brings feelings of meaninglessness, lethargy, misery, depression, lack of attention and withdrawal.

The cells that produce dopamine are distributed along three quite distinct riverbeds of the brain. These are subject to periodic flashfloods that dramatically change your behaviour. As they are interconnected, a surge through one channel can bring about activity in another. Few of us experience the extreme behavioural symptoms this can cause, but we all know those sudden moments of eccentric behaviour that cannot be easily explained in rational terms. This demonstrates how little conscious choice we have over much of our behaviour. Our conscious feelings are often a response to secondary chemical effects that have been instigated milliseconds before by the unconscious emotional system. The system might register danger; the heart rate rises and you respond to the pumping heart and not to the original stimulus. We are acted *upon* rather than being in control of our emotions. Once the rivers of chemicals begin to rise, or drain away, we are truly helpless bystanders on the river bank – witnesses of our own unconscious tides.

The old Taoist teaching of "go with the flow" is, in reality, one we cannot help but accept. Don't fight the current, but learn to be alert to the unconscious forces that determine so much of who we are and how we act. A deep acceptance of this natural condition immediately relaxes a person, for then there is no reason to feel guilty about patterns of behaviour that are probably largely beyond our conscious control.

ASSESSMENT

Identify those feelings you might have had when you were under real or imagined stress. Select from the brief lists below those states with which you most identify. If the score of one column exceeds the other by three or more, you are likely to be strongly influenced by the ebb and flow of your powerful dopamine tides.

EBB
Feeling of meaninglessness
Lethargy
Dulled feeling of inertia
Depression and misery
Social withdrawal
Lack of concentration and attention
Craving to fill inner emptiness
Difficulty in self-starting
Tremors and dreary states
Sense of numbness and void
Paralysis and lack of energy

FLOW
Sense of significance
Uncontrolled movement
Restlessness
Hallucinations
Paranoia
Agitation
Over-excitement
Euphoric states that don't last
Manic exaggeration
Sense of fullness
Energetic over-action

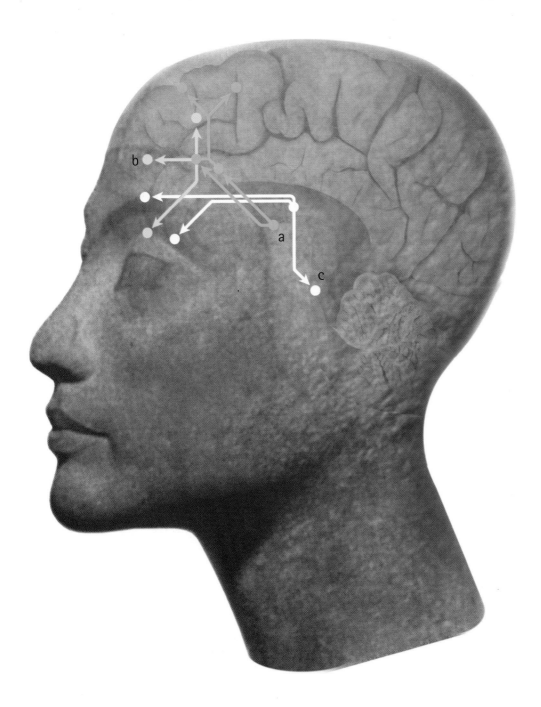

THE THREE MAIN RIVERS OF DOPAMINE AND THEIR EFFECTS

(a) From a nucleus in the brainstem this route travels up through an area which controls automatic movement. It continues to the motor cortex that sends messages to the body. A surge of dopamine here gives us the impetus to move. A lack of dopamine produces dysfunctions in our movement.

(b) This route covers the area of the pre-frontal cortex, which is responsible for our conscious desire to act. Lack of dopamine in this area is thought to cause lethargy and depressions that rob us of our will to do anything.

(c) This route starts in the brainstem and ends in the cortical area devoted to emotions. Too much dopamine and you can become manic — too little and you are likely to become miserable.

41

ARE YOU PHOBIC?

IN SOME FORM OR ANOTHER we all harbour irrational fears that are completely disproportionate to the actual degree of threat. Usually known as phobias, these conditioned fears leave the conscious mind as an impotent bystander.

An irrational terror of butterflies, for example, can seriously disrupt a person's life during the summer months. While the subject can rationally accept there is nothing harmful in the insect, he or she experiences a mindless panic as soon as one flutters innocently past.

Neural research[22] suggests that a phobia is caused by a glitch in the messages to and from the emotional centre. As shown in the illustration, information entering the thalamus is normally shunted in two directions. One is a slow route to the cortex, while the other is what the neurologist Joseph LeDoux calls the "dirty route". This shortcut effectively means that the amygdala has advance warning that something potentially threatening might be happening. In milliseconds the vague fluttering of wings has been checked against its tiny unconscious memory store and bingo! – something vague but threatening appears to be there. The amygdala instigates frenzied action to avoid the threat by signalling the hypothalamus to either fight or flight. The subject rushes into the house and shuts all the doors. About this time, information has been passed to the amygdala from the conscious brain which has checked its records on butterflies and sent the results along the more leisurely route. "Nothing to worry about", is the message. "Stand very still and we can watch this harmless and beautiful creature." The amygdala is having nothing of this. Having caused such an avalanche of stress hormones microseconds before, it is now really over-excited, and so frenzied that it is still at panic stations.

How did this tiny memory get burned into its neurons? It could be some chance event, such as being slapped as a child just at the moment you saw a butterfly for the first time.

A conditioned circuit of fear was born at that moment. You may therefore re-experience the unconscious trauma and nothing will convince you otherwise. Many of us who suffer from vague anxieties and groundless fears share the same essential ingredients as those generated by butterfly-terror.

Incoming signals are dealt with by the thalamus (a) which sends one signal to the amygdala (b). The second signal is sent via the cortex (c) by a long route to the amygdala. But by the time the conscious thought returns, the amygdala has already made the adjustments through the shortcut (d) and we experience the effects as if it was an original emotion.

ASSESSMENT

Check the list on the right for some of your most abiding social anxieties. While some of these can actually turn into phobias, you will recognize that most are pretty groundless and out of all proportion to any actual danger. Some of us fear authority, others having to make a speech or asking someone for a date.

Reconsider your fears in the light of the physiological explanation on this page and attempt to remember it when next you have to deal with an anxiety or phobia. You may not be able to control such powerful conditioned cycles, but an understanding of their possible causes and an acceptance that they will have to run their course actually reduces the stress levels and the frantic panic of the amygdala. Fear is one thing, but a fear of the fear increases it a hundredfold.

ANXIETIES AND PHOBIAS	NOT ANXIOUS	ANXIOUS	TERRIFIED
1. Talking to those in authority.	☐	☐	☐
2. Introducing yourself to a group.	☐	☐	☐
3. Someone asking you the way.	☐	☐	☐
4. Staying at home alone.	☐	☐	☐
5. Being watched while working.	☐	☐	☐
6. Complaining about restaurant food.	☐	☐	☐
7. Asking someone directions.	☐	☐	☐
8. Asking a friend for a date.	☐	☐	☐
9. Having a coffee in a cafe alone.	☐	☐	☐
10. Being praised in front of others.	☐	☐	☐
11. Going to the cinema alone.	☐	☐	☐
12. Going to a dance or the disco.	☐	☐	☐
13. Telling people about yourself.	☐	☐	☐
14. Walking in a crowded street.	☐	☐	☐
15. Sitting facing people on the train.	☐	☐	☐
16. Going for a job interview.	☐	☐	☐
17. Telling someone to do something.	☐	☐	☐
18. Going to a party.	☐	☐	☐
19. Making conversation and small talk.	☐	☐	☐
20. Eating a meal in a restaurant alone.	☐	☐	☐
21. Going to a friend's house for a meal.	☐	☐	☐
22. Being in warm, enclosed spaces.	☐	☐	☐
23. Facing criticism from others.	☐	☐	☐
24. Being given a present.	☐	☐	☐
25. Telling a person who queue jumps to go to the back.	☐	☐	☐

Key: A score of 20 or more in the left-hand column shows you are unusually calm and easy-going. A score of 15 or more in the middle column reveals you are just like most of us.

Over 10 in the right-hand column suggests your best strategy is to take time to relax, understand the mechanism of phobias and accept them. True acceptance, relaxation and a sense of humour are the keys.

42

WHICH MARY ARE YOU?

THERE IS HISTORICAL EVIDENCE to support the idea that the Temple in Jerusalem had a tower representing the Great Goddess in her triple aspect long before the advent of Christianity. The name of this goddess was Mari.[23] She appeared as a maiden, a nymph and a crone. The Christian New Testament also tells of three Marys – Mary the mother of Christ, Mary the annointer of Christ, and Mary Magdalene or "she of the temple tower" who was believed to be his favourite disciple.[24] This triple aspect can be seen as true for every woman. Here the characterization is encapsulated in an archetypal form revealing the three stages of the female life-cycle – the pre-menstrual maiden, the fertile menstrual nymph and childbearer and the post-menopausal matriarch.

It is no coincidence that the assessments concerned with the emotional brain are oriented towards women. The female has considerable physiological advantages over the male as far as emotional responses are concerned. It has been observed, for instance, that the right-hand hemisphere of a woman lights up with a heightened alertness in the limbic system when emotional stimuli are administered.

The other, and perhaps more significant, difference between men and women is the direct link that exists between the limbic system and the womb. From the age of about eleven until four decades later the female is locked into the life-tides and cycles of reproduction and nurturing. Willing, or carried kicking and screaming, women have to pass through a series of dramatic initiations that are totally alien to the male.

Only a woman can experience the onset of menstruation, the acute pain of childbirth, the suckling and nurturing of the child, and the final passage through difficult years adjusting to the withdrawal of the powerful hormonal tides created by the emotional brain. For some this is an ecstatic and life-fulfilling period of their lives. Yet there are others, especially in these modern times, who wish for the freedom and simplicity of the male's lot. But it is only as a woman that you have the real possibility of becoming conscious of the inner workings of the life-cycle.

While part of the whole female life-cycle, each of these three modes can also be seen as an independent archetype.

ASSESSMENT

While each of these three female modes are a part of the whole sequence of the life-cycle, they can also be seen as archetypes. These are designated the Maiden, the Nymph and the Matriarch.

Consider whether one of the three types or stages definitely appeals to you, irrespective of your age. For instance, you might be a thirty-something career woman with children of your own and yet long for the relative freedom and uncomplicated state of the maiden. This sense of being equal and independent in a male world might be the essential core of your personality. Keep your chosen image in mind when you turn to the next page.

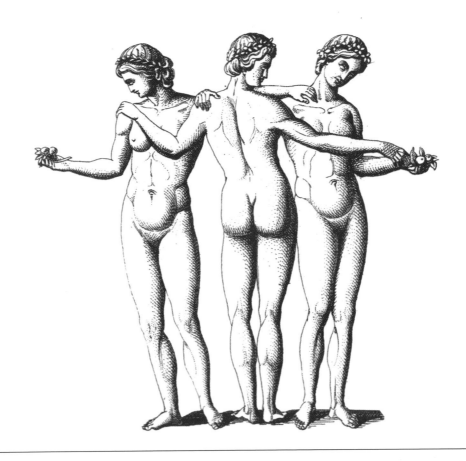

THE THREE MARYS

THE MAIDEN

The innocent girl-child who is almost indistinguishable from the boy-child.

Her aspirations are a quest for knowledge and discovery. Free of any responsibilities and of the moon's tides, she relates easily to the male world. She is fiercely independent in her thinking and is steadfastly unattached. Sex is at most an exciting and romantic idea, yet has no emotional, or overpowering life-charge. Idealized roles, a strong ambition, independence, the power of the shamaness, and the potency of accomplishment make this type's dreams.

THE NYMPH

The menstrual, nubile and child-bearing woman.

This type freely enters the female cycles, celebrating a new-found sense of potential and richness. She also embraces the obligation of being a biological channel for the continuation of life, of renewal and rebirth.
This is the inner experience of life-giving, of mystical marriages, relationships and interdependence with the male counterpart.

THE MATRIARCH

The archetypal female who has the power of wisdom and experience.

She is the ruler, the great mother who can either follow the Empress path of the outer, phenomenal world of politics, social planning, growth and nurturing, or the numinous path of the spiritual, in which she enters the realm of the sacred from an essentially female viewpoint, independent of the male.

43

THE GODDESS WHEEL

JUNGIAN PSYCHOLOGY, with its rich mythical and archetypal imagery, has given birth to a variety of therapy systems. The unique feminine language of the Goddess Wheel is a powerful example.[25]

In this particular assessment your inner states and behaviour, as well as those of the women around you, can be intuitively recognized within a mythic setting. Each of six Greek goddesses is seen as the psychological expression of a dynamic, ever-changing female character type. Each of the three female modes from the previous page is represented by two figures – one essentially extrovert and the other introvert. By translating our everyday experiences into a mythic realm we return to a richer and more emotionally charged setting, bringing to life the deeper meaning of the archetypes.

APHRODITE

(Outward going/menstrual)

The archetypical goddess of love, relationships, sensuality, romance, the arts and inspiration. Aphrodite is sexual and interdependent, requiring the other as a source of pleasure in the life-cycle.
She embodies feeling through the senses with an acute awareness of beauty.

PERSEPHONE

(Inward looking/menstrual)

The archetypal medium concerned with the spirit world, the occult, visionary and mystical experience, death and transfiguration. Persephone rules the passages to the underworld and the unconscious mind, and is in contact with the life-cycles at an intuitive level. Less in touch with her sexuality, she lives in the twilight world of dreams. She embodies feeling through intuition.

ATHENE

(Outward going/pre-menstrual)

She is the most intellectual of the six, concerned with all aspects of city and urban life. She rules technology, science, education and all things of the mind. In the modern world she is the ambitious career woman who relates easily to the male world.
Athene embodies feeling through the intellect.

HERA

(Outward going/menopause)

The archetype of power, sovereignty and rulership. As Zeus' wife, Hera presides over marriage, partnership and power. Abiding by social morality and traditional values, she is the Empress who rules in equality with the Emperor. The supreme extrovert, Hera embodies feeling through power and outward display.

ARTEMIS

(Inward looking/pre-menstrual)

The antithesis of the man-made world of Athene, Artemis is the goddess of untamed nature.
She is concerned with the instinctual blood nature of the life-cycle; she is the shamaness of the physical world. Artemis embodies feeling through the moon and natural instinct.

DEMETER

(Inward looking/menopause)

The archetype of motherhood, of the inner experience of the whole life-cycle of reproduction and life giving. Demeter embodies all aspects of growth, from the seed to the flower. She needs to nurture and care for all young organic growing things. She embodies feeling through nurturing and the womb.

ASSESSMENT

The illustration features three pairs of extrovert and introvert Greek goddesses. Trust your intuition to choose which of the six goddesses best describes you.

Even though the descriptions are defined by the chronology of the life-cycle, your choice of goddess does not necessarily have to correspond to your actual age.

MAIDEN	Athene ~ *Extrovert*	
	Artemis ~ *Introvert*	
NYMPH	Venus ~ *Extrovert*	
	Persephone ~ *Introvert*	
MATRIARCH	Hera ~ *Extrovert*	
	Demeter ~ *Introvert*	

44

WHO IS YOUR INNER PARTNER?

ONE OF THE MOST REVEALING typological systems[26] shows each goddess relating to the male principle, either to its outward display, or its inner manifestation as the animus. The animus is the masculine component within every woman which finds outward expression in the choice of a complementary partner.

The choice of a male companion is thus often an indication of the shape of the inner male, or of those masculine principles towards which each goddess type tends to gravitate.

Yet it is also a reverse mirror, for the man can see his own female anima reflected in the particular coupling.

The following descriptions are typical of many of the workshops and therapies for women that have appeared over the last two decades.

APHRODITE

Relates to the male principle as either a lover or warrior. She enjoys male virility above all else. This powerful life-force can be expressed in either sexuality or creativity as Aphrodite often acts as *la femme inspiratrice* or muse to the objects of her love. Animus ~ A vital and energetic lover like Ares, the Greek god of war.

PERSEPHONE

Relates to the inner man, involuntarily inviting highly powerful and sometimes destructive partners like her own Lord of the Underworld. Her conscious choice, however, is for less threatening men whom she can easily manipulate through her psychic gifts. Her sexuality is largely subsumed into the mystical experience. Animus ~ A dark shadow lover like Hades.

ATHENE

Relates to the male who is likely to be viewed as a heroic companion in arms. He is likely to be in authority ~ the Zeus-like father figure ~ idealized as a personal or even impersonal authority in the form of a corporation, an institution, or a political or spiritual ideal. Animus ~ A strong patriarchal figure like Zeus.

HERA

Relates as an equal partner who expects to share the man's worldly power and prestige. She is likely to be completely monogamous, attracted as she is to the masculine energy of rulership. Requires a husband who subscribes to marriage and social dominance. Animus ~ A strong marital partner, preferably as powerful as Zeus.

ARTEMIS

Has such a powerful male energy that she seldom needs any complementary relationship of interdependence. She does, however, enjoy a male companion who respects her need for independence and freedom. Often sexually reticent, she requires a man to be reserved and patient. Animus ~ A friend, companion or brother figure like Apollo.

DEMETER

Relates to men, not through sexuality for its own sake, but as a means to procreate. Requires a mate to be reliable, offering the security of a protected nest to allow her overabundant mother energies to flower. However, she tends to mother all men, turning them into sons, and thus creates heroes. Animus ~ Son/hero like the mythical teacher of agriculture, Triptolemus.

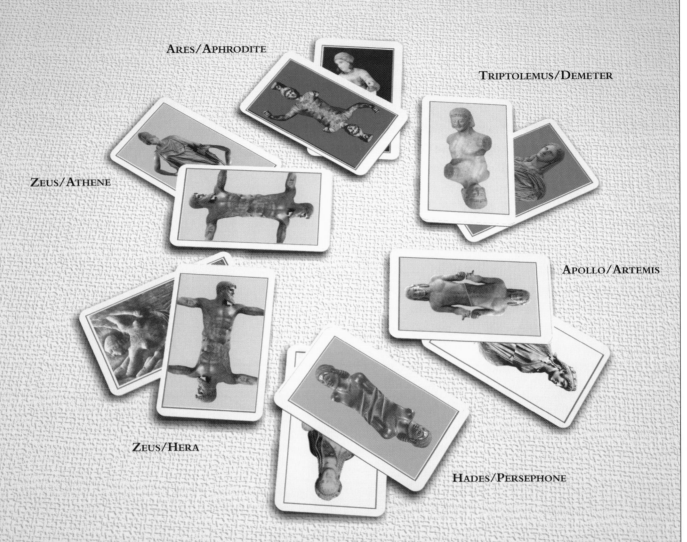

ARES/APHRODITE

TRIPTOLEMUS/DEMETER

ZEUS/ATHENE

APOLLO/ARTEMIS

ZEUS/HERA

HADES/PERSEPHONE

ASSESSMENT

The list opposite indicates the nature of the animus of each goddess type and the male to whom she is most likely to respond. If you are a woman, you can make an assessment by choosing the goddess who most resembles you. Observe whether the companions you find most attractive in your own life fit the description of the animus of your chosen goddess type. If this is the case, it confirms that your reading of both the goddess and her male companion is accurate. If you are a man, check which goddess most appeals to you and then observe whether her animus is a fair description of your general character.

It is likely that you will choose the pair that corresponds to your own female side – your anima. It has long been established that we all have the tendency to project our own animus or anima onto our chosen partners.

45

EYE OF THE WOMB

THIS SIMPLE MANDALA of four types might finally sharpen a woman's image in the mirror. The Maiden, the Nymph, the Child Bearer and the Wise Woman are inextricably linked, both in essence and in time. While a man is hardly affected by nature's life-cycle, a woman experiences the entire spectrum of its demanding tides. These flows are the chemicals and hormones created by your unconscious limbic brain.

This diagram represents a holistic blueprint of past, present and future, located within your limbic area waiting to be triggered. Each woman tends towards one polarity or another during certain times of her life, and yet the psychological phases don't always fit either their appointed times, or the physical cycles. A post-menopausal woman might long to bear a child; her abundant, pregnant energy has to be transformed in some creative activity, or one of personal rebirth. A young mother suddenly longs for the freedom of the maiden, instead of fulfilling the insistent demands of child nurturing. Some women will do everything they can to avoid what they see as a biological cage – becoming the career woman who has entered her father's world in which freedom from the life-tides is taken for granted. Such a person might keep men, or even her own body, at a distance in order to pursue her chosen vocation unhindered. An Athene figure might rail against the monthly reminder that freedom from her cycle comes at a cost. This type, which is increasingly expressed today, has a complex and highly evolved attitude which values achievement, independence and the pursuit of a career above submission to the hormonal flow leading to the cradle.

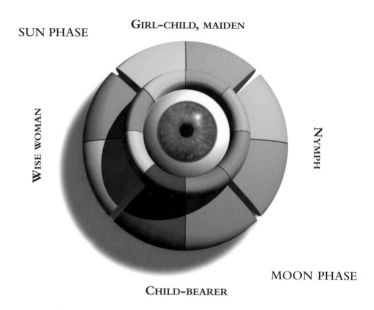

SUN PHASE   GIRL-CHILD, MAIDEN   NYMPH

WISE WOMAN

CHILD-BEARER   MOON PHASE

ASSESSMENT

The four axes of the mandala on the opposite page represent the four stages in a woman's life that are controlled at an unconscious level in the emotional brain. While each stage is part of a sequence in time, it is also the blueprint of a chosen lifestyle. Try to assess your own character from the descriptions and to identify whether you are either joyfully accepting, or heroically resisting the enforced forty-odd years of hormonal activity.

While each stage can be seen as an essential type, few women remain in one aspect for long. Yet many women do find that their psychological attitudes do not always synchronize with their physical and hormonal changes – some being totally inappropriate to the present moment.

GIRL-CHILD, MAIDEN *LIFE-EXPLORER*

Outward orientation
Intellectual curiosity, body oriented, boyish behaviour, exploratory, competitive, bond-link with father. Relates to the father's world, fascinated with the phenomenal world, assertive, aggressive, adventurous, independent.

Inward orientation
Enjoyment of being alone, love of beauty, fascination with the numinous worlds of imagination, concerned with exploring emotional themes, romantic, visionary, enjoys fantasy and creative imagination. Relates to mother, outwardly passive and receptive, yet often rebellious inside.

WISE WOMAN *LIFE-REFLECTOR*

Outward orientation
Released from the biological cycle, this woman is free to follow her inclinations. Re-empowered, she is like the girl-child again with the experience of the moon's sphere of influence. A worldly wise woman respecting traditional values and the continuing cohesiveness of both small and large communities. Strongly moral, an empress, stateswoman, diplomat, matriarch, councillor and judge.

Inward orientation
The body becomes a sacred vessel. This is the wise woman as the spiritual mother, mystic and shamaness. She knows through direct experience and celebrates the holistic process of the life-cycle. Remains deeply in touch with her emotional centre.

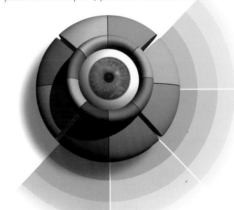

NYMPH, MENSTRUAL *LIFE-RELATING*

Outward orientation
Preoccupation with a profession, career, knowledge, intellect, relating to the patriarchal world. Fascinated with the man-made world of the city. Independent, sees menstruation as a necessary ill but is resistant to it. Puts career before family life, is ambitious, a female bachelor, sexually independent, and seeks friendships rather than shared bonding. Sees the body as a desirable object to adorn and be adorned.

Inward orientation
Concern with the wild and untamed aspect of nature. A shamaness and witch, intuitive, instinctual, favouring nature rather than the man-made. Emphasizes the body more than the head. Embraces the moon-cycles deeply and instinctively. Feels the body as a sacred and beautiful love object. Is concerned with the male in order to release sensual and sexual tension.

CHILD-BEARER *LIFE-GIVER*

Outward orientation
Fulfilment in child-bearing, nourishing and caring for infants. Embraces her role within the life-giving cycle, finds physical pleasure in menstruation and the reproductive processes. A natural lover of all organic growth, from seed to flower. The protector of the family, the home, clan, tribe, marriage and traditional cohesion in the larger community. Traditional and conservative.

Inward orientation
Sense of the mystical beauty of the inner life-cycles. Most potentially aware of the emotional tides but often swept away in hormonal storms. Deeply intuitive in all matters of the moon. Sees the body as a sacred vessel.

46

GRAIL SYMBOLS OF THE MALE ARCHETYPES

KING

KNIGHT

LOVER/
TROUBADOR

MAGE

ASSESSMENT

These archetypes are not static principles; rather they are like ingredients that are constantly in the process of being added in different proportions. These combinations determine your make-up at the present moment.

Assign a number between 1 and 7 for each of the types; 1 being not identified, 7 being strongly identified, while 4 is mid-point. The combination of these four will give you a very clear indication of your own character at this point in time. It is important to recognize that each type is always in transition, always restless, seeking to integrate and harmonize the whole.

PERHAPS CARL GUSTAV JUNG'S greatest gift to the twentieth century was the re-invention of the mandala, both as a diagram of axes showing the relationship of archetypal polarities and as a mythological map for our time. In this next popular typology,[27] found in many forms and therapies, we discover four aspects of the essential male psychological and emotional potential.

The four masculine concepts of King, Knight, Mage and Lover/Troubador can be seen in myth, legend, literature, drama and the media figures of modern times. Perhaps these figures are most clearly seen in the legend of the Holy Grail. The story of the Grail hinges upon the fact that we are moulded by the programmes of our particular societies and religions. We lose the natural ability to respond to our real feelings because they are overwritten by social codes of behaviour. The hero of the Grail finally discovers his own natural feelings through his quest for the Grail, and in doing so heals the wounded Fisher King, which is another aspect of himself.

Men, by virtue of their neurological hard-wiring, appear to have greater difficulty in getting in touch with their emotions than women. However, the very nature of myth creates an emotional charge far in excess of what the story appears to be saying, and is perfectly suited to those of this sensibility. Mythical characters encapsulate archetypes that we respond to unconsciously with our feelings, untouched by what the male-oriented cortex has to say.

By identifying which of these four archetypes best fits your own personality, you will begin to understand which of the four aspects determines much of your unconscious behaviour and lifestyle.

THE DISC

THE SWORD

THE SPEAR

THE CHALICE

King ~ *Principle of leadership, visionary and traditional*

This is the father energy, the overlord and god. The ruler of the realms of both the conscious and unconscious brain ~ the bringer of order out of chaos and anarchy. If the inner father falters, is weak or absent then this is revealed in dysfunctional families, tribes and peoples. This state is reflected in the Grail legend in which the Fisher King was maimed, and because of this his realm had turned into a Wasteland. A king in his rightful power will feel centred and be able to view others calmly and dispassionately.

Knight ~ *Principle of change and transformation*

This archetype reaches clarity through living with an awareness of his imminent death. Every deed is done as if it were to be the last. The Knight avoids self-reflection and must follow a stringent programme of discipline and self control. Austere and economical he never expends more energy than required. He is committed to something beyond himself, whether nation, God or tribe. This makes all personal relationships relative and less important than his loyalty to his cause. Once again the Grail knights exhibited this, but the inherent weakness of the type is that, because they are so unreflective and lack the intimacy of personal love, they tend to stick with rules of acceptable behaviour rather than being able to access their own hearts. The Knight requires an outer quest, set within the worthy ideals and the tangible spiritual goals of his chosen commitment. This determines the zeal with which he will attack and destroy anything that stands in the way of that commitment. His decisions don't depend upon personal or emotional relatedness but on the ideal itself. In this he can become a robot, just as happened to Perceval, the hero of the Grail. Only by the contacting the Lover/Troubador did he manage to redeem himself.

Mage ~ *Principle of communication*

The Mage is the repository of knowledge. He is the initiator into the mysteries. He is the archetype of awareness and insight, the silent observer of the mysteries. This is the mysterious figure of Merlin who in some accounts is responsible for the appearance of the Holy Grail itself, while in others he is a shadowy onlooker. This is the magician who is able to give direction to the other archetypes and give them a sense of purpose. It is this figure who can energize these types for both good and bad. The Mage is the channeller of the Self's power, and through its technology and knowledge is able to regulate the psyche as a whole. This is the creator, the maker, the alchemist, the shaman and the scientist.

Lover/Troubador ~ *Principle of relationships*

The Lover/Troubador is the archetype of love and ecstatic joy, but also of pain and anguish. Pain cannot be avoided if there is to be any vitality and depth to joy. The Troubador sings of the pain of love. He feels for himself and is sensitive to how others feel. Close to the unconscious, he is at ease within the emotional territory. He choses to live and express the sense of connectedness he feels within through feeling and through his relationships with others. He is alive and passionate, sensual and sexual, vital in the world of the senses, and true to his intuitive feelings about others. Only when Perceval moves to his Troubador side does he break the mould of the robotic warrior knight he has become and finally asks a true question, full of his own feelings, of the Fisher King ~ and promptly the Wasteland is restored to its natural state.

47

COURTESAN ~ THE INDULGER

WE NOW COME to three basic emotional responses to the outside world which can best be described as moving towards, moving against and moving away from.[28] Each will be examined separately, for we all carry unique combinations of each of these behavioural patterns within us. Once again, remember that the questions in the assessments are more "poetic" than scientific. They offer indications of our basic attitudes toward the environment and those who live in it. The profiles are as true for others as they are for you, and you may start to recognize similar patterns to your own in the behaviour of other people. These basic emotional attitudes have helped to create sensitivities and values as well as to establish habitual anxieties and inhibitions.

The first type is the individual whose strategies are dedicated to moving towards others. The whole psychological drive of the Courtesan is one that involves acting upon another's wishes, and there is an implied docile submissiveness, rather than a genuine desire to please.

This is caused by an overwhelming need for affection and intimacy, often with one particular companion. The Courtesan feels surrounded by threatening forces that must be appeased. However, those perceived as most aggressive and thus most to be feared are the very people the "compliant indulger" needs most to be liked by. In the compulsive desire to belong and be liked, this type tends to overrate his or her shared interests with others. All behaviour arises from the compelling need to be accepted, approved of and appreciated. By attempting to fulfil others' imagined expectations, this type usually loses sight of his or her own feelings.

But this is not the only inherent difficulty the Courtesan encounters. In assuming and actually living the role of being

The over-compliant Courtesan – moving towards others – typifies the first of three emotional defence mechanisms

unselfish, undemanding, over-considerate and grateful, always taking a subordinate role, Courtesans are surprised at how they appear to bear no grudge and are easily reconciled when someone does something to hurt them. They will go out of their way to accept blame when it is inappropriate, will accuse themselves rather than others of inefficiency or some lapse or lack of judgment, and will credit others with being superior, more attractive and more worthwhile than themselves.

Inwardly they feel weak and helpless, are dependent upon the opinion of others, rate themselves and their performance almost entirely on the approval or disapproval of those they regard as their superiors – which is just about everyone – and fall apart when threatened with even mild criticism, rejection or abandonment. They feel most expansive with values like goodness, sympathy, unselfishness, humility, love.

They contract inwardly and are fearful of ambition, power wielding, egotism, insensitivity and callousness. Curiously these negative values also excite them, for they feel the power and apparent strength they imply. This often reinforces their dependence upon aggressive and assertive companions.

ASSESSMENT

Do you:
1. *often feel as if you are used by others?*
2. *feel the need to control others, especially those who have obvious weaknesses of character?*
3. *prefer to let others win at a game when they obviously want to?*
4. *feel that only the fittest and the strong deserve to survive?*
5. *long for close human intimacy?*
6. *tend to see others as mostly hostile, even though they may hide it well?*
7. *feel that everyone should be trusted until they prove otherwise?*
8. *often feel resentful at an insult and if the opportunity arises, pay the other back in kind?*
9. *find criticism of your person or your work hard to take and often hurtful?*
10. *seldom feel helpless and weak?*
11. *fear being abandoned or deserted by your friends?*
12. *tend to confront people rather than avoiding a scene?*
13. *prefer being with one special person who understands you rather than finding exciting new partners?*
14. *seek redress for some wrong done to you?*
15. *leave the limelight for others who seem to need it?*
16. *enjoy being the centre of attention?*
17. *feel surprised at how easily you forgive an insult and are able to seek reconciliation?*
18. *find it difficult to sympathize with another's viewpoint?*
19. *feel many people share and appreciate your views?*
20. *tend to suspect others' motives and find most people essentially untrustworthy?*

Key: *Answer "yes" to 6 or more of the odd numbered questions and "no" to 6 or more of the even numbered questions, and you are likely to have a strong element of the Courtesan in your makeup. But, bear in mind this is only the first of three attitudes and it is common to have a combination of the three.*

48

WARRIOR ~ IN PURSUIT OF POWER

THE SECOND MODALITY, that of moving against, is clearly evident in a tendency to see everyone as potentially hostile and similar to oneself, combined with the refusal to acknowledge that this might not be the case.

This type lives by the Darwinian creed that only the fittest survive and that the weak are overcome by the strong. In the mind of the Warrior this point of view conveniently justifies the pursuit of self-interest and self-preservation as being part of natural selection. It also highlights his, or her, absolute need for power – the power to control other people as well as the environment that is so keenly felt to be a potential threat. This does not always mean wielding direct and obvious power as a leader. It can take the form of the more skilful manipulations of the king-maker and the power behind the throne.

This type is usually highly competitive and a motivated achiever. The appeal is often not the achievement itself, but rather what it can lead to – not satisfaction in the work itself, but as a means of control and power, and that power must be over others. Thus the integrity of the Warrior, or what might be seen as his centre of gravity, actually lies outside himself, for it relies upon others' affirmation of his success, status and prestige. This is coupled with a strong need to exploit and manipulate others with few uncomfortable qualms of conscience. At its most extreme, the characterization of the Warrior is that of the psychopath. Most situations are milked for what he can get out of them. The firm belief that all other people are just like him in their motivation, forces him to be suspicious even of friends. He finds it difficult to make friends – that is to say, to enjoy companions irrespective of the need to use them. He also finds it difficult to feel love or affection for anyone else.

His inability to be playful or simply to enjoy situations for no ulterior reason, can make this type cold, empty and

The controlling Warrior moves against the world.

inwardly poor, which in turn generates an even harsher cycle of behaviour.

The Warrior tends to regard feeling with suspicion, or as a sign of weakness or sentimentality. Personal relationships are based upon self-gratification and advancement, desirability, social attractiveness, prestige and status. He is usually a very bad loser, and regards admitting that he might be wrong as a serious weakness.

The Warrior feels most expansive with values like power, money and a fighting spirit. In the realm of combat he can be extraordinarily courageous.

The Warrior contracts and feels trapped when confronting weakness, cowardice, appeasement and over-emotional feelings in himself or in others.

Remember this characterization is one of extremes. It appears so completely dark because it is one of three negative strategies to cope with the emotion of fear arising from dealings with others and the outside world. The previous type, the Courtesan, dealt with the potential threat of others by appeasing them; the Warrior's strategy is through control, and you will see, on the next page, that the third method of dealing with this fear is by withdrawing to some safe ground and by not becoming involved.

Combinations of these strategies gradually build up from childhood experiences, becoming so habitual that they effectively become our unconscious modes of behaviour. The neurological pathways of the emotional brain are built around these habits. Neurotransmitters are released around this habitual pattern. But once you are alerted to them you will be able to recognize them both in yourself and others, and they will automatically begin to change.

ASSESSMENT

Do you:
1. *hate to plan ahead with clear future goals?*
2. *realize that you have to be realistic and look after your own interests first?*
3. *prefer to stay away from people?*
4. *like going out with a partner who is considered highly attractive by others?*
5. *not care about what others think of your partner?*
6. *feel that strong emotions can often be disruptive when pursuing important goals?*
7. *dislike being in situations where you are in control and have to instruct others what to do?*
8. *regard over-emotional outbursts as weak and uncontrolled sentimentality?*
9. *feel you are a poor leader?*
10. *consider competitiveness a healthy and natural state?*
11. *hate competitive games and sports?*
12. *think that most people have similar motives to you but maybe hide them from others?*
13. *prefer to let someone else be the leader of a team?*
14. *like to be the centre of attention?*
15. *prefer to remain in the background at a party and help the hostess?*
16. *quickly assess if situations are to your advantage or not?*
17. *feel confused when someone wants to do something unexpectedly kind for you?*
18. *sometimes become aggressive or rude when irritated?*
19. *prefer to serve, rather than be served by someone else?*
20. *need others' admiration to give you a sense of self-worth?*

Key: Answer "no" *to more than 7 of the odd numbered questions and* "yes" *to more than 7 of the even numbered questions and you are definitely a Warrior. Reverse the* "yes" *and* "no" *and you are definitely not.*

49

OBSERVER ~ THE NON-INVOLVED

THIS PSYCHOLOGICAL STRATEGY in relation to others reveals itself in the creation of emotional distance coupled with a complete determination not to become involved. When the world is felt to be leaning into you, getting too close for comfort, a claustrophobic anxiety appears. In fact, any form of identification or involvement is always perceived as over-involvement.

The Observer requires privacy and isolation. To this end he or she constructs an invisible wall around him- or herself through which no one may enter. Within these confines this type is perfectly self-sufficient, resourceful and independent. However, anxiety is always lurking, in case someone or something becomes indispensable, with the attendant danger of being trapped by it. The horror of being caged or imprisoned through identification with someone else ensures there is seldom a personal attachment that could create such a situation.

Rather than letting someone or something come too close, this type adopts an attitude of indifference – preferring nothing to really matter much, rather than to allow others to touch too deeply. The detached Observer would even sacrifice situations that were potentially enjoyable rather than risk dependence on another. Even food, drink and comfort are eschewed if they involve a lifestyle that requires time and energy to maintain. Here we find strenuous avoidance of anything that might create any hint of dependence, including illness.

An example of how these types might be completely misunderstood is when they hate being fussed over when ill, only requiring the absolute minimum of care to bring them back to health. However, when they apply the same principle to people who love being looked after, they are seen as heartless and uncaring.

The anxious Observer avoids involvement with the world.

Invariably the Observer prefers to work alone and, if possible, even to eat and sleep alone, and really dislikes group happenings or "sharings". There is a preference to acquire knowledge first-hand and not to rely on what others have already discovered. This can be an advantage, but it can also be taken to extremes, like refusing to take advice from those who are willing to share and really can help.

Because of the need to examine everything for him- or herself as if for the first time, there is a certain integrity in the strategy of this type. The Observer will not be an unthinking robot, taking everyone else's word for things. Independent self-experience is essential. Yet, this overwhelming need to be self-sufficient and detached is not always positive. The strategy can become a negative avoidance of being influenced or obligated in any way, rather than positive independence for its own sake.

There is also a tendency to feel a certain superiority in his or her splendid isolation, a profound sense of being unique among others, without the need to be competitive or assertive about it.

Overall this type experiences independence, the isolation of the observer and self-sufficiency as expansive. Over-identification with another person, a cause or a thing is essentially experienced as a contraction of the spirit.

ASSESSMENT

Do you:
1. *feel the need to put an emotional distance between yourself and others?*
2. *hate isolation?*
3. *feel the world sometimes intrudes too much into your life?*
4. *ever feel desperately lonely if you are not interacting with others?*
5. *prefer to be a witness watching the antics of others as if from on top of a hill?*
6. *need others around in order to fully enjoy an event?*
7. *feel a real need to be completely self-sufficient?*
8. *feel the need to be competitive and be successful?*
9. *hate to feel dependent on others, especially when you are ill or handicapped?*
10. *often become identified with your emotions and respond passionately during any confrontation?*
11. *prefer to discover things for yourself rather than use what is already known or take someone's word for it?*
12. *seldom feel superior to others?*
13. *tend to hide your real talents?*
14. *seldom feel that people want to interfere with you?*
15. *envision yourself as a solitary tree on the top of a hill rather than part of a group nestled in the valley?*
16. *like people asking questions about your personal life?*
17. *sometimes feel you are being taken for granted?*
18. *ask people directions rather than bother to find a place on your own?*
19. *value independence above almost everything else?*
20. *accept that there are times when you need the help of others?*

Key: *Answer "yes" to more than 7 of the even numbered questions or "no" to more than 7 of the odd numbered questions and you apparently fit this type like a glove.*

50

INDIFFERENCE AND COMPASSION

IT HAS BEEN DISCOVERED THAT DURING INFANCY there is a very short period in which a stimulus is needed to trigger our ability to feel emotions in later life. Many children orphaned at an early age are often found to have a complete lack of warmth towards others, even when their adoptive parents do all they possibly can to give them love. Such children respond with the indifference most often associated with psychopathy.

In a popular newspaper questionnaire about the behaviour of husbands, thousands of women reported that their spouses exhibited all the classic symptoms of the psychopath – they were violent and aggressive, deceitful, emotionally frozen, with a complete lack of any sense of remorse or conscience. A later scientific study[29] revealed that one in every six managers in the United Kingdom also met the diagnostic criteria for psychopathy!

The inability to sense emotions in others, or to feel it ourselves, is a dysfunction that occurs in that centre of anxiety and stress – the amygdala. In brain scans of those who apparently have no emotions, the amygdala shows little response when the subject is exposed to emotionally stressful information. It is thought that a successful bonding between mother and infant is a contributing factor to ensuring a normal functioning of this vital part of the limbic system.[30]

Compassion arises as one develops the ability to step inside someone else's emotional shoes. At such times, brain scans show the activity around the amygdala to be dampened, while the right-hand side of the brain literally lights up. Compassion and indifference are extremes, but they point to your own natural tendencies – of either having a strong emotional field, or one that is cooler and more detached. Remember there is no judgment involved. Both have their weaknesses and strengths.

ASSESSMENT

Do you:

1. *prefer to be a dead hero rather than a living coward?*
2. *feel you are very sensitive to your surroundings?*
3. *enjoy watching aggressive sports, like boxing, on TV?*
4. *feel that poor fools should not be parted from their money?*
5. *feel that many people are too vague or soft in their opinions?*
6. *consider it best to trust your feelings at all times?*
7. *think discussing ethics and morals is a waste of time?*
8. *seldom have fantasies bordering on the sadistic?*
9. *never totally involve yourself when meeting others?*
10. *often say something shocking just to see how others react?*
11. *feel the statement "Every man for himself" is terrible?*
12. *use your body violently when you are really angry?*
13. *avoid telling someone that he or she annoys you?*
14. *prefer to give orders rather than take them?*
15. *avoid seeing a disaster movie in which many people are killed even if it is obviously staged?*
16. *get irritated with people who often talk of falling in love?*
17. *avoid the rifle shoot at a funfair?*
18. *think you would shoot at a burglar who is escaping with one of your prized possessions?*
19. *feel that being in love is far more important than long-term success and the attainment of your ambitions?*
20. *feel you are a poor organizer and a hopeless manipulator of other people?*

Key: You have a naturally compassionate approach to life if you answer "yes" to more than 7 of the even numbered questions and "no" to more than 7 of the odd numbered questions. Reverse the "yes" and "no" and you are beginning to exhibit a markedly cool and detached attitude bordering on indifference.

The waking have one world in common;
sleepers have each a private world of his own.

Heraclitus

51

ARE YOU AN EXTROVERT OR AN INTROVERT?

EARLY IN THE TWENTIETH CENTURY Carl Gustav Jung proposed a psychological typology[31] which could be expressed in the mandala-like form we have already seen in assessment number 35. Many of Jung's protégés and later followers have used his model extensively in their own work, as seen in a powerful wheel of human behaviour devised by Professor H. J. Eysenck.[32] In order to understand its workings more closely we must examine what is meant by the terms extrovert and introvert.

Extroversion is characterized by attention being given to the external, surrounding world. It is object-oriented. Thus a typical extrovert's behaviour is an outward display most strongly influenced by the environment, the events and the people that surround him or her. Generally this is an optimistic and often cheery view of life, but perhaps a little shallow in its carefree nature, for the extrovert strenuously avoids any self-reflection, or examination of interior motives.

Introversion, on the other hand, is directing the attention towards the subject rather than the object. Jung even went so far as to say that an introvert was in continual retreat from the object. This type avoids gatherings like the plague, has difficulty in mixing with others and remains as much as possible aloof from external happenings. This aloofness is partly because the outer world seems too negative and overpowering. Others tend to sense this in introverts and so find difficulty in making contact. This then confirms the introvert's over-critical view that the world is full of untrustworthy, unworthy and menacing influences. The introvert confronts this apparent threat with pedantry, seriousness, caution, distrust and harsh judgments. He, or she, is often pessimistic and anxious, feeling unaccepted, unacceptable or simply inferior.

Yet the world within the introvert's shell is a delight – his or her own company the best and safest of choices. In the quietude of their inner space introverts can flourish, preferring to work, philosophize and follow their personal quests. The virtual reality of their inner worlds tends to displace objective reality. If outer stresses become too much, they batten down the hatches and withdraw. Relating happens only when their drawbridge of distrust can be lowered.

It is as well to remember that Jung himself insisted that he was not providing us with easy labels to stick on people, but a useful platform, which he called a critical psychology, from which to view the diversity of psychological concepts. Likewise, the assessments in this small volume are not intended to typecast the readers but to give some psychological insight into habitual ways of approaching the world and themselves.

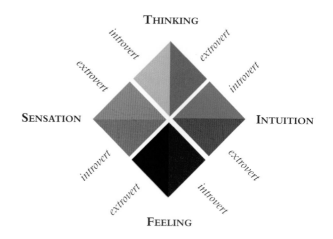

Sensation ~ *establishes what apparently exists.*
Thinking ~ *establishes its meaning and significance.*
Feeling ~ *establishes its intrinsic value.*
Intuition ~ *questions where it has come from and where it is going.*

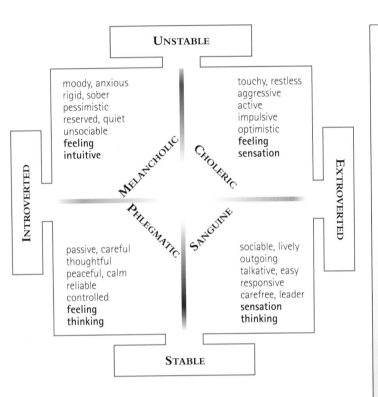

UNSTABLE

moody, anxious
rigid, sober
pessimistic
reserved, quiet
unsociable
feeling
intuitive

touchy, restless
aggressive
active
impulsive
optimistic
feeling
sensation

INTROVERTED

MELANCHOLIC

CHOLERIC

PHLEGMATIC

SANGUINE

EXTROVERTED

passive, careful
thoughtful
peaceful, calm
reliable
controlled
feeling
thinking

sociable, lively
outgoing
talkative, easy
responsive
carefree, leader
sensation
thinking

STABLE

The diagram on the left shows the four polarities of how you approach existence, each having an introspective and outgoing aspect, totalling eight types. The mandala above shows how these polarities can be extended to include stability and instability, and thus shows the four ancient types of the melancholic, choleric, phlegmatic and sanguine person. You might compare your results from assessment 23 with this version to see if the tests confirm your attitudes.

ASSESSMENT

Do you:

1. *like to have quiet time alone with your thoughts?*
2. *get frustrated and irritated in traffic jams?*
3. *like to follow a few interests in depth rather than continually seek new ones?*
4. *feel you are continually on the go?*
5. *prefer telephoning rather than meeting a business client?*
6. *feel annoyed with slow drivers?*
7. *feel uncomfortable when someone moves too close to you when talking?*
8. *like to participate in a theatrical performance rather than watching it?*
9. *prefer vacations that are restful rather than action-packed?*
10. *enjoy many exciting things happening at the same time?*
11. *usually try to avoid meeting people?*
12. *prefer characters in a novel to act rather than talk?*
13. *wish you could sometimes let your hair down?*
14. *agree with the statement "The more, the merrier"?*
15. *enjoy contemplating your life?*
16. *often feel you are bursting with energy and have to act immediately?*
17. *prefer to work alone?*
18. *prefer work that needs immediate action rather than challenging thought?*
19. *tend to be over-modest when relating personal stories to a group of friends?*
20. *enjoy getting a little rowdy with amiable friends or even strangers?*

Key: *If you answer "yes" to more than 8 of the even numbered questions and "no" to more than 8 of the odd numbered questions, you are likely to have an extroverted approach to life. Reverse the "yes" and "no" and the outcome suggests you are highly introspective in your attitudes.*

52

ARE YOU STABLE?

T HE MANDALA ON THE PREVIOUS PAGE introduced the concept of stability and instability, or your overall adjustment to the environment and the people around you. Psychometrists who normally devise such tests usually create many separate indicators of a person's self-esteem, levels of anxiety, obsessiveness, independence, neurotic obsessions over health, the sense of well-being and feelings of guilt.

The assessment on this page gives a more general overview of our overall tendency toward balance or imbalance. But we have to be very wary about sticking labels on ourselves. Sometimes the apparent balanced condition could equally well be described as insensitive, over-adjusted, conservative and complacent, while imbalance could read as over-sensitive, rebellious, revolutionary and disablingly aware. We tend to use such words as if they are reality, while in fact they only give indications of the inexpressible condition of being human. Instability and adjustment are relative to whichever idea of normality is current.[33] The madman of one age is the eccentric of another, and the norm of yet another.

ASSESSMENT

Answer each of the questions listed below.

Do you:

1. sometimes feel guilty about things?
2. usually stay calm and don't easily get upset?
3. feel you are aware of not being able to do things as well as others?
4. feel strong and unworried by illness?
5. sometimes think you are a failure?
6. almost always feel cheerful and happy?
7. seem to have more headaches than your friends?
8. feel you are influenced by what others say?
9. often wish that you were someone else?
10. often apologize for something that is not entirely your fault?
11. wish you had been born with a silver spoon in your mouth?
12. worry about becoming sick or catching a disease?
13. think that others tend to disapprove of you?
14. feel you are more anxiety prone than most of your acquaintances?
15. find it difficult to laugh as much as most other people?
16. avoid having your photograph taken?
17. find it hard to relax easily when sitting or lying down?
18. get upset at others' unjustified criticism?
19. feel a bit cheated about how life has treated you?
20. have certain rituals and routines that you don't like disrupting?
21. get the feeling that people tend to use you?
22. read horoscopes or books hoping to gain some guidance in life?
23. feel you are a fitful sleeper.?
24. mostly feel calm and content in what you do?
25. describe yourself as a real perfectionist?
26. find it difficult to know which rules to follow in this rapidly changing world?
27. tend to hoard many useless or even broken things "just in case"?
28. feel you are not satisfied with what you have made of your life?
29. feel ashamed by some of the things you have done?
30. feel you are easily startled by someone's sudden appearance or an unexpected noise?

Key: *If you answer "yes" to less than 10 of these questions you are probably reasonably well balanced.*
If your score is over 20 it appears that not only are you introspective, and probably melancholic, but also that you have a tendency to be somewhat unbalanced in your attitudes and behaviour. But take heart, the higher scores are more common than the lower.

53

HOW WELL DO YOU COPE WITH EMOTIONAL STRESS?

OUR EMOTIONAL RESPONSES TO STRESS are perhaps the most revealing indications of our ability to function well. Well-being, or normality, is often defined by psychologists as just that – the ability to interact effectively with our environment. This includes the ability to adapt to new situations when habitual ways fail us.

However, we all carry ancient, hard-wired instructions for dealing with a potentially hostile environment. These early warning systems of possible threat from the wild are now mostly the inappropriate habitual responses of our limbic system, yet we still react to them with a sense of impending doom.

Increasingly, stress translates into anxiety. In fact, stress and anxiety in the modern world are almost synonymous. Anxiety is frozen fear – a fear we can do nothing to alleviate through immediate action. The aroused emotional brain floods the whole system with chemicals and we are stuck with an overload of, say, adrenalin, with no woolly mammoth to attack, but a thoughtless car driver who speeds away out of our reach.

Some psychologists regard anxiety as an aspect of arousal. Thus some people respond to flying a glider with excitement, others only with a sense of terror and anxiety. The following assessment indicates how you might deal with stress.

ASSESSMENT

Answer these questions as quickly as you can.

1. When you are excited does your breathing change:
   A) very seldom. B) occasionally. C) usually.
2. When you are worried, what do others see in your face:
   A) you are unaffected. B) you tend to go pale and slightly drawn. C) you go noticeably white and very drawn.
3. If you are about to do something hazardous, do you:
   A) get a churning sensation in the stomach, begin to quiver, and break into a sweat? B) get at least one of these symptoms? C) seldom even get one or any of them?
4. Compared with others is your reaction time:
   A) very fast. B) average. C) slow.
5. You are waiting for an important meeting, an interview or a date. Does your:
   A) pulse increase a little more than usual?
   B) pulse show no discernable change from normal?
   C) heart beat strongly and your pulse race?
6. You are waiting for a friend to get ready and you could miss your train. Do you:
   A) keep reminding her of the time; become frantic, pacing up and down; get in the car and rev it up? B) tell her you will be late for the train and stay around to make sure she hurries? C) tell her once you will be late unless she hurries up and then wait in the car?
7. Do you get physically sick before important functions, like travelling in an airplane, or making a speech?
   A) almost always. B) never. C) very seldom.
8. While concentrating hard someone startles you. Do you:
   A) hardly react at all? B) jump out of your skin and find your heart beating loudly? C) react briefly but quickly resume what you were doing?
9. You are awoken from sleep by a strange noise. Do you:
   A) wake up immediately being totally aware of your surroundings and ready to act? B) take a long time to wake up and finally take your bearings? C) awaken but take a few seconds to become aware of where you are and what is happening?
10. You have been waiting an hour to receive a possibly negative medical report. Would you:
    A) be slightly apprehensive but reasonably calm?
    B) be anxious; beginning to get a bit worried and irritated at the delay? C) have a full-blown panic attack?
11. You are in a rage with a stupid and dangerous driver. Does your face:
    A) become beetroot red in colour, hot and flushed?
    B) slightly flushed? C) stay the same as usual?
12. How did you respond to the instruction at the beginning of the questionnaire:
    A) immediately reacted by doing this section as quickly as possible. B) wondered why the questions were supposedly so important? C) didn't notice.

$A=0, B=1, C=2$

1. A0	B1	C2		7. A2	B0	C1
2. A0	B1	C2		8. A0	B2	C1
3. A3	B1	C0		9. A2	B0	C1
4. A2	B1	C0		10. A0	B1	C2
5. A1	B0	C2		11. A2	B1	C0
6. A2	B1	C0		12. A2	B1	C0

Key: If you score 15–24 you would have survived as an elder tribesperson 35,000 years ago, but today you are probably living in an almost chronic state of anxiety. If you score 7–14 you have a fairly normal, reasonably adapted response to modern stress. If you score 6 or less you are superbly adapted to living in the modern world and would probably do well working in New York, London or Mexico City.

54

DO YOUR CLOUDS HAVE SILVER LININGS?

OPTIMISM SUGGESTS THAT WE LIVE in the best of all possible worlds, with a tendency to expect the best and see the best in all things. By contrast pessimism expects the worst and sees the worst in all things. The pessimistic doctrine – that this world is, by its nature, corrupt and that our sojourn in it is a preparation for some other existence – is, of course, religious in its source. In fact, few of the major religions are at all optimistic about the present, so it is a real bonus that any of us can remain optimistic at all.

In neurological terms, optimism, and the sense of meaning and well-being that accompanies it, is in part caused by a dampening of the activity of the amygdala in the limbic system. Pessimism, often associated with depression, anxiety and low energy, is thought to occur when the neurotransmitters of the limbic system fail to check bursts of activity in the amygdala.

In the following assessment the optimistic person is seen as unusually cheerful and joyous. He or she is highly satisfied with their existence, generally finds life rewarding and is obviously at peace with him- or herself and the world. In contrast, the pessimist is characteristically depressed, gloomy and disappointed with his or her existence. All clouds are storm-laden, without any hint of a silver lining. Pessimists usually have low self-esteem, believing they are unattractive failures. Much of this has been clinically shown to be caused by being pessimistic *about* being pessimistic. Within the normal range of emotions these assessments are designed to cover (which does not include depressive illness), we often need little more than a conscious jolt to emerge from our self-induced and self-perpetuating attitude of mind.

ASSESSMENT

Do you:
1. *describe a half-bottle of wonderful wine as being half-full rather than half-empty?*
2. *enjoy gambling on a fairly regular basis?*
3. *enjoy dreaming about what you might do if you won the lottery?*
4. *go on holiday without booking a hotel beforehand?*
5. *feel your motto is to spend today, for tomorrow might never come?*
6. *very carefully lock up before going to bed?*
7. *feel you are someone who wears rose-tinted glasses?*
8. *love getting surprises?*
9. *feel that essentially most people are honest?*
10. *always have something to look forward to?*
11. *feel you sometimes are on a lucky streak?*
12. *never feel it just isn't worth getting up in the morning?*
13. *never worry about whether your transport will fail and you will be late for an appointment?*
14. *never bother to carry an extra article of clothing "just in case"?*
15. *feel surprised when there is a hitch and things don't work out according to your plan?*
16. *feel delighted by the unexpected?*
17. *feel things seldom seem hopeless?*
18. *feel your future looks inviting?*
19. *not care about growing old?*
20. *have a hunch that existence will take care of you?*

Key: *Answer "yes" to more than 10 of the questions and you are like most of us in your outlook. Answer "yes" to more than 16 and you are decidedly optimistic. Answer "no" to more than 16 and you would do well to take stock of why you are so pessimistic and what can be done about it.*

55

DO YOU PLEAD GUILTY OR NOT GUILTY?

THE PROPENSITY TO FEEL guilty or anxious about our behaviour is a character trait that is commonly found today. Most of us are uneasy about certain aspects of our personalities. Often we blame ourselves even when our behaviour hardly merits any punishment whatsoever. A certain level of guilt is, of course, necessary for some awareness of conscience. Indeed, its complete absence would be symptomatic of the extremes of psychopathy. Excessive self-abasement or recrimination, on the other hand, reveal an equally neurotic and unbalanced attitude.

Those who have persistent feelings of guilt often have an over-zealous religious background, with ideals of behaviour that cannot be matched in real life. However, this is by no means the only cause. In terms of the activity of the brain itself, the presence of an overriding sense of guilt could equally be caused by the limbic system with – once again the villain of the piece – an over-active amygdala that is continually being kept on an uneasy alert twenty-four hours a day.

ASSESSMENT

Do you:
1. feel you have spent much of your life doing things you don't really enjoy?
2. hate your present job?
3. feel bad if you let other people down?
4. worry about other people's opinion of you or your actions?
5. avoid doing things that might upset your friends?
6. find it difficult to sleep until noon at weekends, even when there is nothing urgent to do?
7. spend time in a shop trying on clothes and then feel bad if you leave without buying anything?
8. send birthday cards to people you don't really like?
9. feel upset if someone unexpectedly found you doing something intimate and private?
10. dress in clothes that will please others?
11. feel bad when you think of times you have been rude or thoughtless?
12. find yourself apologizing for something that is not really your fault?
13. say sorry when someone steps on your foot?
14. feel you have let down your parents by not living up to their expectations?
15. agree with the concept of original sin – that you are born a sinner who must be redeemed?
16. feel that we all need some social or religious control over our natural instincts?
17. feel that Roman Catholics are right to have regular confessions of their sins?
18. sense a general disapproval from others about your person or behaviour?
19. feel that you should be punished for past sins?
20. often pray for forgiveness?

Key: Answer "yes" to 16 or more of the questions and you can be sure that at some time someone has programmed both you and your emotional centre to feel guilty.
A score of 4–6 would suggest a healthy conscience.
A score of under 3 suggests you are either enlightened or a psychopath!

HOW GOOD ARE YOU AT LETTING GO?

EARLY IN ANY CHILD'S DEVELOPMENT an emotional link is apparently established between the act of evacuating the bowels or the bladder and the reward of the subsequent physical sense of well-being. However, there is also the possibility of a smack, punishment, or the social admonition "Not here and certainly not now!"

The anal zone, as Freud was quick to point out, is the prime location for a display of contradictory impulses. The sphincter is the battleground for two conflicting modes in the child – that of retention on the one hand and elimination on the other. It establishes its determined rule during that stubborn period every parent recognizes and dreads, between the ages of two and three, when the child will put all his being into a hug one moment only to push the mother away aggressively a few seconds later.

Socially this can be seen as the stage of learning to hold on and to let go. It is part of the child's expansion of boundaries and control, in this case that of the muscles, their flexing, extension, rigidity and relaxation.

If the emotional conditioning tends to favour one mode above another, the child quickly becomes habitual in that pattern with all the strategies connected with it. These patterns of behaviour can polarize, and are carried unconsciously into adult life only to pop up in the most unexpected ways – in possessiveness, rigidity, clinging, hoarding, oral obsessions, stubbornness and the inability to let go of things.[34]

This assessment is devised to make you aware of how you might have retained some vestige of your childhood. The questionnaire and your own intuition will serve as a guide.

ASSESSMENT

Do you:

1. think it unwise to borrow from friends?
2. save for a rainy day?
3. feel that your friends consider you a bit of a miser?
4. fret when you owe someone money?
5. feel you would invest most of any money you won?
6. always read your bank balance carefully?
7. believe in making plans for retirement early?
8. feel that instalment plans represent a risk?
9. make sure you have a secret stash of cash somewhere?
10. make sure you are well insured?
11. hate paying bills more than anything else?
12. feel reluctant to lend someone any money?
13. usually have a shrewd idea of how much money you have on you?
14. feel you have self-control?
15. wish that sometimes you could let your hair down and go wild – but don't?
16. tend to keep useless things?
17. feel you are a compulsive collector of certain things?
18. feel you are considered a bit possessive by your friends and partners?
19. hate having to get rid of your old car?
20. feel that others consider you to be rigid and stubborn?

Key: *Answering "yes" to less than 6 of the questions shows you are able to let go easily. Answering "yes" to 16 or more of the questions reveals that you tend to hold onto things, and probably have a strong desire to be in control of events. You seem to find it very difficult to let your hair down and allow yourself to go a bit crazy. And you probably like gold! Answering "yes" to more than 6 but less than 16 of the questions suggests you balance the two extremes quite well.*

57

ARE YOU A ROMANTIC?

IN 1185, AT THE HEIGHT OF the most chivalrous period of European history, Andreas Capellanus wrote his classic treatise *On the Art of Honourable Loving.*[35] In it he parodied the great Roman poet Ovid's guide to seduction *The Art of Loving,* written over a thousand years before.

To the French courts of the time Andreas' outrageous parody was considered screamingly funny, yet his "Rules of Love" were still adopted as a code of courtly behaviour befitting any would-be lover. His romantic treatise unconsciously demonstrates how deep emotions can be expressed through a set of conscious, rational ideals. It gives the illusion of *feeling,* but in reality it is *thinking about feeling.* Andreas' rules, shown opposite, could almost be an assessment in themselves, but if you would like to confirm your own romantic tendencies you must answer the questions in the assessment on the right.

ASSESSMENT

Do you:
1. *believe in the concept of soul mates?*
2. *believe in love at first sight?*
3. *tend to be tearful, or get a lump in the throat when seeing a sentimental movie?*
4. *carry a photo of your beloved with you?*
5. *dream of a long weekend alone with your lover in a secluded hotel with candlelit dinners?*
6. *know the colour of your lover's eyes?*
7. *remember the date, or the hour, when you first met?*
8. *secretly keep your lover's letters?*
9. *keep a photograph album?*
10. *like buying or receiving flowers?*
11. *remember your first kiss?*
12. *feel joyful when your partner remembers an anniversary?*
13. *enjoy reading novels with a strong fantasy element?*
14. *like books with a strong nostalgic flavour?*
15. *sometimes prefer the dream of romance to the reality?*
16. *keep mementos of good times?*
17. *prefer reading fiction to non-fiction?*
18. *enjoy learning about historic periods in which chivalry was important?*
19. *subscribe to the motto "heart before head"?*
20. *feel that women are more emotional than men?*
21. *find the 1930s postcard on the left rather silly?*
22. *find the postcard charming, nostalgic and evocative of a more romantic epoch?*

Key: *If you answer "yes" to 5 or less of the questions you are definitely a person in whom the head rules the heart.*
A positive answer for 6–9 of the questions would be a great score for men but under average for women, while a positive answer for 10–20 of the questions pictures you as a truly incurable romantic.

The Rules of Love, by Andreas Capellanus, 1185.

1. The state of marriage does not necessarily excuse anyone from loving.
2. He who does not feel jealousy is incapable of loving.
3. No one can love two people at the same time.
4. It is well-known that love is either growing or declining.
5. Whatever a lover takes from his lover's will has no savour.
6. A male does not fall in love until he has reached full manhood.
7. A mourning of two years for a deceased lover is required by the survivor.
8. No one should be prevented from loving save by reason of his or her own death.
9. No one can love save they are compelled by the eloquence of love.
10. Love is accustomed to be an exile from the house of avarice.
11. It is unseemly to love anyone whom you would be ashamed to marry.
12. A true lover only desires the passionate embraces of his beloved.
13. Love that is made public rarely lasts.
14. Love easily obtained is of little value; difficulty in obtaining it makes it precious.
15. Every lover regularly turns pale in the presence of the beloved.
16. On suddenly catching sight of the beloved, the heart begins to palpitate.
17. A new love drives out the old.
18. A good character alone makes someone worthy of love.
19. If love lessens, it soon fails and rarely recovers.
20. A man in love is always fearful.
21. The feeling of love is always increased by true jealousy.
22. A suspicious lover and the sensation of love is increased.
23. A man tormented by the thought of love, eats and sleeps little.
24. Everything a lover does ends in the thought of the beloved.
25. A true lover considers nothing good but what he thinks will please his beloved.
26. Love can deny nothing to love.
27. A lover cannot have too much of his beloved's consolations
28. The smallest supposition compels a lover to suspect his beloved of doing wrong.
29. A man troubled by excessive lust does not usually love.
30. A true lover is continually, without interruption, obsessed by the image of his beloved.
31. Nothing forbids one woman being loved by two men, or one man by two women.

58

ARE YOU A SENSUALIST?

SEXUAL DRIVES have very clear neurological sources. They appear to centre on the area of the hypothalamus, which then expands to include the whole limbic system, the cortex, and then the body. The sexual reward of the final crescendo is an orgasmic tidal wave of the neuro-transmitter dopamine followed by a flood of the hormone oxytocin, which creates a feeling of relaxation and calm. So when you imagine that sex is very much an affair of the thighs, or the heart, you might consider that as far as the brain is concerned, sex is about the biggest explosive reward it can ever hope for.[36]

The actual brain circuitry, and the distinct areas that are stimulated, differ radically between the male and female. In males the name of this heightened game is found in the andro-gen-rich and sensitive zones around the preoptic area of the hypothalamus, which is bloated to about two-and-a-half times its size in the female brain. However, signals from a stimulated amygdala give the male response an overtone of assertion and aggression.

The sexual behaviour of the female is stimulated in the oestrogen-rich and sensitive zones of the ventro-medial nucle-us of the hypothalamus, which again is larger and more developed than its male counterpart. In females the location is the same spot that plays a major role in registering hunger.

The release of hormones like oxytocin create, not just a sense of well-being, but a sense of bonding, so it is not surpris-ing to find that many of these chemicals are also associated with addiction.

ASSESSMENT

Do you:
1. *find sex without love unsatisfactory?*
2. *feel satisfied with your sex life?*
3. *only very rarely think about sex?*
4. *feel you can become sexually excited anywhere?*
5. *feel you have never really had problems about sex?*
6. *have more thoughts of sex than most people?*
7. *have few hangups about unusual sex?*
8. *often have overpowering sexual feelings?*
9. *seldom feel nervous in the company of the opposite sex?*
10. *seldom feel anxious about sex?*
11. *dislike the feeling of sometimes humiliating your partner?*
12. *think you could never be hostile to your partner?*
13. *find the idea of whipping your partner repulsive?*
14. *find sex a very important activity in life?*
15. *dislike being rough, aggressive or biting your sex partner?*
16. *find nakedness beautiful and natural?*
17. *find tenderness more important than bone-marrow-melting sex?*
18. *prefer to yield to your partner's sexual rhythm rather than dominate it?*
19. *like to be conscious of every nuance of making love rather than totally letting go?*
20. *enjoy bonding with one partner rather than just enjoying many carefree encounters?*

Key: *If you answer "yes" to more than 10 of the questions you will have a natural acceptance and healthy enjoyment of sex. If you answer "yes" to more than 14 questions you will be non-aggressive and, even more probably, a woman. Answering "no" to more than 10 questions shows the strong male-oriented and assertive tendency associated with the action of the amygdala.*

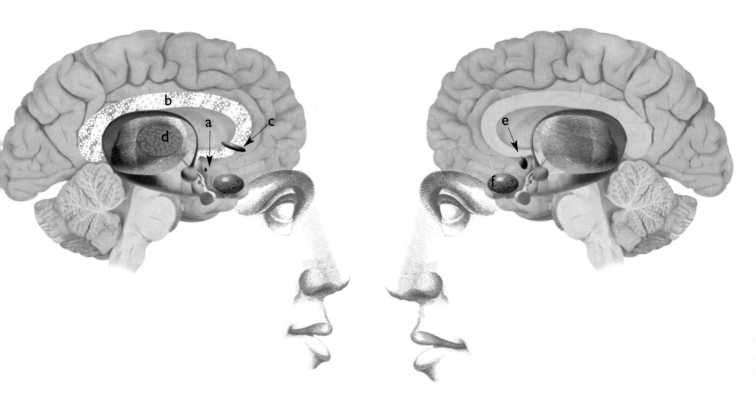

THE FEMALE BRAIN

Female sexual behaviour apparently arises in the ventro-medial nucleus (a), the same zone responsible for instigating hunger and appetite. This is an area rich in oestrogen-sensitive neurons. The dense fibres of the collosum (b), and those of the smaller anterior commissure (c), that link the two hemispheres of the brain are far larger in women. This explains why women are more in touch with their more emotional right-hand brains. The two spheres of the thalamus (d), are joined more densely in women.

THE MALE BRAIN

The area of the medial preoptic (e) is over two-and-a-half times larger in the male. It is located in a zone that is more sensitive to male hormones than any other. At the same time signals are received from the amygdala (f) which might explain why sex in the male is sometimes linked with aggression. The sexual responses in the male appear to be of a much narrower waveband and more focused than in the woman, who has access to a far wider spectrum of emotions and rich feelings.

59

ARE YOU IMAGINATIVE?

ONE OF THE MOST STARTLING IMPLICATIONS of present research on the nature of our brain is the discovery that the two hemispheres function as separate spheres of consciousness, each with its own agenda and personality. It could be said that an intuitive person has greater access to both hemispheres.[37]

A difficulty in distinguishing between what is real and what is visionary, what is internally or externally generated, is characteristic of the intuitive type. This is coupled with a lack of confidence to act on what is intuitively felt. Most psychics have encountered this problem at some time, for many of their visionary experiences can be explained in simple mechanical terms.

There are certain areas of the brain which, when stimulated, will produce intensely real and inspired visions. One area of the emotional system, sometimes called "The God Spot", triggers a euphoric feeling of being in a divine presence. The auditory cortex and speech areas can yield inner voices that are most likely a feedback of your own thoughts. However, such pragmatic explanations do not account for the sheer diversity of experience that the intuitive type apparently channels.

To live in the world of imagination is natural to this type. It is fascinated with and recognizes all the esoteric disciplines and experiences. Many people of this type had special talents or psychic gifts as children, such as the gift or condition of synaesthesia, in which sound, sight, smell, touch and taste all blend, so a person sees a smell or hears a colour.

The basic problem for the intuitive type is that the emotional charge behind the imaginative vision makes it almost impossible for it to distinguish what is real. It is the difficulty experienced by all those who are psychically gifted.

ASSESSMENT

Do you:
1. *sometimes know when someone will telephone before they actually do?*
2. *sometimes sense that someone is thinking of you?*
3. *believe that some people can channel energy?*
4. *have any experiences of something miraculous?*
5. *feel you have some healing powers?*
6. *believe in life after death?*
7. *recall an out-of-body experience?*
8. *believe that out-of-body experiences are real?*
9. *experience unexpected visions about others?*
10. *have the ability to see auras or vague apparitions around people?*
11. *value imagination above all else?*
12. *experience the everyday world as a bit flat?*
13. *sometimes see in psychedelic colours?*
14. *believe some people are mediums for spiritual messages?*
15. *remember experiencing déjà vu?*
16. *trust your intuition?*
17. *recall having been, or like to be, hypnotized?*
18. *believe in a sixth sense?*
19. *ever taste a colour, smell a sound, or see a taste?*
20. *prefer fantasy fiction to non-fiction?*

Key: The questionnaire is obviously loaded, but if you answer "yes" to 15 questions or more you are likely to have strong leanings toward intuition and imagination.
Answering "no" to 13 questions or more suggests you distrust your own imagination and prefer a more pragmatic approach to life.

60

DO YOU THINK WITH YOUR FEELINGS?

LOOKING BACK THROUGHOUT HISTORY we find that some of the greatest lyrical poets and writers who spent their lives eloquently eulogizing love were often the least able to realize or experience it. It is said that real lovers are not going to waste their time *talking* about love when they can love.

People who live through their emotions find it difficult to distinguish whether they think feelings, or feel thoughts. This accounts for the absolute need of the emotional type to take time to reflect upon what they feel. While this is usually achieved through silent contemplation, the process can be accelerated by talking to a trusted friend or lover. Once some clarity is found, there is a sense of release, and only then can any action be taken. By being deeply attentive to their feelings this type can share its profound understandings and insights into the human condition with others.

For these people the life and world of feelings is valued above all other concerns. But they have an overriding need to learn how to extrapolate objective meaning from their essentially subjective experiences. This is their fundamental quest. The ensuing integrity is bought at a price, however. Emotional sensitivity means that they are subject to a wide band of mood swings and have erratic energy. In attempting to participate fully with such diverse feelings, their sense of self can be lost, becoming fragmented and unbalanced. And as all encounters with other people are personalized, it often happens that the feelings of others are experienced as if they were their own. This type of person will always need some physical way of releasing his or her pent-up emotions, either in exhaustive games or by just walking off the excess energy.

ASSESSMENT

Do you:
1. *find that others say they find you very emotional?*
2. *feel bursts of unaccountable joy at seeing someone?*
3. *often think about love or a lover?*
4. *sometimes start crying without knowing whether you are happy or sad?*
5. *feel as if a floodgate of emotion is about to be opened?*
6. *seem to feel extremes of emotion more than most people?*
7. *find it difficult to break off a love affair?*
8. *sometimes find it impossible to be reasonable?*
9. *sometimes feel overawed by an inexpressible beauty?*
10. *often find yourself falling in love?*
11. *really need to understand your thoughts and feelings?*
12. *like to talk over your feelings with a real friend?*
13. *feel helpless when trying to describe your feelings?*
14. *find sudden breakthroughs and insights?*
15. *enjoy sitting silently, taking pleasure in your thoughts?*
16. *feel that most people are scared by emotions?*
17. *often feel over-stressed?*
18. *need some simple physical activity to release emotions?*
19. *have moods of happiness and sadness simultaneously?*
20. *find you are over-sensitive to the moods of others?*

Key: *If you answer "yes" to more than 15 of the questions you are almost certainly someone who "thinks" with his, or her, feelings. Those who answer "no" to 15 or more of the questions are likely to be out of touch with their emotions.*

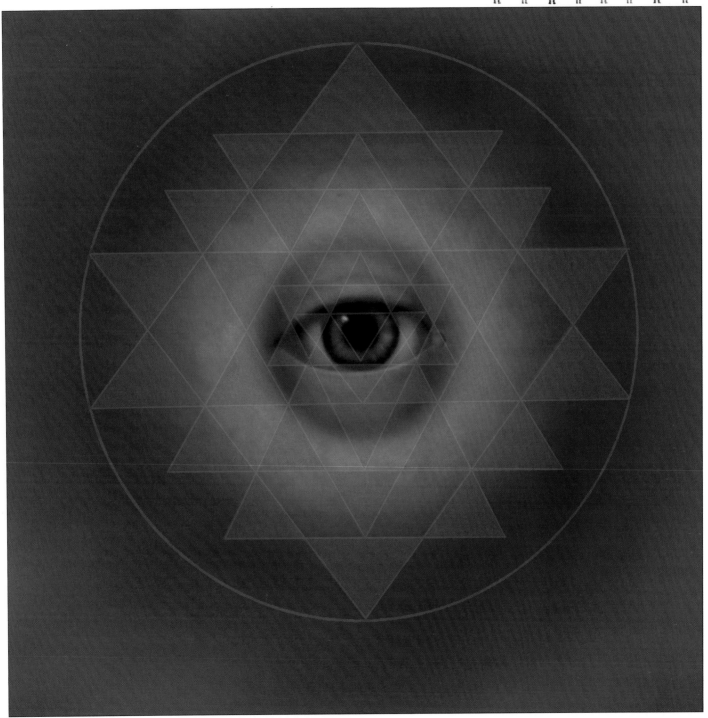

61

TRUST IN GOD BUT TETHER YOUR CAMEL?

THIS SAYING BY Mullah Nasruddin, the legendary Sufi master and jester, tells us that both trust and doubt are pathways to God. How trustful or doubting are you? To some extent that depends on your brain's biochemical and neurological makeup. Our brain is constantly codifying and reconstructing an inner model of the real world around us. The outcome of this translation of outer phenomena into an inner construct is that effectively each of us lives in a totally different virtual environment. Neurological research reveals that we live in very separate worlds, each of which would be totally alien to anyone else. Our assessments so far confirm that each of us views the world as if through our own custom-made lenses. However, we learn to behave as if there were a common and collective average world out there. This is mainly accomplished by a common sign system that defines what we experience – language. But the cost of fitting into a perceptual community is that we begin to experience the world as a set of labels. A rose becomes a noun – a fixed and agreed upon shared label for a unique living, flowering happening. Without language we would be alone within our individual space bubbles, unable to communicate with each other. Yet the idea that we can actually cross the borders of our individual inner worlds through language alone remains an illusion.

However, there are unspoken feelings that somehow do allow us to commune across the gap. We call these trust, or love, compassion, understanding and bonding. These feelings have been found to be triggered by chemicals such as oxytocin, which is released when many animals mate and care for their offspring. It has the effect of forging neural links that imprint an urgent message of bonding. It is as effective with humans as it is with, say, swans. It creates bonding pathways in the brain between lovers, parents and children. The effects have not always

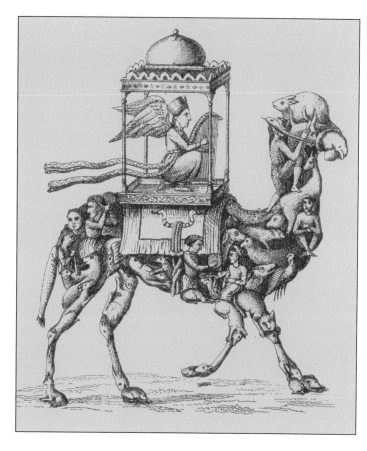

been welcomed as, in retrospect, bonding is often felt as an intrusion, as if we have lost part of our independent identity. In fact this might really be happening, as research suggests that oxytocin does rewrite some of the neural pathways. Anyone who has fallen in love recognizes the symptoms. Yet it is the very basis of love and trust.

Bonding can happen with individuals, children, family and tribe. Its chemistry can flow in any direction where there is shared activity – your fellow students, your gang, your team, your nation, your corporation. And the trust and love that

bonding brings can also create a great sense of joy, happiness and meaning.

This very simple assessment shows how trusting you are. It can also help you to celebrate your chemistry, whether you are accepting of the fact that you are seldom in control of your feelings, or whether you distrust anything that robs you of your independence and of that sense of being in charge of your actions and emotions. There is no need to judge yourself harshly if you honestly do not feel either trust or bonding.

There are two distinct mystical paths. One abides by the positive – "Yes this. Yes that too". This is the way of devotion, trust and prayer, such as practiced by the Sufi mystics of Islam, Christian mystics like St. Francis, or the devotees of Krishna in India. At the opposite pole there is the path of the negative – "No it is not this. No it is not that either." This is the way of Buddhism and Zen. It is the path of casting aside all that isn't true or real. Both ways are valid. And so, too, are attitudes of trust and non-trust. It totally depends on the individual. Only when behaviour becomes rigidly fixed and obsessively unyielding does it merit being called unhealthy or pathological.

ASSESSMENT

Would you say that:
1. *love and trust are probably just the effect of chemicals?*
2. *love and trust are far more than the effect of chemicals?*
3. *after making love you often feel less attracted to a lover?*
4. *after sex you feel closer than ever to your partner?*
5. *you prefer friends for their objective merits; not how you intuitively feel for them?*
6. *you can bond with animals just as well as people?*
7. *a friend or business acquaintance has to earn your trust?*
8. *you find people trustworthy until they prove otherwise?*
9. *love is just an idea dreamed up by the romantics?*
10. *a world without love, even flawed, is bleak indeed?*
11. *you dislike over-sentimentality in birthday cards?*
12. *you become a bit misty-eyed seeing a mare bonding with its new foal?*
13. *fluffy chicks seem too sentimental at an Easter service?*
14. *you enjoy the sight of a young creature being born?*
15. *you agree with the principle of trusting in God but ensuring your assets are secure – just in case?*
16. *you would trust in God and to hell with the camel?*

Key: Score "yes" to 5 or more even numbered questions, and "no" to more than 5 odd numbered questions, and you have a very healthy amount of oxytocin running around your system. You really enjoy the sense of bonding. You are probably trusting in your behaviour and are more than likely to be mostly happy. The reverse score of "no" to even and "yes" to odd numbered questions suggests you are sharper in your judgements, clearer when dealing with used-car salesmen, but a little on the indifferent side when it comes to strong emotions.

62

ENTERING THE DARKROOM?

THROUGHOUT THIS SECTION you have been reminded of two major features of the emotional brain. First, that it is largely unconscious in what it does, and second, that we are at the mercy of those chemicals and neurotransmitters that stream throughout our system without our conscious permission.

You may find it increasingly difficult, in the modern world, where the appearance of composure is a premium, to really access your emotional nature. At best you probably sense a gulf to be bridged; at worst your subconscious is a darkroom seething with feelings you just don't want to confront. Many therapists maintain the major reason for the apparent failure to address emotional issues is that we dare not enter that darkroom without being in command. Yet, you might well ask, as far as emotions are concerned are we ever in the driving seat?

Consider *falling* in love. Is it something you can do deliberately, like *making* love? Powerful emotions are spontaneous; they cannot be done, and if this is attempted they are immediately detected as false.

Happiness, joy, and compassion cannot be manufactured. They happen without your permission. You have to just allow yourself to be swept along by your emotions. But the modern mind is hellbent on doing things – it is programmed to take charge, from early toilet training to controlling emotions, in order to fit into the norms and beliefs of society.

Paradoxically, the whole market economy is based on the desire to possess and yet we all appear terrified of being possessed ourselves. This is the dilemma of any life in which the need to control becomes chronic. Anything that is out of our control makes us anxious and fearful. This causes us to put more emphasis on the head, where at least there is the appearance of being in command of our actions. Any suspicion that we might lose ourselves, become unconscious, or might no longer be who we think we are, largely prevents us from remaining open and vulnerable to a life overflowing with emotions.

In completing the last twenty assessments you will have become aware that everyone develops strategies to deal with emotions – through intuition, raw feelings, the senses, thinking, or a distinctive blend of all of them. What have you discovered so far about how you accept or deny your own feelings?

ASSESSMENT

Do you:
1. *follow wherever your emotions take you?*
2. *think you need to control some types of emotion?*
3. *allow emotions a large role in your life?*
4. *consider it dangerous to be out of control?*
5. *feel you could lose yourself falling in love with someone?*
6. *feel that discussing emotions is often just self indulgence?*
7. *feel that you could almost become one with your lover?*
8. *need to keep a certain independence in a relationship?*
9. *consider it important always to understand and express your emotions?*
10. *feel that being engulfed by unconscious emotions is a sure road to madness?*
11. *feel you should trust your naturally emerging emotions?*
12. *see nothing odd in the phrase "making" love?*

Key: *If you answer "yes" to 4 or more of the odd numbered questions it suggests you are open to your emotions and are generally trusting. If you answer "yes" to 4 or more of the even numbered questions it suggests you keep your feelings at a distance. Neither trait is either right or wrong; it just indicates your particular strategy. Only when an attitude becomes obsessively rigid and inflexible should the alarm bells start ringing.*

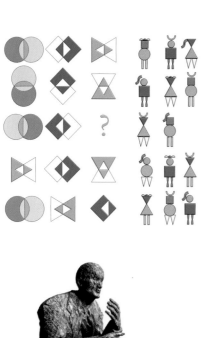

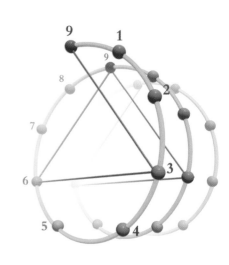

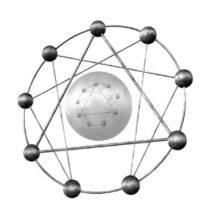

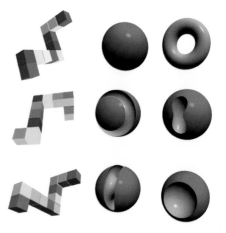

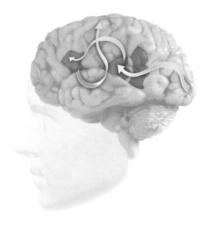

PART III

Thinking types

THE CEREBRAL CORTEX IS THE LATEST evolutionary development within the human brain. This part of the brain has gifted us with consciousness of ourselves and the ability to say "I think therefore I am". It is evident that our present era is dominated by the thinking type. Most of our technology tends to favour the thinker above the sensual and emotional types. Our educational systems reward those who use their cortex rather than their bodies or their feeling centres. Virtually all intelligence tests are designed with thinking types in mind. These people are often happiest thinking *about* action rather than acting. They enjoy ideas and virtual realities more than direct experience. Some of the assessments that follow are based on psychometric tests that are quite demanding. But don't panic. They are only designed to reveal what you *really* excel at.

63

HOW DO YOU THINK YOU THINK?

PERHAPS ONE OF THE STRANGEST FACTS to emerge from recent neurological research[38] is that you could travel the length and breadth of the territory of the brain and yet, for well over two-thirds of your journey, never encounter consciousness at all. While virtually the whole brain is always active, you would only find a very small percentage of it that you could identify as "you", a conscious and aware entity. Ask people in which part of the body they feel they are centred, or where they physically exist, and the majority will point to just above and between the eyes. Their intuition is confirmed by the findings of modern neurology backed up by brain-scanning techniques. The frontal lobes are the seat of self-awareness, where Descartes could confidently say "I think, therefore I am."

In most everyday activities the brain is on automatic – when riding bicycles, driving cars, calculating distances and numbers and making coffee. We don't need to be constantly aware of what we are doing unless something unexpected, like the milk boiling over, suddenly galvanizes those frontal lobes into action.

The illustrations opposite show the relatively small size of this region, although it stretches back into the brain with many "bridges", like the pre-motor cortex, to the larger territories. Just behind the frontal lobe is the area known as the pre-frontal cortex, where ideas are chewed over, strategies are devised and decisions are made over actions to be taken. Below this is the area where emotions are registered and meaning is assigned to events and experience.

The diagrams on the opposite page only give approximate areas of major brain activity but can act as useful guides in the following six tests.

WHERE YOU ARE CONSCIOUS

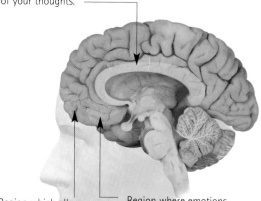

Region of attention and where you are aware of your thoughts.

Region which allows you to put on hold your immediate urges and desires and plan for the future.

Region where emotions are experienced and assimilated and meaning and significance arise.

ASSESSMENT

From the brief descriptions on these pages you can locate those areas of the brain which become active while you are carrying out certain tasks. Over the next few pages you will be asked to use your brain in different and often difficult ways. You will find some of the tests relatively easy while others might stretch your ability. While engaged on each assessment you might imagine the locations where your brain is in action during that particular task. It is possible to sense those areas.
The overall significance of the six major assessments of your abilities will be examined after you have done the tests.

WHERE YOU PROCESS INFORMATION

The area of the frontal lobe is the site of consciousness where "we think, therefore we are".

Touching and sensations

Spatial awareness

If the human brain was simple enough for us to understand, we'd be so simple we couldn't.

Anon.

Smell

Vision

Taste

Hearing

Coordination

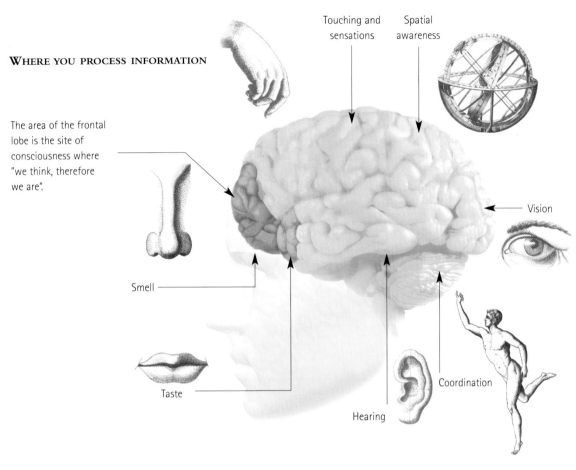

Left	Right	Left	Right	Left	Right	Left	Right

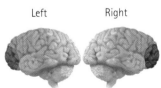

Areas of the cortex which deal with conscious thinking.

Areas of movement and sensation.

Areas of visual processing.

Areas concerned with language.

ANALYTICAL   **NUMERICAL**

MECHANICAL   **SPATIAL**

VISUAL

VERBAL

64

VERBAL REASONING

THE NEXT SIX ASSESSMENTS are in the form of psychometric tests that are not designed to be easy. Most readers will find that in many of them they will score below what is given as good or outstanding. But you will probably find at least one in which you do well.

The whole purpose of these particular tests is to discover what you are good at – not your average abilities. Don't take them too seriously, and take your time doing them. You may be surprised to discover abilities you never thought you had.

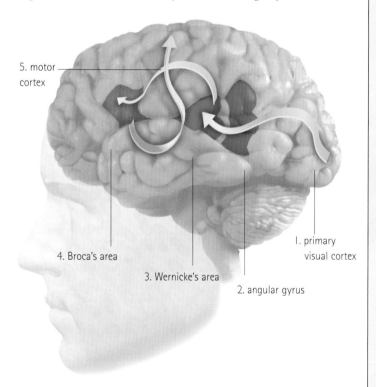

5. motor cortex

4. Broca's area

3. Wernicke's area

2. angular gyrus

1. primary visual cortex

As you read this page your primary visual cortex (1) feeds information to the angular gyrus (2), which bridges word recognition and the language centres of the Wernicke's (3) and Broca's (4) areas. It also sends information to the motor cortex (5) to activate the muscles so you can write down your answers.[39]

ASSESSMENT

After reading the introduction to test 63, answer the following without hurrying:

1. *Which one of these jumbled words does not fit? (clue ~ white water) a. llaesug b. wasn c. tabslarso d. orwc*

2. *Which, in sequence, is the penultimate letter in CALM a. C b. A c. L d. M*

3. *Concupiscence is to covet as consecrate is to: a. desire b. need c. lust d. abstinence*

4. *Which is the odd woman out? a. martrist b. naroa c. neb d. naan*

5. *Which is definitely not a metaphor? a. simile b. metonymy c. metamer d. synecdoche*

6. *Sea is to puddle as deep is to: a. ocean b. lake c. shallow d. expansive*

7. *Never is to seldom as always is to: a. sometimes b. perhaps c. invariably d. occasional*

8. *Which is the odd one out? a. probity b. integrity c. honour d. duplicity*

9. *Which one of these just doesn't fit? a. exonerated b. vindicated c. denounced d. absolved*

10. *Which four letter word can you put after these letters to make a new word for each?*

SP
B
D
T
TH

(? ? ? ?)

11. Insert a word which means the same as the two outside the brackets. Design (? ? ? ? ?) Project

12. Insert a word which completes the first word and starts the second. be (? ? ? ? ?) hazel

13. Which doesn't fit?
a. god b. gronad c. tar d. lerisruq e. ousme

14. A clue from the bottom line gives a four letter word that can prefix all three at the top.
_ _ _ _ maiden _ _ _ _ some _ _ _ _ basin
a. headstrong b. handsome c. shipshape d. sail away

15. Fill in the word
service (r e e d) pedant
tomb (_ _ _ _) essential

16. Insert a word which completes the word beginning (be) and starts the word ending with (ing)
(be) _ _ _ _ (ing)

17. Dynamism is the opposite of:
a. entropy b. electricity c. slow d. resistance

18. Age is to childhood as wine is to:
a. wisdom b. bottle c. grapes d. innocence

19. Hawk is to dove as assassin is to:
a. terrorist b. victim c. eagle d. dovecote

20. Lateral is to linear as box is to:
a. perspective b. plane c. sphere d. line

21. Incoherence is to rational as sullenness is to:
a. affectionate b. saturnine c. cantankerous d. irascible

22. Malevolent is to spiteful as separation is to:
a. fragmentation b. confluence c. solidarity d. conjunction

23. Antiseptic is to sanitized as evening is to:
a. noon b. dusk c. fledgling d. reveille

24. Quixotic is to eccentric as evidence is to:
a. testimonial b. contradiction c. disproof d. rebuttal

25. Which is the odd one out?
a. ocean b. harbour c. beach d. cove

26. Which is the odd month out?
a. August b. September c. October d. November

27. Which word doesn't fit?
a. lustre b. sparkle c. nimbus d. penumbra

28. Insert a word completing the first and starting the second.
(Clue: Country)   Indig (_ _ _ _ _ _) al

29. Insert a word completing the first and starting the second.
(Clue: India)   Bl (_ _ _) ing

30. Which is the odd one out?
a. dichotomy b. synergy c. complicity d. union

Score 18 or over and you are obviously good with words.
Score over 24 and you are gifted, probably do diagramless and acrostic puzzles or are in publishing or word-oriented work.

ANSWERS

1. (d)	11. PLAN	21. (a)
2. (L)	12. WITCH	22. (a)
3. (d)	13. DRAGON	23. (b)
4. (d)	14. HAND	24. (a)
5. (c)	15. MOSS	25. (a)
6. (c)	16. LONG	26. (a)
7. (c)	17. (d)	27. (d)
8. (d)	18. (c)	28. NATION
9. (c)	19. (b)	29. INK
10. READ	20. (b)	30. (a)

PERCEPTUAL REASONING

These are designed to test your perceptual abilities.

1. When these two figures are combined what is the result?

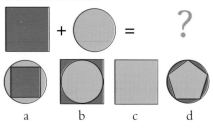

a   b   c   d

2. Which in this sequence is the odd one out?

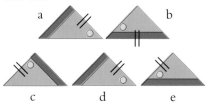

c   d   e

3. Which doesn't fit?

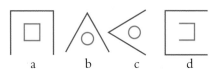

a   b   c   d

4. Which number from the bottom row would be the next in this sequence?

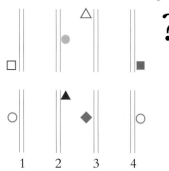

1   2   3   4

5. Which arrow completes the line?

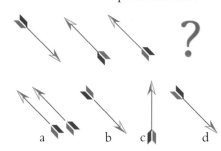

a   b   c   d

6. Which image completes this sequence?

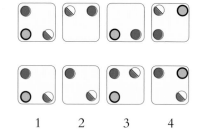

1   2   3   4

7. Which is the odd one in this sequence?

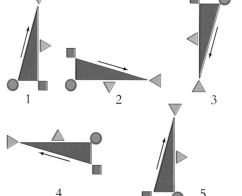

8. Which image below completes this sequence?

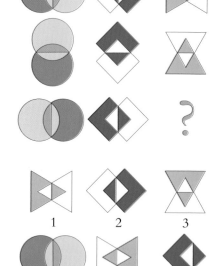

1   2   3
4   5   6

9. Which is the next in this sequence?

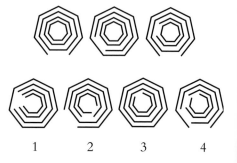

1   2   3   4

10. Complete this sequence.

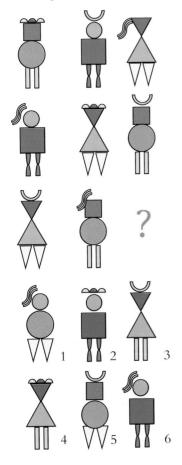

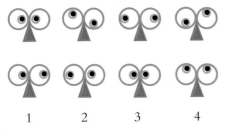

11. Which comes next in this sequence?

12. Which comes next in this sequence?

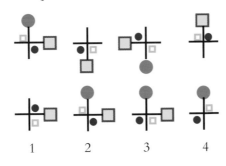

13. Which comes next in this sequence?

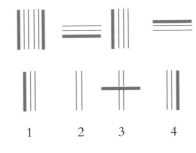

14. Which comes next in this sequence?

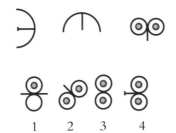

15. Which comes next in this sequence?

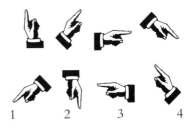

16. Which comes next in this sequence?

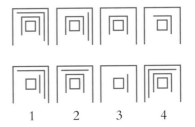

66

MECHANICAL REASONING

ASSESSMENT

Imagine the different components of this kinetic machine on the left in motion, then answer the questions below about the movement of its various parts.

Fig. I

1. *Wheel A moves in a anti-clockwise direction. Does the end of arm B*
   (a) move directly up and down the track,
   (b) move along the half circle track,
   (c) get stuck, jamming the machine?

Fig. II

2. *Wheel A moves in a anti-clockwise direction. Does the large wheel C*
   (a) move anti-clockwise, (b) clockwise, (c) oscillate between the two, (d) so that the first wheel jams with the arm?
3. *Does the wheel D (a) move clockwise, (b) anti-clockwise, (c) remain static?*
4. *Does wheel E move (a) clockwise, (b) anti-clockwise, (c) remain static?*

Fig. III

5. *Which way does the large cog rotate? (a) Clockwise, (b) anti-clockwise?*
6. *Does the small cog on the far right-hand rotate (a) anti-clockwise, (b) clockwise?*
7. *Does the right eye: (a) turn towards the left eye, (b) turn towards the right eye, (c) remain stationary?*
8. *Does the left eye: (a) turn towards the right eye, (b) turn towards the left eye, (c) remain stationary?*

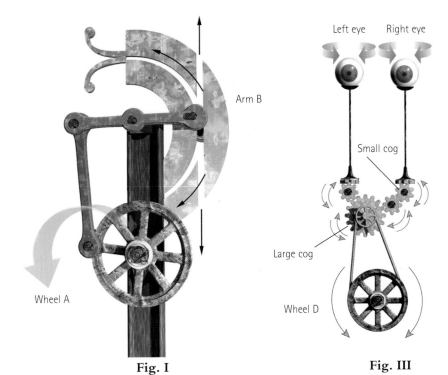

Fig. I

Fig. III

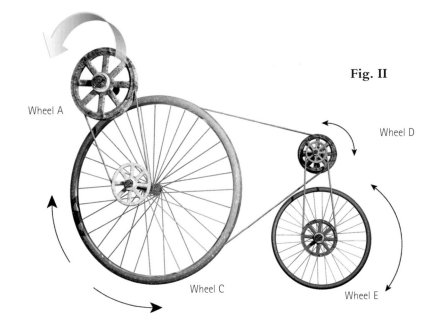

Fig. II

67

REASONING IN SPACE

These are designed to test your spatial awareness and abilities. Take your time.

1. Two shapes, a positive sphere and a negative ring, interact to create a third shape. Select those shapes which are possible from their combinations.

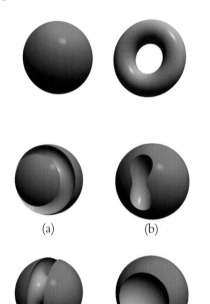

(a)   (b)

(c)   (d)

2. When this flat image is built in 3D which solid below can it make?

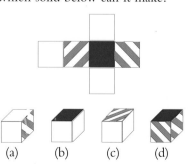

(a)   (b)   (c)   (d)

3. Which solid below can be made from this flat design?

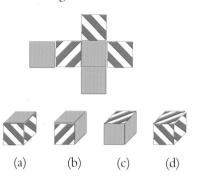

(a)   (b)   (c)   (d)

4. Which solid below can be made from this flat design?

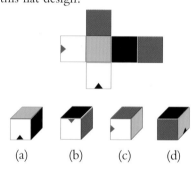

(a)   (b)   (c)   (d)

5. Which solid below can be made from this flat design?

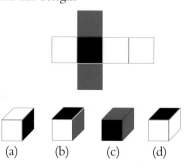

(a)   (b)   (c)   (d)

6. A large positive shape and a small negative shape interact leaving a third shape. Select from below those which are possible.

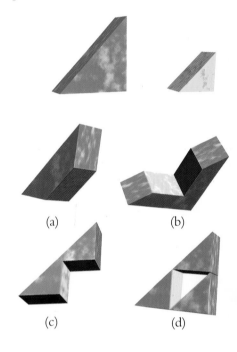

(a)   (b)

(c)   (d)

7. Which solid below can be made from this flat design?

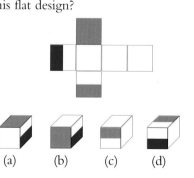

(a)   (b)   (c)   (d)

8. If the white shape were laid over the blue which shape would be possible?

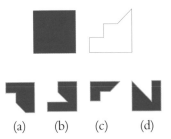

(a)   (b)   (c)   (d)

9. Which solid below can be made from this flat design with no overlaps?

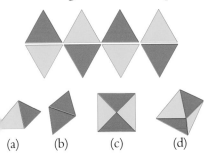

(a)   (b)   (c)   (d)

10. Which solid below can be made from this flat design?

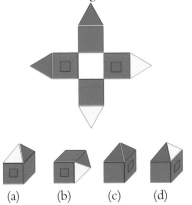

(a)   (b)   (c)   (d)

11. The positive white block interacts with the negative purple shape. Which possible shapes are formed?

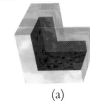

(a)   (b)   (c)   (d)

12. Spot the odd one out.

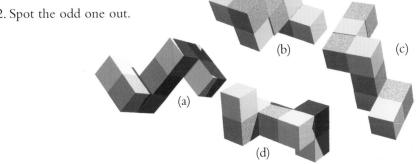

(b)   (c)   (a)   (d)

13. Which solids below cannot be made from this flat design?

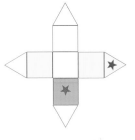

(a)   (b)   (c)   (d)

A score of over 15 reveals a good spatial sense. A score of over 22 shows you are gifted, and also extremely observant as many of the questions had multiple answers.

ANSWERS

1. (a),(b),(c)
2. (a),(c)
3. (a),(c)
4. (a),(c)
5. (b)
6. (a),(b),(d)
7. (b),(c)
8. (a),(b),(c)
9. (c),(d)
10. (b),(d)
11. (b),(d)
12. (c)
13. (b),(d)

x=0

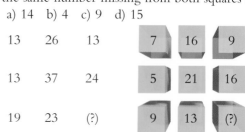

NUMERICAL REASONING

1. What is the missing number?   5 8 13 21 34 (?)

2. What is the missing number?

3	5	9	15
5	8	15	(?)

3. The diagonal of a rectangle is five inches with one side being four inches long. What is the perimeter?
        a) 12   b) 14   c) 16   d) 18

4. A group of 60 has 36 boys. What is the percentage of girls?
        a) 20%   b) 24%   c) 40%   d) 48%

5. Maggie is two years older than Tom. Twelve years ago she was twice as old as Tom. How old is Maggie now?
        a) 14   b) 16   c) 20   d) 32

6. What is the missing number?

13	7	6
27	13	14
39	13	(?)

7. Identify the missing number: 5   11   21   (?)   85

8. Which number completes the circle?
        a) 9   b) 7   c) 16   d) 96

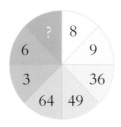

9. Find the same number missing from both squares below:
        a) 14   b) 4   c) 9   d) 15

13	26	13
13	37	24
19	23	(?)

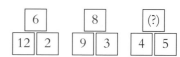

10. Which is the largest number?
        a) 41/80   b) 17/32   c) 25/48   d) 21/40

11. Complete the last number in the squares:

12. Complete the number on the last domino:

13. What is the number on the far right?
        a) 150   b) 149   c) 56   d) 121

14. What is the missing number below on the right?
   a) 5   b) 14   c) 16   d) 19

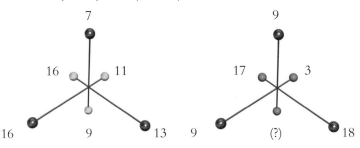

15. What is the missing number on the right?
   a) 15   b) 10   c) 13   d) 12

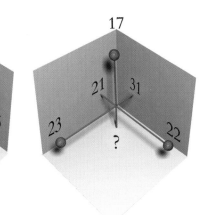

16. What is the missing number below?
   a) 5   b) 14   c) 18   d) 19

17. What is the missing number on the right?
   a) 20   b) 9   c) 16   d) 14

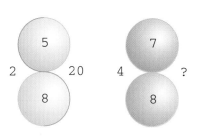

69

HOW GOOD ARE YOU AT ANALYSIS?

THE FOLLOWING ASSESSMENTS will give some indication of how you think, and how you assemble information in order to form logical conclusions and strategies.

Sam and James wear glasses. James and Peter love to play football. Who is most likely to break his glasses?

1. a) James   b) Sam   c) Peter

Judith is fatter than Jenny. Sarah is fatter than Judith.

2. Who is fattest?

3. Who is thinnest?

Choose two of the statements below that confirm that "The Dale is north of Riverside".

4. a) Riverside is south of Beeching.
   b) The Dale is north of Beeching.
   c) Beeching is east of Mirkwood.
   d) Riverside is southwest of Mirkwood.

Newtown is larger than Oldham. Seatown is larger than Newtown.

5. Which is the largest of the three?

Choose two of the statements below that confirm that "Maggie is playing hockey".

6. a) Maggie always plays on the ice rink.
   b) Maggie is on the ice rink.
   c) Hockey is played on the ice rink in spring.
   d) Everyone on the ice rink is playing hockey.

Choose two of the statements below that confirm that "Penny is blonde and beautiful". (The girls are either blonde or brunette.)

7. a) Penny and Paula are beautiful.
   b) Paula and Julie are not blonde.
   c) Julie and Betty are not beautiful.
   d) Betty and Penny are not brunettes.

In the last 100 metres of a race Ben is in front, Ned is second, Tom is third and Tony is last. At 50 metres from the finish Ben changes position with Tom. At the finish Tom changes position with Ned.

8. Who is last in the race?

9. Who wins the race?

Choose two of the statements below that confirm that "Tom runs faster than Tony".

10. a) Ned won the last race.
    b) Tom can run further than Ned.
    c) Tom can run as fast as Ned.
    d) Ned runs faster than Tony.

Choose two of the statements below that confirm that "It is Saturday today".

11. a) September began on a Saturday this year.
    b) Five days ago it was Tuesday.
    c) It is the 8th of September today.
    d) The 9th of September was on a Monday last year.

In a rock band Jimmy plays the synthesizer but not the guitar. Tessa plays the guitar and the drums. Dave also plays the drums but cannot play the synthesizer. Joe plays the guitar but not the drums.

If each of the performers plays two of three instruments then which one could take over from Tessa if she is sick?

12. a) Jimmy   b) Dave   c) Joe

There are six families living in an apartment building which has three floors. The apartments are arranged so that even-numbered apartments have a door on the right while odd-numbered ones have a door on the left. Apartments 1 and 2 are on the first floor; 3 and 4 are on the second; and 5 and 6 are on the top floor. The Simpsons have a door to the right and are living between two families.

13. What is the number of their apartment?

The Smiths live next door to the Simpsons. The Gables live in an even-numbered apartment with the Browns below them. Both the Butchers and the Fishers live next to families whose names start with different letters.

14. In which apartment do the Butchers reside?

15. Who lives next door to the Browns?

16. Who lives above the Simpsons?

17. Who lives in apartment number 1?

18. Who lives at number 6?

19. Who lives on the first floor next to the Fishers?

20. Who can hear the Butchers dancing above them?

Albert and his wife Collette organize a dinner party. They invite their old, rather withdrawn friend, Jason, because they know he is the lover of the shy introvert, Susan. The trouble is that they have also invited Dennis, who is attracted to Susan. Both Susan and the hosts' old friend dislike Dennis and Dennis hates Susan's admirer. So Albert invites Diana, who likes Dennis but is jealous of Susan. The host seats himself at the head of the table (1, in the figure top right) with Susan to his left and Dennis as far away from Susan as possible. The hostess decides to seat herself between Dennis and her old friend and makes sure Diana sits next to Dennis.

21. When Susan shyly looks at her lover does she have to look to either left or right?

22. When Dennis asks the host to pass the wine around the table does it have to be touched by anyone who dislikes him?

23. If Dennis is talking to Collette can Diana talk to a man next to her?

24. Which seat is surrounded by those most friendly?

25. Which seats next to one another do Albert and Collette fear might create the most friction?

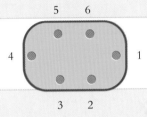

70

ARE YOU DOING WHAT YOU DO BEST?

HAVING COMPLETED THE LAST SIX ASSESSMENTS you will have some idea of what your talents and abilities appear to be. However, this does not give you much of an overall picture of the nature of your reasoning and how you might make it work best for you.

Many of us are in occupations that have been forced on us in one way or another. We remain like one of the world's greatest surgeons who, as he retired, bemoaned the fact that he'd had to follow his father's choice and so never became a dancer.

Often we have no idea of how precious our familiar gifts are. The following are only indications of those activities which you might re-evaluate in the light of your own findings.

SPATIAL REASONING

The ability to visualize solid three-dimensional objects and space from two-dimensional visual information.

VERBAL REASONING

The ability to reason with both spoken and written words.

TECHNICAL REASONING

The ability to respond to objects and situations within the changing environment in practical and direct ways.

NUMERICAL REASONING

The ability to think in numbers, although it should be understood this is not identical with mathematical reasoning.

ANALYTICAL REASONING

The ability to think logically, making meaningful connections, organizing structures and strategies from seemingly chaotic information.

PERCEPTUAL REASONING

The ability to think in abstract symbols and ideas.

ASSESSMENT

Choose the combination of talent that best describes you from the list below, and see whether it corresponds with your work:

Thinking in words and numbers.
The ability to manipulate and express overviews ~ senior administrators, organizational heads, economists, managers.

Thinking perceptionally and in words.
The ability to theorize ~ the natural sciences, eco-biologists, ecologists, lyricists.

Thinking in words and spatial concepts.
The ability to express aspects of three dimensions in words and word concepts in space ~ photojournalists, creative directors, film directors, film and TV cameramen, design consultants, publishers, multi-media directors.

Thinking analytically and in words.
The ability to analyse in words ~ philosophers, psychologists, lawyers, management consultants, science journalists, critics, science editors.

Thinking in numerical and perceptual mode.
The ability to think in fundamentally original ways about the phenomenal world ~ the mathematical sciences, theoretical physicists, chemists, astronomers, musicians.

Thinking in numerical and technical ways.
The ability to think in practical yet numerical modes ~ all aspects of applied science, technicians, toolmakers, structural engineers, design engineers.

Thinking in numerical and spatial ways.
The ability to visualize three dimensions with a feel for numbers ~ surveying, architecture, construction, information technology, graphic multi-media programming, 3D modellers.

Thinking in numerical and analytical ways.
The ability to think analytically, yet with a number bias ~ statisticians, stockbrokers, systems analysts, method-based musicians.

Thinking in perceptual and spatial mode.
The ability to think in space and time and overviews ~ constructional and kinetic sculptors, psychometrists, artists, scientific illustrators, "spatial" musicians, synaesthetes.

Thinking in perceptual and technical ways.
The ability to bring theory into practice ~ inventors, laboratory technicians, engineers, applied arts and sciences.

Thinking in perceptual and analytical ways.
The ability to think critically in abstract theory ~ all aspects of pure science, philosophy, the understanding of underlying reasons for the way things are.

Thinking in spatial and technical ways.
The ability to visualize three dimensions in a practical way ~ modelmakers, carpenters, builders, printers, electronics engineers, technical illustrators, music technicians.

Thinking in spatial and perceptual ways.
The ability to visualize three dimensions in abstract and theoretical terms ~ 3D designers, sculptors, painters, musicians, pilots, multi-media directors.

Thinking in spatial and analytical ways.
The ability to visualize, analyse overviews and three dimensions ~ graphics programmers, 3D modellers, economists, computer graphics, electronic engineers, civil/structural engineers.

Thinking in technical and analytical ways.
The ability to think in the most practical yet analytical way ~ information technicians, quality controllers, programmers, construction consultants, mechanical engineers, mechanics.

71

DO YOU THINK LIKE A MALE OR A FEMALE?

ARE THERE REALLY any hard-wired differences between the brains of men and women that reveal an entirely different way of thinking?

The evidence, from research carried out in the last few decades, is not conclusive. However, it does suggest that, for instance, the right-hand hemisphere of the cortex is generally thicker in males than in females. When shown emotionally charged images during brain scans, the emotional centres in women's brains light up, while the males hardly register at all.

The thick cluster of fibres that link the two halves of the brain are on average larger in women than in men, which may account for the fact that women tend to use both hemispheres when solving a problem while men appear to be more focused on the left-hand side.

It is thought that the difference between the sexes is caused by certain hormones released at critical stages during fetal neurological development. It is known, for instance, that androgen, often associated with male development, does increase spatial performance when administered to females.

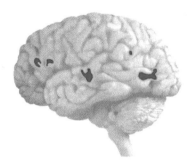

MALE BRAIN

When asked to think of something emotional, men do not generate much activity in their emotional centres. In comparing the sexes, it is found that on average men are:

1. better at mathematical reasoning, although not so good at actual calculation.
2. more skilled in tasks that have a spatial dimension.
3. better at detecting the figure from a disguised background as in camouflage.
4. superior in mentally rotating objects.
5. better at hitting targets accurately.
6. better at distinguishing embedded shapes within complex patterns.
7. faster at analysing complex data.
8. more gifted at understanding objects in terms of physical causality.

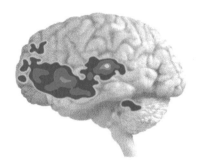

FEMALE BRAIN

When asked to think of something emotional, women generate far more activity in their emotional centres. In comparing the sexes, it is found that on average women are:

1. more empathetic, cooperative and better judges of other peoples' behaviour.
2. more likely to develop their language skills faster than men, being better at spelling and understanding subtle nuances of meaning.
3. better at matching items.
4. better at generating ideas, especially through words.
5. quicker in tests that require matching like with like.
6. better able to spot objects missing in a display like in the four illustrations opposite.
7. better at mathematical calculations.
8. far more skilled in delicate manual tasks.

The lists on the opposite page can confirm whether you tend to think as a male or as a female. Try the three tests below. You have ten seconds for each one.

(a)
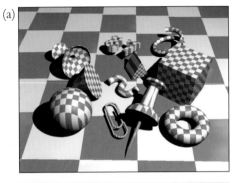

(b)

(c)

(d)

1. Spot the missing object.

2. Which is the odd one out?

(a) (b) (c)
(d) (e) (f)

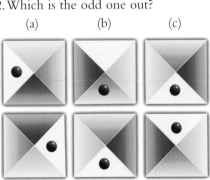

3. Which is the odd one out?

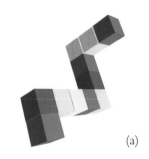

(a)

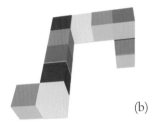

(b)

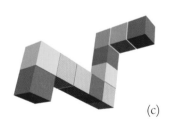

(c)

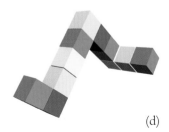

(d)

ANSWERS

1. **(d).** *The small prism is missing. If you found it within less than ten seconds you are most likely to be a woman, or at least think like a female. You are also quick.*

2. **(b).** *All the other balls are on a light background. Males do well turning images in their mind.*

3. **(d).** *The three cubes at the end are oriented to the left of the main figure. In the other three they are to the right. If you are a man and took too long on the first test you will probably be able to feel superior in this one. Invariably women take longer.*

72

WHO ARE YOU AT WORK?

A NUMBER OF TYPOLOGIES and behavioural tests have been developed over the years to assist business management to make decisions about personnel. Most of these deal with strategies that people tend to use in everyday interactions with the organization, clients and other employees.

These are patterns of behaviour that have become familiar and habitual, and are likely to be highly predictable in situations of stress or negative tensions.

This particular model[40] is typical of the genre; it consists of a fourfold type but contains a novel variant on the theme of yielding/dominant and reserved/outgoing.

The questions below are descriptions of the four styles of interpersonal relationships. Answer all the questions to discover who you might be.

THE DIRECTOR

Do you:

1. feel most comfortable making decisions?
2. prefer to make difficult decisions alone?
3. find it difficult to delegate responsibility?
4. tend to counter-attack when strongly criticized?
5. like to be in control?

Would you say that:

6. you can be a bit insensitive to others?
7. you are competitive and often goal-oriented?
8. you are resourceful and a good strategist?
9. you are assertive?
10. others think you are sometimes autocratic and domineering?
11. you prefer immediate action to long deliberations?
12. you tend to state your opinions freely?

THE COUNSELLOR

Do you:

1. acquiesce when someone tries to force an opinion?
2. prefer to be part of a team rather than go it alone?
3. enjoy supporting others toward a common goal?
4. like to participate in a project with many others?
5. feel the process is more important than reaching the actual goal?

Would you say that:

6. you could be described as outgoing yet unassuming?
7. you listen readily and are genuinely interested in others?
8. you tend to withdraw when you are ignored?
9. you tend to give in when aggressively challenged?
10. you are very sociable?
11. you are known by your associates to be cooperative?
12. find it difficult to implement unpopular decisions?

THE REVIEWER

Do you:

1. consider yourself to be reserved with others?
2. feel that your main orientation is towards thinking?
3. generally prefer to work alone?
4. mostly prefer to avoid conflict and argument?
5. find it difficult to delegate responsibility?

Would you say that:

6. you tend to be controlled?
7. you are generally non-confrontational?
8. you are good at planning and organizing?
9. you are good at examining facts and analysing problems?
10. you are a good listener?
11. become resigned when others don't listen to your advice?
12. tend to withdraw when you are rebuffed?

THE DOMINATOR

Do you:

1. tend to get emotional in your dealings with others?
2. show your feelings easily?
3. like to get your own way?
4. often use your "gut feeling" when making decisions?
5. thrive on the interplay between yourself and others?

Would you say that:

6. you can be quite persuasive?
7. you can get carried away with projects and ideas?
8. you are ambitious?
9. you are assertive and even confrontational?
10. you get irritated when no one listens to you?
11. you get aggressive when challenged?
12. you get stubborn when others obstruct your efforts?

ASSESSMENT

If you answer "yes" to more than 8 questions for any of the four modes there is a high probability that you fit this type. Most people score highly in at least two of the modes, it being unusual for anyone to fit only one type.

From the nature of the questions you not only can get a clear picture of your own overall traits, but also those of your colleagues and fellow employees.

Armed with this information you should be able to negotiate your workplace with consummate skill.

73

HOW DO YOU FUNCTION WITHIN THE CORPORATE BODY?

THE LAST ASSESSMENT dealt with four essential kinds of behaviour at work. The four types on this page are yet another way[41] of looking at how we all function within our various organizations and workplaces.

This particular typology assesses the leadership qualities for teams and of those who would run corporations, yet it also reveals how we all see ourselves and how we act. Loosely based on a number of psychological and psychometric tests, these questions will gradually fill out the major aspects of each type. Answer the questions for each type.

THE MAKER

Do you:

1. believe in being paid for a job well done?
2. prefer to create or construct rather than to manage a business?
3. find beauty in a well-crafted object or idea?
4. see others in terms of supporting or thwarting your aims ?
5. prefer to work on your own rather than involving others?

Would you say that:

6. you are no good at organizing others to do your work?
7. so long as you get support you don't mind who gives it?
8. you feel self-contained in your chosen work or craft?
9. you are fairly modest and sincere in your beliefs?
10. you avoid the organizational and financial side of work?
11. patrons who support your ideas don't have to be "good"?
12. the act of creation is the most important part of life?

THE SURVIVOR

Do you:

1. feel the need to have some power over your life?
2. agree that life is a case of eat or be eaten?
3. make sure you have a good defence before attacking?
4. dream of building some great empire?
5. tend to feel that your subordinates are a bit inferior?

Would you say that:

6. if you want to get on in life you can't always be honest?
7. you bought this book to find strategies to survive?
8. you are carefully advancing yourself in your job?
9. losers probably deserve what they get?
10. often life and work are not a game but a jungle?
11. others are as competitive as you are but hide it well?
12. a friend who got your job was really your enemy?

THE TEAM PLAYER

Do you:

1. feel good about being part of a powerful, protective company?
2. admire the Japanese concept of corporate loyalty?
3. identify with your company or your team?
4. tend to be supportive of others in your team?
5. thrive on your team's good performance?

Would you say that:

6. you are concerned with the human aspect of your work?
7. you can be a little too submissive in confronting authority?
8. you are very concerned with job security?
9. you share in the glory of your company's achievements?
10. you try to create an ambience of cooperation with staff?
11. you are stimulated by your fellow workers' mutual aims?
12. you would hate to be self-employed?

THE PLAYER OF GAMES

Do you:

1. really love to win?
2. enjoy competitive activity when you are good at it?
3. get impatient with those who are over cautious?
4. like to take risks yourself?
5. see work as a complex and enjoyable game?

Would you say that:

6. you love new ideas and short cuts to a goal?
7. you enjoy discussing tactics and strategies more than most?
8. you motivate others to increase their pace to equal yours?
9. you energize others with your ideas and vision?
10. you feel that only gamesters like you should be leaders?
11. you worry more than those who won't take a risk?
12. you tend to see people in terms of their use towards the goal ?

ASSESSMENT

If you score "yes" more than 7 times for any of the four modes it is highly probable that you fit this type. It also is likely that you will score highly in another of the modes, for once again it is rare that anyone fits a single type. In most modern organizations, from tennis to information technology companies, character is more

subtly blended. The gamester becomes a team player acting on behalf of the organization with which he, or she, identifies. The craftsperson also can become the scientist who will work for whomever will foot the bill for research — be it state, army or corporation.

74

HOW DO YOU RELATE TO THE OUTER WORLD?

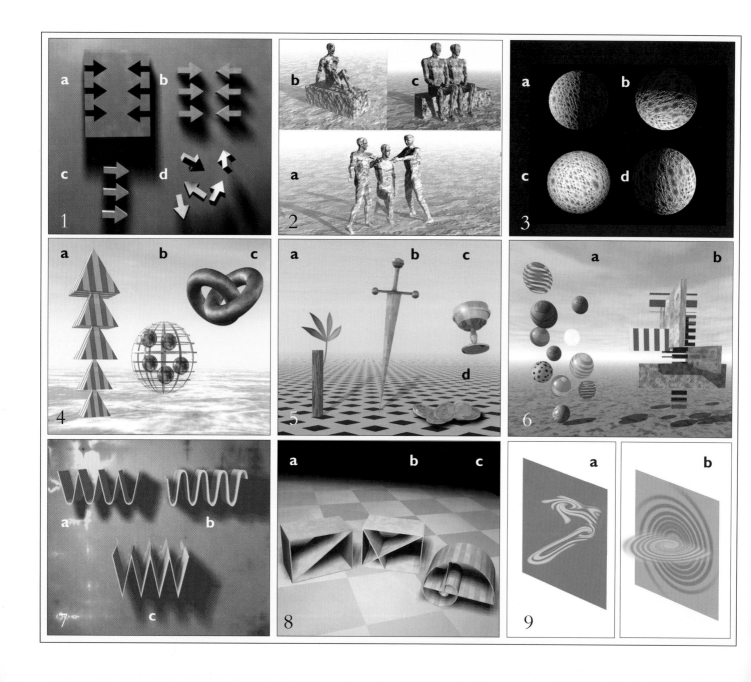

ASSESSMENT

Choose the image which most appeals to you in each of the picture groups on these pages, noting its identifying letter. It is important to do this as quickly as possible without thinking about what they might signify. Only check the results below after you have completed your choice.

This particular test indicates your tendency to relate easily to others or keep them at a distance. Most of us waver in different situations between the two. Socializers are unusually outgoing, impulsive, confident, assertive, active and demonstrative, and really enjoy being the centre of attention. They will score strongly in the first two columns of the table on the right. Loners tend to be more passive, reflective, reserved, sensitive and serious-minded, preferring solo activities like reading, to those of socializing or being the centre of attention. They will typically score better in the middle and third columns.

Key: *If you score higher than 6 in any of the columns on the right ("Relating", "Average", "Withdrawing") it shows a decided tendency toward that type of behaviour. If you score right down the center you are average.*

	RELATING	AVERAGE	WITHDRAWING
1	a	b	c
2	b	a	c
3	ad	b	c
4	a	c	b
5	bd		ac
6	a		b
7	a	c	b
8	c	a	b
9	a		b
10	a	c	b

75

ASSESS YOUR ENNEAGRAM TYPE

ASSESSMENT

Check below to see which personality type most corresponds to your self-image. Once you have selected your type, you can use the key at the bottom of the page to discover which of the nine enneagram types set out on the opposite page it corresponds with.

TYPE A
Positive aspects: self-assured, authentic, confident, popular, tends to stand out in company, ambitious, efficient, image-conscious, pragmatic, career-oriented.
Negative aspects: competitive, narcissistic, arrogant, devious, exhibitionist, self-promoting, sadistic, deceptive, calculating, pretentious.

TYPE B
Positive aspects: creative, inspired, intuitive, humorous, emotional, romantic, artistic, imaginative, introspective, a dreamer, self-absorbed.
Negative aspects: moody, effete, melancholy, self-pitying, alienated, depressed, self-destructive, despairing, precious, self-indulgent.

TYPE C
Positive aspects: independent, cooperative, lovable, loyal, reliable, responsible, trustworthy, trusting, traditionalist, dutiful, committed, organized.
Negative aspects: over-obedient to authority, indecisive, defensive, insecure, over-dependent, anxious, paranoid, masochistic, ambivalent, cautious.

TYPE D
Positive aspects: content, receptive, stable, peaceful, optimistic, genuine, accommodating, good-natured, easy-going, patient, self-possessed.
Negative aspects: complacent, unreflective, neglectful, ineffectual, avoiding conflicts, oblivious, ostrich-like behaviour, over-habitual.

TYPE E
Positive aspects: discerning, wise, realistic, tolerant, rational, fair, ethical, strong personal integrity, moral, idealist, reformer, crusader.
Negative aspects: judgmental, opinionated, self-righteous, overly critical, condemnatory, punitive, over-perfectionist, preachy.

TYPE F
Positive aspects: altruistic, caring, empathic, compassionate, concerned, generous, helpful, demonstrative, well-intentioned, self-sacrificing.
Negative aspects: patronizing, overwhelming need to be indispensable to others, manipulative, creating guilt in others, coercive, "victim/martyr" role, self-deceptive.

TYPE G
Positive aspects: Perceptive, insightful, visionary, discoverer, pioneer, innovative, knowledgeable, original, intellectual, observant, analytical.
Negative aspects: extremist, reclusive, phobic, cynical, obsessed by theories and ideas, eccentric, loses contact with environment.

TYPE H
Positive aspects: joyful, responsive, grateful, multi-talented, enthusiastic, lively, extroverted, hyperactive, dazzlingly gifted, vivacious.
Negative aspects: dilettantish, excessive, greedy, obnoxious, addictive, obsessive need for new experience, debauched, self-centred.

TYPE I
Positive aspects: courageous, self-assertive, confident, strong, an inspirational leader, authoritative, commanding, honourable, enterprising.
Negative aspects: bullying, aggressive, wilful, dominating, intimidating, confrontational, dictatorial, megalomaniac, belligerent, violent.

Key: A=3, B=4, C=6, D=9, E=1, F=2, G=5, H=7, I=8

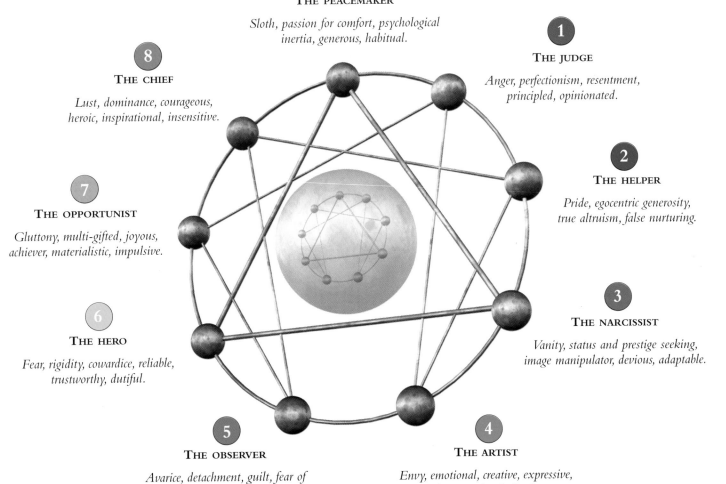

THE NINE ENNEAGRAM TYPES AND THEIR MAJOR MOTIVATIONS

9

THE PEACEMAKER

Sloth, passion for comfort, psychological inertia, generous, habitual.

1

THE JUDGE

Anger, perfectionism, resentment, principled, opinionated.

8

THE CHIEF

Lust, dominance, courageous, heroic, inspirational, insensitive.

2

THE HELPER

Pride, egocentric generosity, true altruism, false nurturing.

7

THE OPPORTUNIST

Gluttony, multi-gifted, joyous, achiever, materialistic, impulsive.

3

THE NARCISSIST

Vanity, status and prestige seeking, image manipulator, devious, adaptable.

6

THE HERO

Fear, rigidity, cowardice, reliable, trustworthy, dutiful.

5

THE OBSERVER

Avarice, detachment, guilt, fear of engulfment, visionary, perceptive.

4

THE ARTIST

Envy, emotional, creative, expressive, masochistic, melancholic, dreamy.

1. Needs to be right and justify his or her position. Strives to be as perfect as possible and help others to be the same.

2. Needs to be loved, needed and appreciated; to express feelings for others, and to have others reciprocate and acknowledge his, or her, worth.

3. Needs affirmation, attention. Wants to be outstanding and to impress and to distinguish him/herself in the eyes of others.

4. Needs to understand and express the self and its powerful feelings; to creatively manifest strong emotional responses to the world.

5. Wants to understand the world but gathers knowledge about the environment to protect the self from the awesome experience of it.

6. Needs security, to be liked and the approval and love of others in order to combat an overwhelming sense of insecurity and frozen fear.

7. The strategy to avert a sense of anxiety is to be as active and multi-achieving as possible; to do and to have more and more of all and everything.

8. Needs to prevail over self, others and the environment; to have an impact upon history and to do everything his, or her, own way.

9. A preservationist at any price; an overriding desire to merge with others, so avoiding conflicts and tensions. Self-forgetfulness through habit.

76

THE ENNEAGRAM

ORIGINALLY INTRODUCED TO THE West in this century by Gurdjieff[32], the nine-sided "diagram of all life" is claimed to have been used in the Middle East for over four thousand years. Sufis, like the Naqshbandi dervishes, are known to have used similar devices in order to transform the spiritual seeker. Gurdjieff himself saw it as a symbol of the dynamic movement of the cosmos, but during the last four decades, the enneagram has been adapted by therapists as a useful psychological template describing nine essential types. The following pages can only be considered an abbreviated introduction to the system, of which there are many variants.[43]

Essentially we carry all the nine tendencies displayed on the large diagram opposite and move around the circle daily. Gurdjieff once remarked that "It is the greatest mistake to believe that the human being always remains a constant unity. He continually changes; he rarely stays the same for a single hour."

While this is true, there appear to be defensive, habitual and entrenched strongholds that we scuttle back to whenever the going gets tough. Many of us get obsessively stuck at one point and refuse to budge from what we see as familiar and comfortable. For instance, the Observer strategy (type number 5) prefers to view the world as if through a peephole in the fence, avoiding actual contact with whatever is happening on the other side, yet longing to engage in the games taking place there.

The beauty of the enneagram system is that once each point can be recognized for what it is – a neurotic defense entrenchment which defines the personality – then its fixed nature changes to become one of nine movable feasts which reveal basic approaches to life.

Each type has the choice of moving on a path towards becoming either more neurotic or more healthy. This means that a neurotic Observer under stress tends to move towards type 7, taking on some of that type's worst characteristics and becoming erratic, impulsive and hyperactive. The Observer's main need is to move from *thinking about* doing to *actual* doing, so in moving toward type 8 he, or she, moves from knowledge to direct experience.

Jesuit priests, who helped develop the enneagram, see the nine points – or unconscious defence mechanisms – as representing "sin". They incorporate the traditional seven deadly sins into their diagrams. To the Jesuits sin is anything that does not allow a person to live out his, or her, integrated potential; it is the state of unawareness that leads to the cultivation of the ego-centred personality.

On the following pages the enneagram has been presented in three modes – sensing, feeling and thinking. By now you should have a good idea of your orientation and be able to find your type and defensive strategy easily.

As shown in the smaller diagrams on the right there are three shock points that represent the quantum leap between these three different modes. This is symbolized by the triangle (3, 6, 9). Surrounding the triangle on the circle is a six-sided figure (1-2, 4-5, 7-8), with two points to each outer face of the triangle. These show the two thinking, two emotional and two physical types linked by the triangle. Also shown are the directions towards health and neuroticism each type demonstrates.

ASSESSMENT

Does your choice from the previous page correspond with what you now know about the three basic modes of behaviour? Does your overall type – thinking, feeling or sensing – match what you have chosen? Have you become fixed in a particular habitual mode at one point, or are you moving between points?

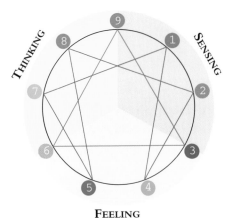

THINKING

SENSING

FEELING

The three basic types.

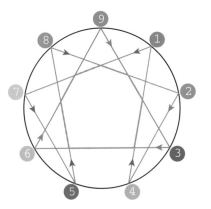

The positive direction of integration showing the routes toward resolving neurotic and fixed patterns of behaviour.

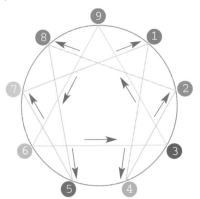

The negative direction of disintegration establishes neurotic and fixed patterns of behaviour.

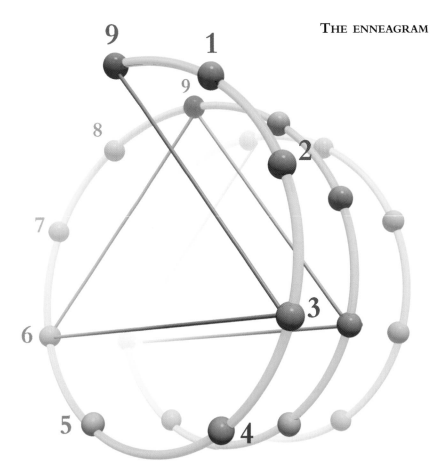

THE ENNEAGRAM

Above right: *The enneagram was intended as a ceaselessly moving, three-dimensional model. Not only are there shock points between the major modes of sensing, feeling and thinking, but at type 9 in each complete revolution, the whole model makes a quantum leap onto a new level. Gurdjieff's model is an ever-changing and dynamic system, while many of the recent psychological enneagram systems tend to regard characteristics as if they are fixed and unmoving.*

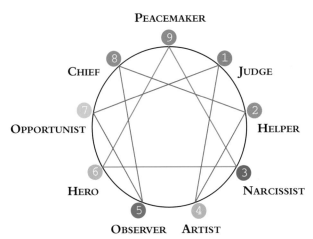

PEACEMAKER

CHIEF

JUDGE

OPPORTUNIST

HELPER

HERO

NARCISSIST

OBSERVER   ARTIST

77

ARE YOU A MATERIAL TYPE?

THE FIRST THREE OF THE NINE POINTS on the enneagram are essentially those outwardly oriented strategies favoured by types who are concerned with the material, phenomenal world. Remember these are the one-sided, focused and fixed standpoints that make up our personalities and dictate both how we view the world and how we interact with it. On this page they are shown as type 1 and type 2 with the shock point, or bridge, of type 3 to the emotional mode. By seeing your chosen strategy you inadvertently reveal the type of focus that keeps you rigid, habitual and unconscious of the true nature of your behaviour.

Type 1 is concerned with recognizing and perfecting outer conditions, while type 2 is characterized by a driven need to find happiness through constant activity. So the attention of these two is on the practical appraisal of the material situation and on the appropriate actions required to achieve goals. Type 3 is the shock point that offers a bridge to the inner dimension that is neglected by too much concern for the phenomenal world of action.

Each personality type is described by its major fixation and virtue – the habitual behaviour patterns, its healthy and neurotic tendencies and its origins in childhood. Understanding that you carry all the possibilities and personality types within you and that certain types lead towards integration while others towards disintegration, can completely transform your whole behaviour and world view.

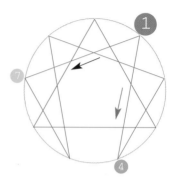

TYPE 1

The Judge, Perfectionist, Reformer, Critic, Entrepreneur.

Fixation: ***Suppressed rage*** *becomes rational anger or resentment.*
Virtue: ***Serenity*** *and a joyful acceptance of perfect imperfection.*

Focus: Attached to material structures, possessions and money. The decision to have rather than be. A need to be right. Strong judgment of both the self and others who do not match ideals makes this type a perfectionist. A constant ethical and moral concern with "shoulds" and "musts". Hard work, thrift, honesty and doing right are valued, but underlying this perfection is a resentment arising from unsatisfied needs.

Childhood background: through a background of criticism and disapproval the child becomes preoccupied with being worthy of love, with being "good". Impulsive or spontaneous intuitions are substituted by rules of correct behaviour.

Aware attention and integration; route towards healing and health:
Good entrepreneur with decisive business sense. Wise, discerning, balanced, realistic, high-principled and ethical. Integration towards point number 7. Learning to relax, becoming playful, taking delight in life without feeling he or she has to be perfect.

Neurotic and unconscious tendency; route to disintegration:
Fear of insecurity especially in finances, tendency to rigidity and inflexibility. Self-righteous, punitive, cruel in his or her need to be right. Disintegration towards point number 4. This creates too much emotional turmoil, making the type neurotic, obsessive, compulsive and contradictory.

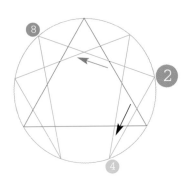

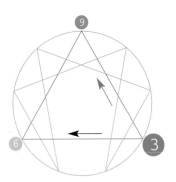

TYPE 2

The Helper, Planner, Shaper, Egocentric Giver.

Fixation: **Pride and flattery;** *they need others to depend on them.*
Virtue: **Humility** *and unconditional generosity.*

Focus: Enjoys planning for the future, for a better world. Love of beauty and art. Focused on others. Being sensitive to others' feelings and needs but feeling that they are not loved for themselves. Fearing this, they spend their lives trying to make people love them by doing things to gain approval. They prefer to give rather than receive, and although they appear to be independent and have no needs of their own, they are actually focused around relationships.

Childhood background: In childhood the type learned to become acutely aware of all the subtlest clues of the most important adults, either over-dominant or needy parents. They found that in order to be loved they had to meet the needs of others.

Aware attention and integration; route towards healing and health: ⟶
Sensitive to others' feelings, cheerful and energetic, giving for the sake of giving, altruistic and caring, unselfish and future oriented with a clear view of what is beautiful and practical.

Neurotic and unconscious tendency; route to disintegration: ⟶
Self-sacrificing intrusives who complain that no one ever appreciates them. Smothering and manipulative. Only giving in order to get something in return. Moving towards point 8 brings a tendency to become dominating, irritable, calculating, with the smouldering resentment that becomes open anger.

TYPE 3

The Narcissist, Status Seeker, Performer, Magician, Actor.

Fixation: **Deceit and vanity;** *identification with outward roles.*
Virtue: **Honesty;** *integrity and acceptance of being a channel.*

Focus: Image-conscious and exhibitionist; competitively concerned with prestige and career; often an attractive, self-assured ideal for others; can be exploitative, narcissistic and over-concerned with outward appearance; can be inner-directed and authentic with a desire to improve self, becoming outstanding in chosen field.

Childhood background: In childhood the type felt they had to achieve in order to be loved and accepted. Only by successfully producing something would they be deemed worthy. They often expect the world to lavish attention on them similar to a mother's high regard. The parent's admiring gaze made them feel important and worthwhile, especially when engaged on some outward activity.

Aware attention and integration; route towards healing and health: ⟶
Self-acceptance of being real to themselves without the need to identify with an external image. By moving towards point 6 they allow themselves to be exposed for what they really are.

Neurotic and unconscious tendency; route to disintegration: ⟶
Neurotic and fixed need for others' applause and admiration. Movement to point 9 intensifies a sense of the unreal and de-personalization. They feel as if they are in a dream and often deteriorate into fragmented, multiple personalities simply because they are out of touch with who they really are.

78

ARE YOU A HEART TYPE?

THE SECOND THREE OF THE NINE POINTS on the enneagram are essentially those strategies that focus inward on feeling. At number 4 the world is viewed almost entirely subjectively and emotionally. At number 5 our intellect is beginning to influence those emotions. At number 6 there is a shock point which thrusts the enneagram firmly toward the head. If you have discovered that the assessments so far have shown you to be an essentially emotional person then pay particular attention to the three enneagram points on this page.

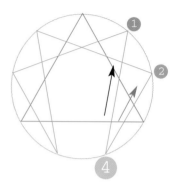

TYPE 4

The Artist, Romantic, Emotional Striver, Expressionist.

Fixation: ***Envy and melancholy;*** *a sense that something is missing.*
Virtue: ***Equanimity;*** *harmony and completion within oneself.*

Focus: The most purely emotional type within the enneagram. The inner world of feelings is deemed far more important than any activity in the outer world. A major hurdle to becoming whole for the type is over-indulgence and self-absorption. Life is a continual drama in which he or she is the director. Creative and inspired, intuitive and self-revealing, the type has an emotional integrity that requires time to assimilate and reflect before acting.

Childhood background: There is an underlying feeling of having been abandoned and separated from unconditional acceptance and love. They feel they must have been unworthy to have been abandoned, yet feel emotionally different from others as they seek the perfect love again.

Aware attention and integration; route towards healing and health: ⟶
Realization of innate worth and depth of emotion. Towards number1 they become more practical and outwardly directed, focusing on objective reality without being overwhelmed by feelings.

Neurotic and unconscious tendency; route to disintegration: ⟶
Melancholic suffering through depth of feelings. Self-indulgent and over-dramatic. Moving towards number 2 they tend to become more dependent on others for the unattainable, perfect love, while being filled with self-hatred trying to escape from themselves. Always longing for the unavailable and extraordinary.

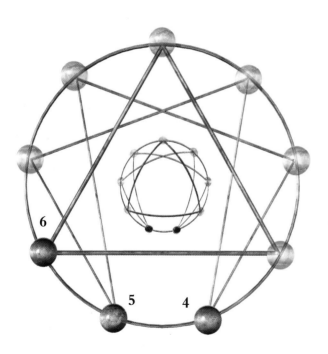

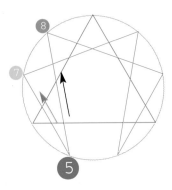

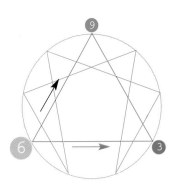

TYPE 5

The Observer, Thinker, Sufferer, Spectator.

Fixation: ***Avarice and stinginess;*** *need for privacy and time.*
Virtue: ***Non-attachment and omniscience;*** *experiential knowing.*

Focus: The withdrawn thinker who suffers from the purposelessness of the world. A visionary and over-viewer, an original thinker who is both insightful and perceptive, who wants to understand the environment, yet needs to find a way of defending him- or herself against the potential threats in it. Has the capacity to heal, yet cannot really act.

Childhood background: In dealing with what is perceived as a threatening world the child withdraws into an imaginative realm where there is safety. In order to avoid pain he, or she, creates a distance from emotions. Is in a state of constant alertness about the environment in order to foresee events and take defensive action against threats. Becomes a watcher through a peephole in the fence.

Aware attention and integration; route towards healing and health: ⟶
Assumes a detached point of view while acting in the world. Movement towards number 8 brings the ability to act and trust in the environment. Acquires courage to act out his or her profound understandings.

Neurotic and unconscious tendency; route to disintegration: ⟶
Withdrawn from the world and action. Becomes a recluse who is isolated from reality. If this type moves to number 7 in order to act, he or she becomes impulsive, erratic and hysterical. Tends to become paranoid with strange ideas and manic activity to divert the anxiety.

TYPE 6

The Hero, Follower, Loyal Trooper, Sceptic.

Fixation: ***Doubt and cowardice;*** *the overwhelming fear of fear.*
Virtue: ***Courage and faith;*** *trusting oneself and existence.*

Focus: Loyal, hard-working, dependable and cautious. Has a problem with authority, being at either extreme of submissiveness or rebellion. So can be either timid or confrontational. Procrastinates, avoiding action, preferring to think about it. Essential emotion is one of frozen fear or anxiety. Sees success as frightening.

Childhood background: In a potentially threatening environment the child learns to be alert to clues for likely aggression, sudden change or threats of violence. Tends to identify with father figure or other authority figures at an early age. Feels secure when pleasing these figures, so the child diligently learns the rules of the parental home at the expense of expressing his or her own desires and needs.

Aware attention and integration; route towards healing and health: ⟶
Recognizing the motives and hidden agendas that influence all relationships, the type moves towards number 9, becoming emotionally more open and discovering the courage to go his or her own way.

Neurotic and unconscious tendency; route to disintegration: ⟶
Cowards die a thousand deaths and the type suffers from constant anxiety and over-compliance. By turning towards number 3 these types turn their suppressed aggression from themselves to others and can become sadistic towards those whose love they need the most.

79

ARE YOU A THINKING TYPE?

THE LAST THREE ENNEAGRAM POINTS are concerned with the intellect. Their prime focus is upon communication and expression. The strategy of a number 7 type attempts to ensure love and success through the power of communication. To this end the type will be entertaining, multi-gifted and well liked. But this ability to be all things to all men often hides a superficiality. Its outward-orientation and need to "do something" means that the type skims the surface of many activities, often lacking real depth. By moving towards the inner contemplation of point number 5 this many-faceted "doer" takes on a more thoughtful and profound aspect.

At point number 8 the intellect is concerned with the power of reason, but is also over-concerned with its controlled action on the environment and others. In this case a movement to number 5 has disastrous consequences, creating a withdrawal into thought and inaction, creating anxiety and paranoia.

At shock point number 9 the whole enneagram is poised for the quantum leap to the next stage, level or cycle. But a tendency to see all sides of a situation creates "fence sitting" and indecision, coupled with avoidance of any conflict. In attempting to descend from the fence and act, the 9 moves towards point number 6, which further increases the sense of distance from his, or her, surroundings and gives a rational base for doing so. By moving to point number 3 there is a reconnection with the world and an empathetic understanding of how others feel without being swamped by the need to over-identify.

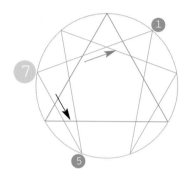

TYPE 7

The Opportunist, Generalist, Optimist, Greedy Epicure.

Fixation: ***Gluttony;*** *superficial experiencing to avoid fear.*
Virtue: ***Sobriety and sacred work;*** *experiencing life at depth.*

Focus: Communicative, versatile with a quick grasp of situations. Enthusiastic, grateful and awed by life's wonders; vivacious, lively and often dazzlingly multi-talented; a "doer" who loves new projects, people and experiences. A dedication to adventure; someone who is excellent at starting a project but poor in finishing. This is an enthusiast who is often likened to the "Renaissance man", capable of turning a hand to anything. But avoids pain at all costs.

Childhood background: A lack of perceived parental love made the child feel insecure and prompted a fear of deprivation. This prime concern is expressed as a demand that as many narcissistic desires are satisfied as possible without any necessary depth of experience.

Aware attention and integration; route towards healing and health: ⟶
Excellent intellectual grasp of situations, with a concern to synthesize and understand the nature of this type's wonder and gratitude to life. Path to integration is towards number 5, which gives a sense of peace, profundity and depth of experience.

Neurotic and unconscious tendency; route to disintegration: ⟶
Becomes over-excited, excessive, superficial with a complete disregard of emotions. Disintegration is towards number 1, which increases the sense of panic, the obsessional need for an outer direction through work. Punishes those who thwart any desires.

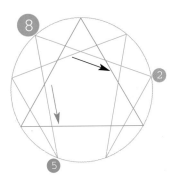

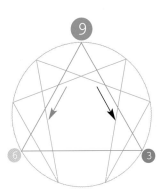

TYPE 8

The Chief, Leader, Boss, Overseer.

Fixation: ***Lust and vengeance;*** *single-minded urge to satisfy needs.*
Virtue: ***Innocence and truth;*** *immediate response to existence.*

Focus: Magnanimous, courageous, self-assertive, confident and strong. A natural born leader who is enterprising, honourable and protective of his or her team. The need to be self-reliant and to prevail over both the environment and others can change healthy, expansive attitudes into dictatorial, combative and ruthless behaviour.

Childhood background: Often the child discovered that to get the parent, usually the mother, to respond to his or her needs, the child would have to be strong and aggressively assertive. The discovery that he or she was stronger than the parent confirmed the child's assumption that he or she could dominate other adults with impunity. Life was then seen in terms of the exercise of power and the survival of the strongest.

Aware attention and integration; route towards healing and health: ⟶
Magnanimity, courage and genuine strength. Moving towards number 2 this type intensifies its creative powers, opening up to others instead of dominating them, and gaining empathetic insights.

Neurotic and unconscious tendency; route to disintegration: ⟶
A desire to rule and dominate others, yet a real fear of being in touch with emotions. A reluctance to either reflect on his or her actions, or confront the unconscious. Moving towards number 5 makes this type more anxious and withdrawn into thought. In such isolation the individual can become paranoid and tormented by past actions.

TYPE 9

Peacemaker, Mediator, Loving Friend.

Fixation: ***Sloth and indolence;*** *inert, self-forgetful and diverted.*
Virtue: ***Action and love;*** *no separation from others.*

Focus: Peaceable, tolerant, accommodating, uncompetitive. Likes to fit in with others yet finds it difficult to know his or her own priorities. Likes a comfortable life but tends to be sluggish and passive. Loses awareness of own agenda and priorities, preferring to merge with others. Replaces essential needs with inessential substitutes.

Childhood background: As a child this type often felt overlooked, or was told not to express what he or she was really feeling. These people learned to forget their anger at not being acknowledged or accepted. Their strategy was to identify with their parents, and often the impetus to differentiate from the adult was minimal simply because this type's emotional needs were being met, even if it meant assuming a subordinate position.

Aware attention and integration; route towards healing and health: ⟶
Generous, open-minded, often empathetic, the type creates harmony in situations. Moving towards number 3 these people become more self-assured, assertive, and develop themselves through creativity.

Neurotic and unconscious tendency; route to disintegration: ⟶
Needy, indecisive, apathetic and over-compliant. Towards number 6 this type rationalizes and excuses its sluggishness and superficiality. Diverts energy to trivial pursuits. Anxious and self-destructive, this type is no longer able to repress aggressive feelings which fuel its self-hatred.

80

How did you learn?

RECENTLY THERE HAS BEEN A REVOLUTION in the way intelligence is now recognized. Howard Gardner[44], a psychologist at Harvard, maintains that all of us demonstrate seven distinct kinds of intelligence. These are:
1. Linguistic. 2. Logical-mathematical. 3. Spatial. 4. Musical. 5. Body-kinesthetic. 6. Interpersonal. 7. Intrapersonal.

Long-established IQ tests use almost identical questions but posed in three distinct ways in order to test verbal, numerical and perceptual skills. It has always been assumed that, like the three "r's" of reading, writing and arithmetic, this combination was an adequate means of testing intelligence.

In the following descriptions of the seven types of learning ability, it is evident that most educationalists have applauded especially the highly linguistic, mathematical and logical thinker. Our present-day society seldom recognizes more than three of these seven when deciding who is bright. Yet, it can be claimed that the four other types can be just as intelligent, but with very different learning styles and skills. If you are one of those who fits these descriptions you have probably suffered from learning difficulties, trying to fit into what were inappropriate methods for you. We are often forced to become clones of the social norm, and in the process lose our own natural and instinctual ways of being ourselves.

Assessment

Read the following profiles. You should discover your own description among the seven categories. Take what seems to apply, and from the various combinations you will see whether you still have the possibility of realizing your potential, given your own unique strengths and weaknesses.

1. Linguistic intelligence

You have always enjoyed playing with words and have noticed you are more skilled in picking up new words, or new languages, than others. You probably read as much as you can, or enjoy inventing and telling stories. You have a great memory for obscure poems, verses, or trivial quotes, and can remember dates, peoples' names and places with ease. You always had high marks for any activity that required verbalizing, like debating, or hearing and seeing words.

For you the phrase "In the beginning was the Word" appears to be the alpha and omega. Your spelling is usually accurate and you are good at doing crossword puzzles or games such as Scrabble. You probably get a kick out of nonsense rhymes and you learn best by verbalizing and playing with words.

2. Logical-mathematical intelligence

This form of intelligence is the gift of abstract thinking. As a child you tended to play with pattern games, especially those involved with logical puzzles. You enjoy creating a sense of order and can play with abstract and logical ideas. You have always found it easy to work out numerical problems in your head and find you have a natural talent for dealing with computers. You probably were continually pestering your parents and teachers with complex philosophical questions that they couldn't answer and at an early age began to beat even adults at strategy games like chess, checkers, or Go.

You have always enjoyed creating experiments in order to understand certain principles and your chemistry set was probably a favourite. You scored high in all subjects that required logical reasoning, especially in the perceptual and numerical questions of an IQ test. You learn best through strategies and puzzles.

3. Spatial intelligence

This form of intelligence centres around the ability to think in images and pictures. You only need to visit a city once and will immediately be able to find your way around on a second trip, even when approaching it from a different direction. You would always be the first to come out of a maze and would have finished a jigsaw puzzle long before anyone else. As a child you spent hours with construction sets and blocks. There is a strong likelihood that you could draw well at an early age, preferring to design on paper, or computer, rather than verbalize an idea. You find delight in

maps and diagrams and can easily understand their underlying principles. When daydreaming or thinking about something, you can usually express the concept in clear visual imagery as accurate drawings, videos, sculpture or photographs. You learn best through designing and making.

4. MUSICAL INTELLIGENCE

This type of intelligence is most easily recognized in an environment in which music is important, or instruments are readily available, but it is sometimes overlooked in less supportive surroundings. As a musically gifted child you probably hummed, or sang to yourself, and could pick up a tune at first hearing. More than likely you could distinguish a musical note and match it if asked to do so. As soon as you hear music you begin to move to its rhythms or join in.

You certainly have strong musical tastes, with distinct loves and hates. Playing an instrument is relatively easy for you and you seldom mind practising. You have a large collection of tapes and CDs if you can afford it, and you feel that a home without some form of sound system is a mausoleum. You will be particularly sensitive to sounds within the environment, from running water to bird song. You have always been an excellent mimic where sound is involved, being able to imitate a favourite pop singer to the delight of friends and family. When studying you like to have music playing in the background and you can always be seen keeping time to its rhythm. You learn best through non-verbal sound and rhythm.

5. BODY-KINESTHETIC INTELLIGENCE

This type processes knowledge and experience through bodily sensations. As a child you were probably always being accused of fidgeting and spent most of your happiest times in a playground. Sitting still at school was torture, and in any tests you probably trusted your gut feelings more than any logical or thought-out solution. You always have had very good motor-coordination, excelling at sports and athletics. You may have been gifted with the skills of a dancer, skater, skier or gymnast. Often this is coupled with the gift of mimicry, through which you can ape other people's gestures and physical mannerisms. In some cases, your motor skills are channelled into a fine craft like pottery or woodworking.

It is likely you need to touch others in order to communicate, and you are always moving, twitching, fidgeting or tapping your feet and hands to real or imagined rhythms. You learn best through moving and acting things out.

6. INTERPERSONAL INTELLIGENCE

This intelligence concerns relating to others. You are probably popular and have many friends. As a child you were often the leader of a gang and are able to organize and manipulate your peers with skill. You are likely to be street-wise, knowing the neighbourhood and all the cliques and groups in town.

Because you have an uncanny talent for intuiting the feelings of others you can mediate between factions and excel in all group activities and team games. This empathy means that you make a trusted counsellor, so you are probably the earpiece for many of your friends. You learn best through engaging in team activities and cooperative ventures.

7. INTRAPERSONAL INTELLIGENCE

This is the essentially private intelligence that does not need the interaction of others to realize its aspirations and goals. You are probably somewhat of a loner, preferring to pursue your own interests and ideas. Most likely you do not enjoy shared activities and are often accused of living in a world of your own. You have a strong sense of your own independent worth and exhibit certain intuitive skills that border on the psychic.

This deep sense of self-worth means that you do especially well on your own; you are a self-starter who, when following through, would ask questions and gain personal experience. You are highly individual in your dress, your behaviour, general attitudes and eccentricities. You will have strong opinions, especially on controversial subjects, and usually an experiential wisdom and integrity that can back those opinions. You learn best through indirect support, while being essentially left to your own agenda, preferring to learn by experience rather than through the words of others.

81

WHAT IS YOUR TYPE OF HUMOUR?

I T IS PERHAPS AN INDICATION of how seriously we take
psychology that few researchers have ever been funded to
investigate the nature of humour. Freud wrote a book
about jokes – and a very serious book at that. There are a few
tests to assess whether you have a sense of humour or not. It is
not the intention of this book to test whether you have a sense
of humour, but the examples opposite can give you an idea. It
is revealing to know what kind of humour you enjoy as this
gives an indication of your general behavioural type.

One of the most useful typologies[45] so far created uses four
categories – nonsensical, satirical, aggressive and sexual. These
four roughly fall into the twin divisions of extrovert and introvert behaviour.

Nonsense humour relies on incongruous elements. As it is
usually free of any aggressive or sexual content, introverts are
more sympathetic to it. Introverts also enjoy satire, even when
ridicule of both persons and institutions can be seen as indirect
aggression.

Extroverts have a tendency to prefer more blatantly aggressive or sexual humour. They are also found, in general, to enjoy
jokes more than their introspective counterparts.

ASSESSMENT

To assess your type of humour read the dozen jokes
below and list those that bring a smile. Check your
type at the end.

1. *The clever cat eats cheese, then breathes down a
   mousehole with baited breath.* (W. C. Fields)
2. *Why do Baptists object to fornication?
   They're afraid it might lead to dancing.*
3. *How do you like children? Boiled.*
4. *Two aunts are talking about their young niece. "What a
   shame she isn't P-R-E-T-T-Y!" spelled out one. The child
   looked up: "Who cares so long as I am C-L-E-V-E-R?"*
5. *What is the difference between erotic and perverted?
   Erotic is when you use a feather, perverted is when you use
   the whole chicken.*
6. *She talks 100 words a minute with gusts up to 130.*
7. *If you want to know why women are called the opposite
   sex – just express an opinion.*
8. *I owe, I owe so off to work I go.* (bumper sticker)
9. *Friend: "Do you ever smoke after sex?"
   Girl: "Don't know – never looked."*
10. *Babies? No problem. Keep one end full and the other
    empty.*
11. *A conservative is someone who believes that nothing
    should be done for the first time.*
12. *Don't worry, sex is hereditary. If your parents didn't have
    it, the chances are you won't either.*

ANSWERS

*There are three jokes for each type. Those who favour satire might
enjoy 2, 4 and 11. Those who prefer nonsense are likely to choose
1, 6 and 8.
The reader who enjoys essentially aggressive jokes will probably
only like 3, 7 and 10, while those who enjoy sexual jokes will
probably prefer 5, 9 and 12.*

"Say what you like but you have to admire the director's split-second decisions".

"and something else. . .I want half the wisdom".

aggressive

satirical

EXTROVERT

INTROVERT

sexual

nonsensical

"Come over here, Tarzan"!

"I have a dream".

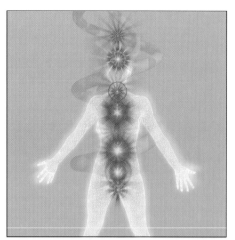

PART IV

Spiritual types

Having explored your physical, emotional and mental make-up you now enter the world of the spirit. Yet even in this transcendent realm we find the three basic human types reappearing. If, for instance, you have found you are a feeling type, you will be drawn, most likely, to those religions or mystical paths that support that tendency.

Within this section the nature of the assessments changes. Your true spiritual type – who you really are – can only be known through direct experience. It is not something that can be discovered casually, or philosophically. Any mystic worthy of his or her chakras will tell you that it is only when your personality, or ego, is abandoned that the Divine can reveal what you truly are. Thus some of the assessments have been replaced by meditations. These ancient techniques have the potential to awaken you to the real self. In order to find that out, you will have to get up from that armchair.

82

You, and the other you!

WE HAVE ALREADY seen in assessment 28 how the left and right cerebral hemispheres have totally different styles of thinking and reasoning. Patients in whom the two brains have been partially severed often behave as if different personalities were operating within one body. In one particular split-brain disorder, nicknamed the "alien hand", the patient buttons his shirt with the right hand only to have it unbuttoned by the left as if by another person. One hand opens a door to enter a room while at the same time the other is trying to close it. Whatever the neurological explanation for this might be, it does demonstrate that two very separate spheres of consciousness, each with its own agenda, appear to be operating within us.

Normally, with the connections between the two hemispheres intact, we experience a single stream of consciousness, with a unity of purpose between each brain half. Neurologists are increasingly sceptical about whether this process is quite as simple as this.[46] Our consciousness tends to be channelled through the dominant half of the brain, leaving the non-dominant half no voice, or equal voting rights. The educational and societal systems in the West tend to favour the logical, analytical and linguistic side, ignoring the contribution of the non-dominant right hemisphere.

Yet, the non-dominant hemisphere can occasionally gain momentary control – for example, when we are tired, stressed or confronting the unexpected, the dominant brain relaxes its grip. And it is in those moments that we may feel we are possessed by a stranger, or that we respond to the world in ways that are completely alien to our normal behaviour. Many so-called spiritual and psychic experiences can be traced to this simple phenomenon. The lists opposite may give you an indication of your other self.

DIFFERING PERCEPTIONS IN THE BRAIN

Keeping both eyes open, visually cover a distant target with your thumb as shown below. Keeping the thumb and object in place, close each eye in turn. The eye that still covers the object is your dominant visual cortex. The right eye is connected to the left hemisphere and the left eye to the right. This small exercise demonstrates the differing nature of the experience of each brain. In the illustration below, the dominant visual cortex cannot see the juggler skeleton while the non-dominant can. Yet your steady and single stream of consciousness would have over-ridden the less dominant viewer, unless it managed to gain momentary control in relaying its shock.

In this example the right eye (left visual brain) is dominant. The left, non-dominant, eye can still see the objects covered by the thumb.

In this example it is the left eye (right visual brain) that dominates. The right, non-dominant, eye can still clearly see the objects.

SPHERE OF CONSCIOUSNESS A

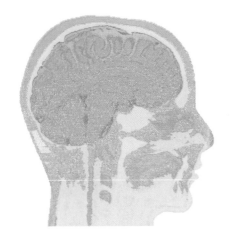

SPHERE OF CONSCIOUSNESS B

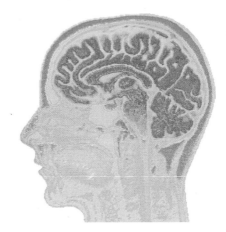

ASSESSMENT

Do you:

1. *feel you are essentially a thinker?*
2. *think convergently, with ideas logically structured?*
3. *feel you are an intellectual and enjoy mental activity?*
4. *feel you behave and think in a rational way?*
5. *enjoy deducing things through processing ideas logically?*
6. *enjoy thinking in logical structures and sequences?*
7. *see objects as if made up of discrete and separate units?*
8. *enjoy playing with abstract ideas?*
9. *have an essentially realistic approach to life?*
10. *tend to seek clear direction in all you do?*
11. *try to differentiate and evaluate things clearly?*
12. *feel you are best at theorizing about things?*
13. *immediately see how things fit in sequence?*
14. *tend to see events in terms of a linear, factual history?*
15. *prefer explicit, direct expression and information?*
16. *view life as an objective reality, independent of the viewer?*
17. *see life taking place through sequences of cause and effect?*
18. *feel you are analytical in your approach to life?*

Do you:

1. *feel you are mostly intuitive in your actions?*
2. *think divergently, in unorthodox ways?*
3. *feel you are a sensualist, enjoying all the senses can offer?*
4. *think in metaphors, seeing odd links between things?*
5. *make leaps of imagination rather than being logical?*
6. *tend to think laterally and by association?*
7. *see the world as a continuous, inseparable whole?*
8. *prefer direct experience rather than thinking about it?*
9. *feel you are essentially impulsive in your actions?*
10. *tend to allow life to take you wherever it wants to go?*
11. *find it difficult to differentiate between things?*
12. *like theorizing about things?*
13. *find life too complex to see any real patterns?*
14. *tend to see life as a multi-faceted and timeless whole?*
15. *accept the tacit or implied without a need for the factual?*
16. *always relate the experience to the experiencer?*
17. *see things as existing or operating in sychronicity?*
18. *feel you are holistic in your approach to life?*

Key: In order to determine which of the two brain personalities is in charge, check the two lists above. They roughly reflect the type of attention to be found in the left and right hemispheres. Whenever you choose a "yes" for one column, the corresponding "no" in the parallel column is an indication of the nature of your non-dominant personality. By answering all the questions you should be able to build up an accurate picture of your dominant sphere of consciousness.

83

ARE YOU OPEN TO UNORTHODOX PHILOSOPHIES?

SIGMUND FREUD AND CARL GUSTAV JUNG are household names throughout the world, renowned as the most important pioneers of human psychology. Yet perhaps the greatest psychologist of this century was George Ivanovitch Gurdjieff, who is little known to most of us. It was Gurdjieff who not only reintroduced the enneagram to the West, but also formulated a sevenfold typology of the soul and spirit reaching far beyond the psychological insights of Freud or Jung.[47]

The essential types that were examined in the enneagram (sensing, feeling and thinking) are included as the first three types of Gurdjieff's sevenfold system. Bridging these to the "higher" three types is number 4. This links the automatic, almost robotic state of semi-sleep of the first three types with the state of awakening.

Gurdjieff insisted that we have to work for our soul; it doesn't come free at birth. The potential of the soul is present, but unless we awaken to the reality of our situation we are not much better than vegetables. His whole work revolved around harmonizing the first three types, or attentions, so that a fourth and natural intuition would be formed.

He maintained that our basic instincts have been meddled with so much that we no longer respond naturally and spontaneously, but react with our particular programming. We tend to mistake direct messages, sending them to the wrong centres. For instance, our sexual energy which naturally arises in the body, is routed through the head. Only when the individual has learned to harmonize the first three centres within himself can the bridge open to the higher centres of awakening. Are you open to unorthodox spiritual typologies such as this? Try answering the questions on the right.

ASSESSMENT

Do you:
1. *have any prior knowledge of unorthodox philosophies?*
2. *feel that Gurdjieff sounds like yet another of those self-styled gurus who tend to attract the unstable?*
3. *feel that the concept that we are not born with a soul but have to work for it might have a degree of truth?*
4. *feel it is both absurd and even sacrilegious to suggest we are born without a soul?*
5. *often feel that you are living in a dream and that at any moment you will awaken?*
6. *find it difficult to comprehend anyone saying that you are actually asleep when you think you are awake?*
7. *often feel that you walk through life like a robot?*
8. *disagree that you are automatic in your behaviour?*
9. *have an urge to change your habitual behaviour and are prepared really to do something about it?*
10. *feel that you are perfectly awake to your surroundings and as alert and conscious as you can be?*
11. *feel that to awaken to your full potential you must work hard and even sacrifice your comfort and security?*
12. *delight in the availability of so many different religious ideas and ways to the truth?*

Key: If you answer "yes" to 5 odd numbered questions or "no" to over 5 even numbered questions you are likely to be attracted to any teaching that suggests ways of awakening from what you are uneasily beginning to feel is just a dream and a set of robotic reponses.
Reversing the score, answering "no" to the odd numbered and "yes" to the even, reveals that you feel uncomfortable with such concepts and prefer more familiar religious concepts.

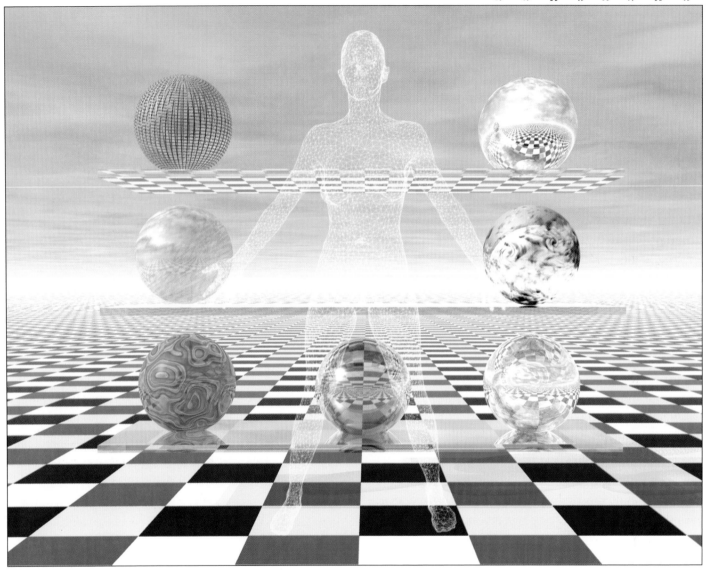

GURDJIEFF'S SEVEN STAGES OF MANKIND

MENTAL CENTRE ~ *Head*		HIGHER MENTAL CENTRE
EMOTIONAL CENTRE ~ *Heart*		HIGHER EMOTIONAL CENTRE
SEXUAL CENTRE ~ *Belly*	INSTINCTIVE CENTRE *The bridge between worlds*	MOVING CENTRE

84

PHILOSOPHIA PERENNIS

THE PERENNIAL PHILOSOPHY, a term first coined by the German philosopher and mathematician Gottfried Wilhelm Leibniz, forms the esoteric core of Hindu, Buddhist, Tao, Sufi and Christian mysticism. Its central teaching implies a transcendental path that moves from body to mind, then from mind to soul, and finally from soul to spirit. One part does not exclude another, however, as the essential message is one of wholeness and unity of being. [48]

A human being can be seen to evolve through seven stages and it is possible to see each type of person as one particular stage on an invisible ladder towards wholeness. It is also possible to view each stage as if it were a type, as if an individual could be identified by his or her focus of attention.

Our present dilemma is that we are caught up in the phenomenal world of science and technology, and in the consuming materialism that fast follows in its wake. So the tendency has been to become fixed at the first stage. However, imbalance is not unique to our time. Other cultures have concentrated their attention on different stages – on more psychic and magical planes rather than those of the material world. The Perennial Philosophy [49] directs our attention to a holistic view of being human and of the responsibility to awaken to our potential. For the whole is ever present, yet seldom realized. It is the pure Nature of every human being, but has to be awakened from its sleep deep within our core.

While this concept was not fully developed in the West, the New Age movement of the 1970s found it a milestone on the road to a spiritual understanding of the Eastern esoteric and metaphysical realms. [50]

ASSESSMENT

Do you:

1. *dislike the esoteric garbage that many so-called spiritual teachers preach to their gullible followers?*
2. *feel that there are many paths to truth?*
3. *prefer the religion of your childhood to any new ideas?*
4. *recognize a truth in the Perennial Philosophy?*
5. *feel that it is better to pray to a familiar God than seek out unknown and mysterious ways?*
6. *feel that the Western religions are a bit childish in their call for blind faith?*
7. *know that the religion you were taught is the only one that is true and that all others are false?*
8. *feel that while you prefer to worship in your own way, there are different religions that are equally true for others?*
9. *feel that the Eastern idea of reincarnation or seven stages of development is a rather primitive illusion?*
10. *sense that the Eastern approach to mysticism is far more intelligent than the beliefs of the Western world?*
11. *feel that the availability of so many different religious ideas is confusing?*
12. *delight in the availability of so many different religious ideas and ways to the truth?*

Key: *If you answer "yes" to 5 even numbered questions or "no" to over 5 odd numbered questions you are likely to be attracted to the teaching of the Perennial Philosophy. Reversing the score, answering "no" to the even numbered and "yes" to the odd, reveals that the concepts on this page are definitely not for you. But you would know that already!*

THE EASTERN LADDER OF BEING – A WESTERN SYNTHESIS

7. ULTIMATE
Absolute enlightenment →

7. ATMAN
The Divine Cosmic Principle ←

SPIRIT

6. SPIRIT, CAUSAL
Sage mind →

6. BUDDHI
The Divine Cosmic Principle ←

5. SOUL, SUBTLE
Saintly mind →

5. MANAS
Individual cosmic intelligence ←

SOUL

4. SOUL, PSYCHIC
Shamanistic, Siddhic powers →

4. SELF
Personal, egoistic consciousness ←

3. ADVANCED MIND
Self-reflective, rational, egoistic, conscious →

3. ASTRAL BODY
Independent consciousness ←

2. MIND
The mammalian brain and early mind →

2. ETHERIC BODY
Life-giving force of the being ←

1. PHYSICAL NATURE
Primitive life forms, early brain →

MATTER

1. PHYSICAL BODY
Mind, emotions, memories, body ←

**THE EVOLUTION OF CONSCIOUSNESS
IN THE UNIVERSE**

**THE EVOLUTION OF CONSCIOUSNESS
IN THE INDIVIDUAL**

85

WHICH OF YOUR SEVEN CHAKRAS ARE ACTIVE?

CHAKRAS ARE TRADITIONALLY UNDERSTOOD as localizations of psychic energy latent within all of us. They have no precise physiological correlation but according to both Hindu and Yoga psychology the first centre appears at the base of the spine, the second below the navel, the third at the navel, the fourth at the heart, the fifth at the throat, the sixth between the eyebrows, and the seventh at the crown of the head.

These descriptions suggest an ideal unfolding of the being and a ladder to ultimate realization. The following exercise can give you a direct experience of these energy wheels, bringing great clarity and a sense of being alive. [51]

MEDITATION

Sit in a lotus position with closed eyes and imagine your base chakra radiating light. Feel the rays surging up to the sex centre. You will begin to feel a certain heat generated there. This is an excellent sign that your imagination has triggered the energy. When that centre becomes a source of light itself, move on to the navel, the heart, throat, between the eyes and to the crown of the head. If the energy is moving strongly in the three last chakras, the head will feel very hot. You may feel dizzy the first time but it will pass. Allow the light to build up at the crown and then allow it to be released upwards to the sky. If you continue the meditation regularly over a period of time you might experience an overwhelming, orgasmic explosion of bliss and insight, or even enter a sleep-like state known as yoga-tandra. This is an extremely powerful meditation. When you do it, ensure there is no interruption and be careful always to complete the sequence through all the centres.

SAHASRARA CHAKRA
The seventh chakra is the last centre of samadhi, of ultimate unfolding and merging with existence. It is the radical state of enlightenment in which the individual disappears as a person and becomes a presence.

AJNA CHAKRA
The sixth chakra type moves into the realms of wisdom. These are the subtle realms of pure ideas in which there is no longer any identification with the body or the egoistic personality.

VISHUDDHA CHAKRA
The fifth chakra is the point of turning inward towards a cosmic viewpoint. Here we encounter the planes of light and energy and an overview of existence through direct experience.

ANAHATA CHAKRA
The fourth is the heart chakra in which love and compassion arise. This is the bridge to the upper levels. The direct experience of awakening our reality and our intuitive state begins here. This is the Jungian type who is in contact with the mythical archetypes. Yet at this point Jung himself would go no further.

MANIPURA CHAKRA
The third chakra is connected to the acquisition of power, and the mastery and control of the self and its identity. This is the Adlerian psychological type.

SVADHISTARA CHAKRA
The second chakra is concerned with the pleasure and procreation principles. This is the sex centre dedicated to gratifying desires. It sits between the two other lower centres as the focal point for those types who remain in the first three. This is the Freudian type.

MULADHARA CHAKRA
For most people all energy is located within the first three chakras which start functioning at birth. The first chakra is concerned with the survival of the individual as a separate entity. The person whose attention is at this spot could best be called the Darwinian type.

Sahasrara chakra

Ajna chakra

Vishuddha chakra

Anahata chakra

Manipura chakra

Svadhistara chakra

Muladhara chakra

86

ARE YOU IN TOUCH WITH YOUR SEVEN BODIES?

IN HINDU TRADITION EVERY INDIVIDUAL is said to have seven bodies, which are known as the *gross*, the *etheric*, the *astral*, the *psychic*, the *bliss*, the *cosmic* and the *nirvanic* bodies. These are connected with their corresponding chakras. While we are all born with the potential for each body to flower, this very seldom happens and in most of us the four higher bodies remain dormant as only a seed or a potential.

Two aspects are given for each chakra centre in the first four bodies – one being unconscious while the other is its transforming and integrating element. The unconscious aspect is the obstacle that must be overcome and transformed in order to harmonize the bodies. The natural time frame of seven years for the development of each body was common to ancient tradition. Today, development has been accelerated so much that, for instance, puberty and early adulthood happen earlier than in the original ideal.

ASSESSMENT

Continue to practise the meditation found on the previous page and you may gradually be able to glimpse, at first hand, some of the descriptions of the seven bodies. The descriptions, on this page give a brief account of each body. Pay particular attention to the description of the fourth body, as this is both the bridge to the higher bodies and also the realm of delusions and spiritual wishful thinking.

THE GROSS BODY ~ *Sthul Sharir*
It is only this body that forms during the first seven years of life. Mystics say that some people never get beyond this stage, claiming no greater ambition than to live to eat. The chakra connected to this body is the *Muladhara*. The natural urge of this body is expressed through sex, while its transformation is claimed to be found in celibacy or *brahmacharya*.

THE ETHERIC BODY ~ *Bhawa Sharir*
The emotional body forms during the second cycle of seven years and is fully developed by the age of fourteen. This point, at which sexual adulthood is achieved, is also when nature, having completed her part, withdraws and leaves the human being to develop on his or her own.

The chakra, known as *Svadhistara*, connected to the etheric or emotional body, has a natural potential for fear, hate and anxiety (clearly corresponding to the action of the amygdala in the physical body). In its transformed state this body expresses compassion, love and fearlessness.

THE ASTRAL BODY ~ *Sukshma Sharir*
This third body develops between the formative years of fourteen to twenty-one. This is the body devoted to reason and the intellect. The chakra associated with this body is *Manipura*. The natural and primary concern of this body is of doubt and thinking which creates the inability to act. When transformed it radiates trust, clear discrimination and awareness.

THE PSYCHIC OR MENTAL BODY ~ *Manas Sharir*
The fourth body is that of the imaginative and subjective realm. It is the territory of the shaman and shamaness, the psychic and the sorcerer. In this dream body it is difficult to distinguish between delusion and reality. The potentially diverting siddhic powers that arise in many meditation techniques like Tantra or Yoga originate from this body. Dreaming takes place here and its ultimate expression can be found in the lucid dream – in which the individual wakes up within a dream while the body remains asleep. The psychic states that have their basis in this body have no actual spiritual value, but they mark the bridge from the corporeal to the spiritual world. This body develops between the age of twenty-one and twenty-eight and the chakra associated with it is *Anahata*. The transformative quality that arises from this body is the ability to see the truth and reality of the situation rather than its dream.

THE BLISS OR SPIRITUAL BODY ~ *Atma Sharir*
This body would normally develop naturally by the age of thirty-five. This is the awakening of the Self or *Atman*. Here all the dualities of the first four bodies cease to be. It is the body of awareness and consciousness and the only obstacle for any further development is an overwhelming ecstasy and sense of fulfilment enjoyed by this body. It is said that many mystics become entangled here at the very onset of their Buddhahood.

The chakra associated with the bliss body is *Vishuddha*, which is located at the throat. This is the soul body and the state of *Moksha* or liberation.

 THE COSMIC BODY ~
Brahma Sharir
The sixth body with its associated
Ajna chakra is where the blissful Self of the
fifth body is left behind and only beingness
remains. There is now no Self that can claim to
be conscious, but only consciousness – only
God, or Brahma, exists. The *Ajna* chakra is
located at the third eye.

THE NIRVANIC BODY ~
Nirvana Sharir
This is the completion of the
seven-times-seven cycle ending at the age of
forty-nine. Associated with the *Sahasrara*, or
crown chakra. The obstacle to further development in the sixth body was Brahma, the
absolute beingness. Once
overcome, this final body is the journey into
non-being, cessation and entering the void
from which all came into existence. About the
last two bodies which transcend all intellectual
thought, nothing really can be said.

*These descriptions of the Eastern tradition
are based on the direct experience of Osho –
one of those rare mystics of this century who
can speak on his own authority based on his
direct experience.*[52]

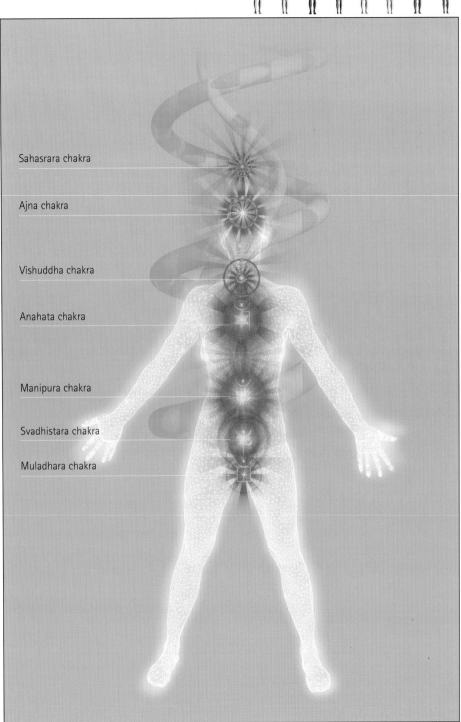

Sahasrara chakra

Ajna chakra

Vishuddha chakra

Anahata chakra

Manipura chakra

Svadhistara chakra

Muladhara chakra

87

ARE YOU A BELIEVER?

I T IS SAID THAT BELIEF IS NEVER one's own, it is always someone else's. Considering that our religions are mostly founded on a principle of faith and belief, this speaks loudly for our rather lazy approach to all things spiritual.

This in no way is a criticism, but a fact. When a child asks those crucial questions, "Where did I come from, who am I, who made me and where am I going when I die?" few of us are courageous enough to answer truthfully that we just don't know. It is easier to quickly polish our particular belief system and present it to the young mind. It is then a rare child who continues to pursue the subject for long, usually being satisfied with the adult's explanation.

The four sets of questions on the right illustrate the major ways of how we continue to approach those questions into adulthood. You can confirm your own approach by choosing the image that appeals to you the most.

Whatever you answer to the assessment, there is no implied value judgment. No one approach is more sacred, or higher, than the others – just different.

ASSESSMENT

Key: If you answer "yes" to the questions in any of the four columns with an excess of 4 for one particular column, you can be sure to have found your basic attitude to the mystery of God and the Divine.

BELIEVER

Do you:

1. feel your chosen religion to be the only true one?
2. feel that it was preordained that you were born into your religion?
3. know that you are here to fulfil God's purpose?
4. see no need to question your faith because its truth is self-evident?
5. feel that firm belief is the most essential religious quality?
6. need clear scriptures outlining rules of religious life?
7. feel that sincere belief will lead you to God?
8. respect the authority of leaders in your church or temple?
9. feel God will reward you in Heaven for deeds on Earth?
10. believe that your soul will survive death?
11. feel other religions are fundamentally false?
12. enjoy worshipping with others of your religion?

AGNOSTIC

Do you:

1. feel it is impossible to tell whether God exists or not?
2. keep an open mind on the subject of God?
3. see that not all versions of God in the world can be right?
4. prefer to not take anyone's word as proof of the existence of God?
5. sense that if there is a God then God is unknowable?
6. feel that only the measurable world can be known?
7. find no convincing reason why there should be a God?
8. feel able to enjoy this world without troubling about God?
9. feel able to accept God as a working hypothesis, but only that?
10. have no reason to believe in a single, male God?
11. feel that most God-oriented religions of prayer are childish?
12. feel those who claim to do God's work delude themselves?

ATHEIST

Do you:

1. feel no need to explain existence through a Creator God?
2. feel that there are simple scientific explanations for the existence of the universe?
3. dislike beliefs based on no verifiable facts?
4. feel that beliefs are nothing more than wish-fulfilment dreams?
5. feel that a benevolent God is not consistent with so much suffering?
6. prefer scientific facts to an imaginary God?
7. feel that the ideas about God are still very immature?
8. suspect that God was made in our image – not the reverse?
9. feel we need God only for the promise of future reward in Heaven?
10. detest people trying to sell you their image of God?
11. feel that those who believe that only their God is omnipotent are daft?
12. prefer the rigours of philosophy to those of religion?

SELF–DISCOVERER

Do you:

1. only trust your direct experience of the Divine?
2. consider that belief is blind and only the blind believe?
3. feel that you should never follow second-hand beliefs?
4. feel the need to question your own nature through first-hand experience?
5. feel you can only know God if you actually meet God?
6. prefer *to be* truth or *to know about* truth?
7. distrust any religion that demands belief as a precondition?
8. sense that you are unusual in your religious attitudes?
9. need to explore who you are and where you have come from?
10. distrust self-appointed messengers from God?
11. find the idea of submitting to a religion distasteful?
12. feel it is better to "know thyself" than to be told who you are?

88

HOW DO YOU APPROACH THE THREE BASIC QUESTIONS?

VIRTUALLY EVERY SCHOOL OF MYSTICISM that has ever existed has had at the core of its teaching the three fundamental questions of existence:

"Where have I come from?"

"Who am I?"

"Where am I going?"

These are not philosophical or superficial questions for the curious. They are radical, existential dilemmas that have to be directly experienced by every seeker of truth on the path of self discovery. But they can be asked in very different ways depending on the individual's particular type, his or her religious or mystical background and social programming. The three columns opposite give a broad view of the conformist believer, the logical atheist and the non-conformist who seeks understanding of the self.

In the first case, those who are attracted to any of the major religious traditions of the Book – Judaism, Christianity or Islam – are essentially outwardly oriented, looking toward a Godhead who is revealed through a chosen messenger. Some Eastern religions also have this attitude, as can be seen in the rich tapestry of Hindu Vedic culture.

The second focus is on the material, phenomenal world of reason, science, philosophy and technology. This is the object-oriented view of existence.

The third is Self-oriented. It includes most of the meditation-based religions of Buddhism, Tao, Hindu Tantra and Yoga.

Mystics tell us that all roads reach the top of the mountain. There is no absolute and right path, only the one you have chosen and that fits your type. However, you may not be aware of the broad spectrum of choice.

We are usually born into a way of life in which religious beliefs are taken for granted. Your tradition may not really suit your particular type at all. Check these three ways of viewing the world and see whether you feel sympathy with other ways of looking at the basic existential questions.

The conformist sees the flower first and foremost – God the Spirit – with the Self as a shadow. The materialist tends to see only the fixed phenomenal world of the vase, while the individual who is on the path to self-discovery sees both God and Self as dreams of the Void.

In the following pages you are about to embark on a journey through the main spiritual attitudes. These are the traditions that favour each of the nine types of the enneagram. So just as personalities are broadly divided into body-oriented, emotional and mental types, we can show a spiritual typology based on the same premises.

Read the different attentions and focuses without any judgment until one of them begins to resonate with your own feelings and ideas.

ASSESSMENT

The three columns opposite correspond to three basic types. They list the most likely explanations given to the original fundamental questions of "Where have I come from?", "Who am I?" and "Where am I going?"

See how many of these fit your own beliefs and ideas.

Do you simply fit one category, or do you find that you agree with many of the points in each column?

From this would you deduce that you are firm and clear in your belief, or that in all honesty you would have to admit to being confused in your religious beliefs?

TRADITIONAL RELIGIOUS BELIEFS

Where have I come from?

I have a soul independent of my body.
My soul was created by God.
My soul has been reincarnated many times.
I have incarnated in many other bodies.
I am reborn in order to learn.
My soul is given to me at birth.

Who am I?

I am born in order to develop my spirit.
I live to fulfill a Divine purpose.
I must be obedient to God's will.
I am here in order to be fully conscious.
I am here to be tested by God.
I am here to awaken from life's dream.

Where am I going?

My soul continues after death.
My soul will be judged by God.
I will reincarnate to fulfil my spiritual goal.
I will be reborn according to my deeds.
I must clear my karmic past to gain freedom.
I will go to Heaven or Hell.

MATERIALIST NON-RELIGIOUS IDEAS

Where have I come from?

There was no existence before birth.
I am part of evolution's game.
I am formed from recycled atoms.
My birth is through chance events.
I am a gene's strategy to create more genes.
I am part of an evolutionary process.

Who am I?

I was born through my parents.
My advantages were the luck of the draw.
Life is just the dream of evolution.
I must live this single life to the full.
I live to survive and survive to live.
Consciousness is a by-product of the brain.

Where am I going?

There is no life after death.
I continue to exist through my children.
I shall exist through what I have made.
My body will disperse and be recycled.
I shall cease to exist save in others' memories.
My genes will continue like clones.

ALTERNATIVE PATHS OF SELF-DISCOVERY

Where have I come from?

I am part of undifferentiated consciousness.
Consciousness exists before birth.
My essential being exists before birth.
I have existed throughout time.
I am part of the cosmic whole.
I must be reborn until I awaken to reality.

Who am I?

I am born as consciousness.
Through habitual strategies I build an ego.
The personality and ego are false selves.
I must awaken to truth of my beingness.
I must discover who I am.
I must become aware that I am dreaming.

Where am I going?

Death/rebirth is a cycle until awakening.
When you awaken there is no death.
Death is an illusion of our minds.
After death one prepares for the next life.
Death is discovery and transformation.
A mystic dies to the ego before bodily death.

89

SAGE AND SORCERER

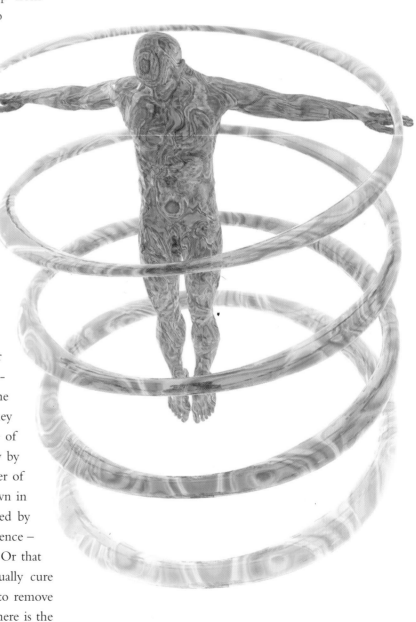

THIS CENTURY HAS SEEN a quantum leap from physics to psychics, from psychology to metaphysics. In the West the metaphysical thinking of the last few decades has created new perspectives on our traditional belief systems.

This sudden explosion of interest in psychic, magical and mystical ways, however, has created confusion rather than enlightenment in many minds. It has also stimulated interest in the indigenous mystical traditions long superseded by Christianity in many cultures. As most of our native traditions were essentially shamanistic it is no surprise that many of the so-called mystical paths are in reality those of the psychic, and not of the mystic.

Yet the very "siddhic powers" that invariably arise when anyone treads the spiritual road are those that any true mystic will avoid like the plague. For while such powers are the very stuff of healing, telepathy, materialization, out-of-body experiences and the control of dreams, they have little spiritual worth. They are the spin-off effects of walking across the bridge of the fourth (dream) body and so are fuelled entirely by the imagination. This is not to say that a practitioner of *Chod* – a visualization/actualization technique known in Tibet in which illusionary dream figures are created by adepts, and which then take on an independent existence – is just an illusion. They are indisputably substantial. Or that the psychic surgeons of the Philippines don't actually cure patients by plunging their hands through the skin to remove damaged or diseased organs. What is in operation here is the

world of mental powers, intimately bound up with the collective dream of our phenomenal world. However miraculous such manipulation of the material world may seem to be, it remains a psychic art, an unknown science, rather than something especially sacred.

The shaman or sorcerer, male or female, is concerned with *empowerment*, not with *awakening*. The power may be for good, as in healing, seeing into the future, substantiation, or telepathy. It can be for personal aggrandizement, like walking across red-hot coals or even over water. It can be for destructive and evil purposes. But it is essentially engaging the awesome powers of imagination.

So what is the essential difference between a sage and a sorcerer, between mysticism and magic? Simply expressed it can be seen as the choice between personal power and truth.

In mysticism the individual disappears and only a presence remains. The identified-self dies and only the truth survives. In the shamanic realm the individual is empowered, for good or bad, for others, for the tribe or for personal gain of knowledge. In spiritual terms the shaman, or shamaness, is only a stage along the path to awakening – an overnight, diverting stop at the most. The seeker must cross the bridge of the dream body to avoid being trapped for lifetimes in dreams.

The problem we all face in the West is that none of us have been spiritually prepared for the amazing multi-coloured coat that is our potential. Names like Freud and Jung, Merlin, Blake, Rasputin, Edgar Cayce and Gautama the Buddha, are all jumbled and synthesized into bright new packages of self-discovery by self-styled therapists, publishers and gurus.

The following questions are designed to crystallize your own position, your own magical or mystical needs at this moment in time. Are you inclined towards empowerment or surrender?

90

THE MALE AND FEMALE SEEKER

BEFORE WE EMBARK ON OUR JOURNEY of the spirit, one factor must be considered. It is said women make the finest disciples but men become the priests. It is true that no woman has ever founded a major religion. The number of women reported to have awakened spiritually is a mere handful compared with the thousands of men. The known female count includes such mystics as the Sufi Rabi'a al-Adawiyya, the Indian mystics Meera and Lallah, the Zen nun Chi'yono, or the Christians Theresa of Avila and Hildegard of Bingen, but they are hardly household names. You will notice that the mystics on the following pages to exemplify the nine major religious and spiritual types are all male. Now if you are generous enough to discount sexual discrimination on the part of the author, what other possible reasons are there for women to be so poorly represented in the spiritual realm?

One clue may be found in the meditations accompanying the nine spiritual types. All are chosen from the *Vigyan Bhairav Tantra*, an ancient text in which the Hindu deity Shiva gives a hundred and twelve techniques of awakening to Devi, his consort. The receptivity of a disciple is not limited to gender – men must be as receptive as women if they are to absorb the master's teachings. Otherwise they make appalling disciples.

What happens when a female disciple awakens is far more difficult to answer. Apparently she remains essentially receptive, so it becomes impossible to pass on what she has discovered. A certain masculine quality is needed in order to *give*. Otherwise the enlightened woman would simply go her way and few would be any the wiser of her awakening. A woman like Rabi'a had a certain male orientation even though she declared, "I have ceased to exist, and have passed out of self. I am one with Him and entirely His." And it was in that masculine spirit that Rabi'a delivered a devastating critique on the whole male-dominated, intellectual edifice of early Islam, effectively laying the foundations of later Sufism. But she was extremely rare.

The enlightened Zen nun Chiy'ono miraculously suffered a sex change, according to Zen records, becoming a male monk in Japan. This confirms the belief in many cultures that a seeker can only become enlightened when born into a male body. Such traditions reflect the fact that, regardless of gender, a masculine mind is needed to impart a teaching.

One anecdote, which perhaps best encapsulates the difference between the male and female mind, is the following tale from Rabi'a's life.

A famous Sufi ascetic made a fourteen-year long pilgrimage to Mecca, religiously praying at every holy site along the way and strictly abiding by the teachings of the Quran. When he eventually reached Mecca the sacred stone, the Ka'ba, was not there. He was told that the Ka'ba, discovering that Rabi'a was also on a pilgrimage, had gone out to meet her. Rabi'a herself was not impressed, commenting that what she had come for was not the house, but the master of the house. The ascetic was furious with Allah that his long austerities and holiness had been ignored in favour of a common slave, and a woman at that. Allah didn't comment.

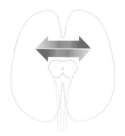 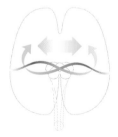

Left: A female mind can multi-track, being far more holistic than its male counterpart. *Right:* A female is more sensitive to hearing, pitch and timbre. She also can listen to two separate conversations at once.

WHY WOMEN ARE MORE LIKELY TO BECOME AWAKENED

The basic template for the wiring of the human mind is female. About six to eight weeks after conception the embryo is either flooded with male hormones, especially testosterone, which creates a male child, or it isn't and the child remains female. Yet this is not an "either or" situation. Sometimes the child receives only minimal doses, so while born a male he has an essentially female brain circuitry. On rarer occasions a female has higher testosterone levels during the formative period and so acquires a more masculine brain pattern in a female body.

The abbreviated list below suggests that a female mind has the advantage when it comes to religion. Why should this be so? It is possible precisely because the female mind is multi-tracked, is more holistic in its approach, has a wider field of vision, is more sensitive to touch and hearing, and is generally more receptive.

These attributes greatly contribute to the ability to intuitively absorb a spiritual teaching. A male brain with its single-minded, goal-focused vision, its analytic spatial need to separate figure from background, its lack of multiple links between the hemispheres and its tendency to compartmentalize, finds it far more difficult to view the world in a holistic and holy way. [53]

1. A female brain can multi-track. It can talk, read, watch TV and even knit at the same time. It is far more holistic than its male counterpart.
2. The female brain is more communicative, so women talk more and tend to build relationships more easily than men.
3. A female brain can also multi-track while talking – switching subjects and moods, while interweaving diverse and unconnected ideas. It has the ability to speak and listen simultaneously. A female brain has thirty percent more links between the two hemispheres than a male brain, allowing both left and right speech centres to operate simultaneously.
4. Female eyes have a greater variety of retina cones which makes them far more sensitive to colours. They also have a far wider angle of peripheral vision than male eyes, and see far better in close-up. Male eyes, on the other hand, have a more focused and long-range vision, which enables them to see far better at a distance.
5. The female brain can hear better than a male brain, and in a resting state its electrical activity is thirty percent greater, while it continues to receive and process information from its surroundings.
6. Women's bodies are more receptive than men's bodies in general, and they are ninety percent more sensitive to touch.

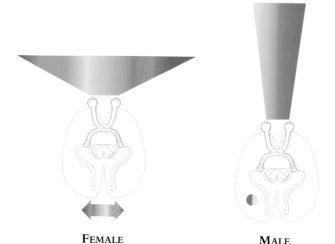

FEMALE   **MALE**

Left: The female discerns a wider spectrum of colours and is better at viewing close up. Visual information is shared by both hemispheres.

Right: A male discerns a narrower and simpler spectrum of colours. Links between hemispheres in a male brain are thirty percent fewer than in a female brain.

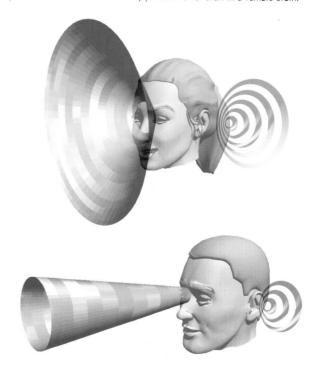

Above: The female has a wider peripheral as well as a wider close-up vision and her hearing is more sensitive than that of a male. The male has a tunnel vision, better suited to distanced viewing, and his hearing is less acute.

91

YOUR TRUE RELIGIOUS TYPE

WE TEND TO SEE OTHER RELIGIONS from the viewpoint of our own. Of those who profess any religious belief, over ninety percent will have chosen the faith they were born into. To an impartial observer this might seem to confirm that most of us prefer ready-made answers, rather than striking out to find the truth on our own. The eight religions featured on the page opposite have millions of adherents, all convinced that their spiritual team is the only one that has the Absolute truth.

In the listings three religious types are shown. Those who predominantly *sense* their way through life, those who *feel* and those who *think* about it. This, admittedly over-simplified, division does demonstrate that the major Western religions of the Book – Judaism, Christianity, and Islam – are all prayer-based, while many of the Eastern religions, more specifically Buddhism, Jainism and Tao, are meditation-oriented.

Using this typology we can see that in a prayer-based religion God is regarded as the true, ultimate reality and seekers try to unite with that reality through their devotion. Mystics of the heart like St Francis of Assisi, the Baal Shem Tov, or Jalal ud-Din Rumi, lost their identity through devotion to something greater than themselves. For them by far the most important religious quality was that of trust.

Compare this with the Eastern religions of meditation. In these the highest spiritual quality is not trust, but doubt. The meditator seeks only that which is real and non-illusory. Everything outside the seeker is seen as a dream from which he or she must awaken. It is the Self that is the goal. Existence and God might only be found once the Self is known. The greatest mystics of these traditions like Lao-Tzu, Patanjali or Gautama the Buddha, simultaneously discovered their true being and the Divine.

It is said there are many roads up the mountain yet they all arrive at the same peak. The one you eventually take depends upon you, your type and your own particular makeup.

You have now probably discovered your basic behavioural patterns, your outlook and general personality type operating in the phenomenal world. Entering the numenal world of the spirit you will find remarkably similar dispositions functioning there. These will be outlined in the next nine assessments.

In order to present each type as clearly as possible, individual mystics, rather than mainstream religions, have been chosen to exemplify a particular path. Their names are unlikely to be familiar to most readers, so their particular teachings may surprise and perhaps touch you, irrespective of your belief.

One of the major hurdles for all of us is laziness when it comes to matters of the spirit. If we spent as much energy at finding God as we do on sex, shopping and working out, we might all be Buddhas. But lack of energy for the spiritual dimension could equally be caused by the fact that our childhood religions fail to excite us. And that could be because their methods simply don't suit our particular type.

ASSESSMENT

The descriptions opposite show how sensing, feeling and thinking types can also be found in the realm of religion. Before turning the page to the first of the body-oriented spiritual types, consider whether your chosen religion or path – be it one that you were born into, or that you chose later in life – really suits your personality type. Remember this table is only a very rough categorization of mainstream religions, rather than individual mystics. Yet it can show those who may be faithful to one religion that there are other ways to approach the reality of the spirit.

 CHRISTIANITY ~ Christians believe in one God who has a special relationship with humankind. Through disobedience humans sinned and God sent his son Jesus Christ to redeem those sins. Eventually all will be resurrected from the dead and judged for their actions. Only faith, good deeds and prayer will truly redeem humanity.

APPROXIMATE NUMBER: 1,400,000,000

BODY TYPE ~ *Mystic practices:* Ascetics

FEELING TYPE ~ *Prayer, devotion:* Orthodoxy, mystics

 JUDAISM ~ Jews believe in one God who made a personal covenant with them, and keeping His holy laws is their part of it. Other peoples are not obliged to observe these laws, only the ethical principles. They await the coming of a Messiah who will bring peace to the world. The dead will be resurrected and judged at that time.

APPROXIMATE NUMBER: 12,800,000

FEELING TYPE ~ *Prayer, devotion:* Orthodox prayer

THINKING TYPE ~ *Meditation:* Kabbalistic meditation

 ISLAM ~ Islam means submission to the will of the one God, Allah, whose last prophet was Muhammed. It was he who recorded the divine message and is the final revelation of God. By prayer and following the Prophet's example followers can hope to live in eternal paradise.

APPROXIMATE NUMBER: 1,200,000,000

BODY TYPE ~ *Mystic practices:* Sufi Dervishes

FEELING TYPE ~ *Prayer, devotion:* Orthodoxy, Sufis

 HINDUISM ~ A cauldron of beliefs originating in India embracing meditation and prayer, including the *Vedas, Upanishads, Mahabharata* and *Ramayana*. Most Hindus believe that each person embodies *atman*, a divine spark of the universal soul which is reborn. Every thing that exists is part of God, including human beings. Every action has an effect, or *karma*, on this and future lives. By accumulating good *karma* one can awaken, breaking free of the cycle of birth and death to achieve eventual union with God.

APPROXIMATE NUMBER: 750,000,000

BODY TYPE ~ *Mystic practices:* Ascetics, Yoga

FEELING TYPE ~ *Prayer, devotion:* Popular Hindu Bhaktis

THINKING TYPE ~ *Meditation*: Mystical Hinduism

 SIKHISM ~ Sikhs believe in one God, who is timeless and without form. He makes himself known only to those who are ready and have sought Him by prayer and good service to others. God's revelation is not confined to Sikhs alone but to all who are devout.

APPROXIMATE NUMBER: 17,000,000

FEELING TYPE ~ *Prayer, devotion:* Prayer and service

 BUDDHISM ~ Buddhists follow the teachings of Gautama the Buddha, or the Awakened One. They believe that they are reborn again and again into a suffering world because of the ties of desire. By meditation and right practices, the power of the mind, with its false idea of self, gradually evaporates enabling the practitioner to escape the wheel of birth and death and awaken to being one with existence.

APPROXIMATE NUMBER: 450,000,000

FEELING TYPE ~ *Prayer, devotion:* Tibetan sects

THINKING TYPE ~ *Meditation:* Basis of Buddhism

 TAO ~ Taoists follow the Way or Path, in alignment with the natural force and principle of the universe. Living in harmony and in balance with the Tao brings peace, happiness and wisdom. By understanding and meditating on the balances of life, the adherent can either prolong life or return to the void from which all and everything arose.

APPROXIMATE NUMBER: 35,000,000

FEELING TYPE ~ *Prayer, devotion:* Deity sects

THINKING TYPE ~ *Meditation:* Original Tao

 SHINTO ~ The ceremonial religion of Japan meaning the Way of the Gods. It is closely linked both to the land and to the continuum of family and ancestors. Appeals are made to Kami, the force of nature, but many ceremonies combine with other beliefs, especially Zen Buddhism.

APPROXIMATE NUMBER: 40,000,000

FEELING TYPE ~ *Prayer, devotion:* Ceremony/worship

THINKING TYPE ~ *Meditation:* Shinto/Zen/Buddhism

92

ARE YOU A YOGI? *(body type)*

WE NOW EMBARK ON THE NINE SPIRITUAL PATHS. One pattern that has reappeared in many of the typologies you have so far encountered is the triad of *sensing, feeling* and *thinking*. The first three parts of this book are arranged as body, emotions and mind. We can apply precisely the same principle to the realm of religion and self-discovery, dividing our approaches to the sacred into three basic paths. These are again sub-divided into three attitudes making up nine in all. It must be understood that such divisions are like painting roads across the sky. These designations have no existential reality. They are only useful indications of your basic attitudes to the Divine.

The sensing, or body-oriented, types see the body and mind as one. If you change the body, you will change the mind. Through persistent physical practices one can alter the patterns of the mind. The three body-oriented sub-types can be seen as the practitioner of Yoga, the Ascetic and the Fakir.

The example is Yoga, which could be called the science of the spirit. In one of the ancient *Upanishads* of India it is said:

When the five senses and the mind are still,
And the reasoning intellect rests in silence,
Then begins the highest path.
This calm steadiness of the senses is called yoga.

While yoga did not originate with Patanjali,[54] it was this sage, living twenty-two centuries ago, who recorded and systematized what was already an ancient knowledge. He defined yoga as "the restraint of the thought-waves of the mind", and in his exposition *The Yoga Sutras* the whole science is unfolded in very terse and simple sentences. The introductory verses are reproduced here with a brief commentary.

Illumination

1. *We now begin the exposition and discipline of yoga.*
   Patanjali saw the body and mind as. Change the body and you change the mind. If the body becomes totally still and centred the mind also becomes still and centred. This requires discipline of mind and body.

2. *Yoga is cessation of the activities of the mind.*
   By definition the mind is the *activity*; it is not a *thing*. It is the constant flow of thoughts within the brain and not the brain itself.

3. *When the mind is quietened, the Witness arises by itself.*
   When activity of thoughts ceases, you, the witness-seer are there.

4. *Otherwise it conforms to the nature of the mind's activities.*
   In other states we identify with the thoughts and memories and so become whatever we are thinking of. Our sense of self changes with each thought.

5. *The modifications of the mind are five. They can be either a source of misery or non-misery.*
   The body and mind are one. The body has five instruments of activity, the mind has five modifications or functions. Our basic

nature is bliss but the mind can only choose misery (being closed) or non-misery (being open). The mind itself cannot give you bliss but it can remain open to allow its natural flow.

6. *They are right knowledge, wrong knowledge, imagination, sleep and memory.*

7. *Right knowledge has three sources: direct cognition, inference and the words of the awakened ones.*

   Direct cognition can only occur when there is no medium, even the senses, between the observer and the observed. Direct knowing comes through meditation. *Inference* is an open hypothesis based on available information. In a state of blind ignorance we need the words of the enlightened ones.

8. *Wrong knowledge is a false conception not corresponding to the thing as it is.*
   We all have preconceptions, prejudices and fixed attitudes which give wrong understanding. Our minds are full of pre-packaged knowledge handed down from others and not our own. We are unable to see the real situation as it is because of the distorting lenses of this programming.

9. *An image conjured up by words without any substance behind it is imagination.*

10. *The modification of the mind which is based on the absence of any content in it is sleep.*

11. *Memory is the calling up of past experiences.*

12. *Their cessation is brought about by persistent inner effort and non-attachment.*
    Yoga is neither quick nor easy but it will reveal results if you persist. The following sutras are self-evident.

13. *Of these two the inner practice is the effort for being firmly established in oneself.*

14. *It becomes firmly grounded on being continued for a long time, without interruption and with reverent devotion.*

15. *The first state of desirelessness is cessation from self-indulgence in the thirst for sensuous pleasures, but only through conscious effort.*

16. *The last state of desirelessness of all desiring is by knowing the innermost nature of the supreme self.*

ASSESSING THE SPIRITUAL PATH

The usual assessments are simply inappropriate when dealing with spirituality. Instead, the next nine assessments are in the form of a meditation. These are taken from the five-thousand-year-old Indian scripture, the Vigyan Bhairav Tantra. *It lists one hundred and twelve techniques given by Shiva to his consort Devi. These are claimed to be all the possible methods for transcending the mind. When Devi asks about the nature of life, consciousness and the cosmos, Shiva does not give her philosophical answers, but techniques for experiencing the Divine directly. This ancient science of transformation can be followed whatever your belief.* Vigyan *means "consciousness",* Bhairav *means "beyond" and* Tantra *is the method. So whichever method attracts you, try it out for a few days and discover whether it works for you.*

MEDITATION

"This experience may dawn between two breaths.
After breath comes in [down] and just before turning up [out]
– the benificence."

Sitting in a relaxed lotus posture, breathe normally and naturally. Be aware of each incoming and outgoing breath. There is a fraction of a second in which you stop breathing – a gap. Neither follow the breath in, nor move ahead of it, just move along with it. Consciousness and breathing become one. Suddenly you will be aware of the gap in which there is no breath. In that gap, suddenly there is the *benificence* – an awakening, a glimpse, a *satori*. But do not expect results overnight. It takes time. Buddha is said to have taken thirteen lives to attain illumination. However, don't despair – he used this method!

93

ARE YOU AN ASCETIC? *(body type)*

TIBETAN BUDDHISM is an exotic brew of the Indian *Vedas,* the *Upanishads,* Yoga, Tantra, the teachings of Buddha and an ancient native shamanic tradition called Bön. It was one of the most powerful practitioners of black magic in the Bön tradition – instrumental in the death of many people, including thirty-five of his relatives – who must rank as the most steadfast and single-minded ascetic in history.

Jetsun Milarepa [55] became a disciple of a Tantric Buddhist master, Marpa, as an act of deep repentance for what he had done. In order to expiate his accumulated sins, he had to endure what must be the most severe austerities ever inflicted on a disciple by an enlightened master. Seven times he was ordered, single-handed, to construct a house on different sites; six times he was told it was useless and had to be demolished and to return the site to its original state. Each time he began his assignment he was promised secret religious instruction on its completion, but each time it was withheld. His whole body was covered in sores and often he despaired, but somehow he continued with the trials and penances imposed by his Guru, Marpa. Eventually he expiated his sins and continued to meditate in a cave, living only on nettles, yet gaining the most phenomenal siddhic powers. It is hardly surprising that he taught unswerving attention and the abandonment of all other concerns in order to awaken.

I have obtained spiritual knowledge through giving up all thought of food, clothing and reputation. Inspired with zeal in my heart, I bore every hardship and inured myself to all sorts of privations of the body; I devoted myself to meditation in the most unfrequented and solitary places. Thus did I obtain knowledge and spiritual experience; do you also follow the path trodden by me and practise devotion as I have done.

Milarepa exemplifies the ascetic's single-minded approach to the awakening of the spirit by working through the body in order to quieten the mind.

Accustomed long to meditating on the secret whispered truths,
I have forgotten all that is said in written or printed books.
Accustomed, as I have been, to the study of the eternal Truth,
I've lost all knowledge of ignorance.
Accustomed to meditating on this life and the next as One,
I have forgotten the dread of birth and death.
Accustomed long to studying, by myself, my own experiences,
I have forgotten the need to seek the opinion of others.
Accustomed long to applying each new experience to my own spiritual growth,
I have forgotten all creeds and dogmas.
Accustomed long to regarding my fleshly body as my hermitage,
I have forgotten the ease and comfort of the monasteries.

…Maintain the state of undistractedness, and distractions will fly away. Dwell alone, and you shall find the Friend. Take the lowest place, and you shall reach the highest. Hasten slowly, and you will arrive sooner. Renounce all worldly goals, and you shall reach the highest goal. If you follow this unfrequented path, you will find the shortest way. If you realize "Sunyata" [the absolute Emptiness], compassion will arise within your hearts; and when you lose all differentiation between yourself and others, then you will be fit to serve others.

As can be seen from these brief extracts, this is not a path for the armchair mystic. It is a severe and arduous route to God requiring courage, time and an almost superhuman persistence.

MEDITATION

*"Feeling pain – gently observe its centre –
the blissful gap!"*

Milarepa spent many years practising the
discipline of *Tum-mo*, the awakening of the
inner fire to heat the body in the sub-zero
temperatures of the mountains. The following
technique is an ancient meditation, very similar
to that used by Milarepa's Kargyütpas sect.

The original technique was to "Pierce part of
your nectar-filled body and gently enter the
piercing", but there is no need to be so
aggressive toward your body. While sitting in
meditation for any time there usually comes a
point at which you become aware of a pain in
your joints or back muscles. Concentrate on
where the pain exists. The more you focus on
the area the more you will notice how the
pain intensifies but at the same time shrinks in
area. Keeping your full attention on the
shrinking point it will suddenly disappear and
you will be filled with an overwhelming bliss
and sense of beingness. The reasoning behind
this method is that when observing you cease
to identify with the pain. As you begin to enter
the pain, as if from far away, you dis-identify
with it and attain an inner silence. Feeling is
transformed into observation which disrupts
identification with the body, so that you are
only conscious of being.

94

ARE YOU A DERVISH? *(body type)*

JALAL ud-DIN RUMI IS PROBABLY the most famous Sufi mystic, either through being known as "the greatest mystical poet of any age" or as the founder of the Order of Whirling Dervishes.

Sufism is the mystical wing of Islam. Often in conflict with their more orthodox leaders, the Sufis none the less agree on most of the traditional tenets of the Islamic faith. Rumi was born in Persia at the beginning of the thirteenth century and became a well respected religious teacher. However, it wasn't until a chance meeting with a love-intoxicated dervish called Shamsud'din Tabriz that he finally awakened. His masterpiece, the *Mathnawi*, has been called the "Persian Quran".[56]

His exuberant and rhapsodic poems talk of the Beloved (God) as if they were love songs. His imagery is only for those who come from the heart. Here is the perfect feeling type whose association with the Whirling Dervishes reveals how the heart can be accessed through a dynamic and bodily technique. While Rumi may have written over twenty-six thousand verses in the *Mathwani* alone, he would insist that, "The speech of tongue may elucidate but speechless love is yet more clear." So the technique of whirling was a far greater vehicle for awakening to the presence of the Divine than mere words. For here was direct existential communion and union with God, the Beloved.

> As waves upon my head the circling curl.
>> So in the sacred dance you weave and whirl.
> The flame upon His cheek as candle bright,
>> Calls that the moth its wings singe at the sight!
> Dance then, oh heart, a whirling circle be,
>> Burn in this flame – is not the candle He?
> When rapture once has caught and burned my heart,
>> Ne'er from the fire could it endure to part! [57]

MEDITATION

"Blessed One, as senses are absorbed in the heart, reach the centre of the lotus."

This whirling meditation is only for those who are body- and feeling-oriented. It is a device to lose your head; while dancing the dancer becomes the dance.

This meditation happens naturally in whirling. The head disappears as you find the experience centring in the heart. The energy and attention of the whirler moves from the heart to the navel, the centrepoint of being. It is best to use loose clothing and have bare feet and navel. To start, cross your arms with the left hand on the right shoulder and the right hand on the left shoulder. Return to this position if you feel dizzy or nauseous. Move in whichever direction seems right. If you whirl in an anticlockwise direction, rotate your left foot in short turns while using your right foot to act as the driving force. Raise the right arm, palm upward as if channelling energy through the body. Discharge it with the left arm lowered, palm down. (Reverse this if moving clockwise.) Keep the eyes open and unfocused so that what you see is blurred and flowing in a single line. Rotate slowly at first, gathering speed after the first fifteen minutes as soon as you feel stabilized and comfortable. Let the dance take over until you become a whirlpool of energy with a silent witness in the centre. At a certain point you will be whirling so fast that the body will fall by itself. Allow it. Don't attempt to control when or how it happens. You will land softly and the ground will absorb your landing. Roll over onto your belly and allow your bare navel to contact the floor and remain in that position for at least fifteen minutes.

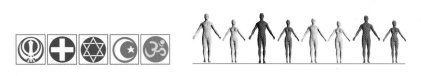

95

ARE YOU A DEVOTEE? *(feeling type)*

THE FIFTEENTH-CENTURY POET Kabir was born in
Benares, India, as a Moslem yet contrived to become
a disciple of the Hindu mystic Ramananda. Thus his
songs are a unique blend of the two religious views and it is
ironic that Hindus and Moslems both claim him as exclusively
their own.

He was a weaver, an illiterate family man who extolled the
simple life. He was contemptuous of the traditional sanctity of
the yogi who "has a great beard and matted locks and smells
like a goat." He saw the spiritual quest not as one of celibacy,
renunciation, and the life-negating austerities practised by
ascetics, monks and sadhus, but as integral to everyday living.
His songs have become the poetic treasures of India, yet they
reach far beyond mere poetry. In the following translations by
Rabindranath Tagore, Kabir sings to God and the God within
us all. He exemplifies the man of feeling. His devotional songs
speak for the Bhakti mystics of India, the Sufis of the Middle
East, the Hassidim of central and eastern Europe or devotional
Christians.

Remember that whatever your religion, at its heart lies the
direct experiences of individual mystics who were the source
of subsequent priestly misinterpretation. This is the reason that
their original and individual words, rather than religions, have
been chosen to represent the nine types.

Are you ready to cut off your head and place your foot on it?
If so, come; Love awaits you!
Love is not grown in a garden, nor sold in the marketplace;
Whether you are a king or servant, the price is your head,
*   and nothing less.*
Yes, the cost of the elixir of love is your head!
Do you hesitate? O miser. It is cheap at that price!

O Friend, where dost thou seek Me?
Lo! I am beside thee.
I am neither in temple nor in mosque: I am neither in Kabba
*   nor in Kailash:*
Neither am I in rites and ceremonies, nor in Yoga and
*   renunciation.*
If thou art a true seeker, thou shalt at once see Me: thou shalt
*   meet Me in a moment of time.*
Kabir says: "O Friend! God is the breath of all breath."

The river and its waves are one surf: where is the difference
*   between the river and its waves?*
When the wave rises, it is the water; and when it falls, it is the
*   same water again. Tell me, Sir, where is the distinction?*
Because it has been named as wave, shall it no longer be
*   considered as water?*
Within the Absolute, the worlds are being told like beads:
Look upon that rosary with the eyes of wisdom.

Tell me, O Swan, your ancient tale.
From what land do you come, O Swan?
*   to what shore will you fly?*
Where would you take your rest, O Swan,
*   and what do you seek?*

Even this morning, O Swan, awake, arise, follow me!
There is a land where no doubt nor sorrow have rule:
*   where the terror of death is no more.*
There the woods of spring are a-bloom, and the fragrant scent
*   "He is I" is borne on the wind:*
There the bee of the heart is deeply immersed, and desires
*   no other joy.*[58]

MEDITATION

"Devote yourself."

Devotion is always to something or someone outside yourself. It is a surrender to the other, of love, caring, prayer and dedication. In dissolving your identity in another there is transformation. As you enter the object of devotion, the ego, the mind and its false sense of self, disappears.

The object is irrelevant. It can be God, a flower or a beloved. It does not matter whether any of these are worthy of your love. Devotion is a way of life. This requires complete trust in life, twenty-four hours a day. But the path of devotion is ultimately freedom.

96

ARE YOU PRAYERFUL? *(feeling type)*

MOST WESTERN RELIGIONS can be said to be religions of prayer. They were founded at a time when people were more centred in their feelings than in thought. In this century the reverse is the case, which means that the older faiths are being challenged by those spiritual concepts of the East which are meditation-based.

One of the greatest poets of prayer was the thirteenth century mystic Fakhrud'din Iraqi. A legend in his region for his devotion to Islam even as a child, he joined a group of dervishes wandering through Persia and India. He wrote the *Lama'at* or *"Glimpses"* on his return to the Middle East. This language of prayer could have equally been created by Theresa of Avila, St. Francis of Assisi, the Sufi mystic Hallaj, the Hassidic sage Baal Shem Tov or the Hindu female mystics Meera and Lallah. It is the universal language of those who are guided by their feelings. It is a song of absolute trust in which there is no distinction between God and the individual.

I asked for news of You from all I met.
  Then I saw You
  ~ Through myself,
  And found we were identical.
Now I blush to think
  I ever searched for signs of You.
"O You who are so unbearably beautiful,
  Whose beloved are You?" I asked
  "My own," He replied;
  "For I am one and one alone –
  Love, lover, beloved, mirror, beauty, eye."

I sought solitude with my loved one,
  Yet find there is no one here but myself.
  And if there were a "someone else",
  Then, truly I should not have attained her.
I am the one I love;
  He whom I love is I
  Two, yet in a single body.
If I have become the Beloved.
  Who is the lover?
Beloved, Love and lover – three in one;
  There is no place for union here,
  So, what is this talk of "separation"?
Hunter, prey, bait and trap;
  Candle, candlestick, flame and moth;
  Beloved, lover, soul and soul's desire;
  Inebriation, drinker, wine and cup ~
All is He!

If You are everything,
  Then, who are all these people?
And if I am nothing,
  What's all this noise about?
You are the totality;
  Everything is You. Agreed!
Then, all that is "other-than You" ~
  What is it?
Oh, indeed I know, nothing exists but You.
  But tell me, whence all this confusion?
Listen riff-raff:
Do you want to be ALL?
Then go ~ go and become nothing! [59]

MEDITATION

"Imagine spirit simultaneously within and around you until the entire universe becomes the spirit."

This is a simple prayer without words. It is best done at night before going to sleep. You can do it in your room, or in warm weather do it under the stars, alone.

Close your eyes and imagine a wide river of spiritual force overflowing around you. Start feeling it within the body as well. Allow your body to sway, to jerk or vibrate. This will show your imagination is beginning to operate. Do not try to dispel this by reasoning. Just allow it to happen. Feel that the whole space around you is de-materializing and becoming pure energy and spirit. Gradually your body becomes just energy and merges with the energy around you. While this is simply your imagination, it is beginning to de-programme your fixed patterns of how you see the world. Continue until you begin to feel that the whole of existence is immaterial, just waves of oceanic energy in which you disappear and merge with an energy that is God, the totality of all there is. At this point a real prayer is born.

This prayerful state will remain in sleep. If you continue to practise this for at least three months you will begin to feel that the whole of existence is really immaterial – just waves of oceanic energy in which you disappear and merge. And that energy is God, the totality of all there is. Prayer is born in the bliss of dissolution as the fixed and solid-seeming self evaporates, leaving just a prayer on the wind.

97

ARE YOU A LOVER? *(feeling type)*

THE BAUL MYSTICS OF BENGAL are virtually unknown outside India.[60] This is hardly surprising as they are always on the road. They have no centre, no mosque or temple or even scriptures. The songs and poetry they sing are unique to each individual but are recorded by others. They seldom travel in big groups. A Baul's possessions are little more than a cloth, a hand-made single-stringed instrument, drums and a begging bowl. He, or she, just dances, sings and celebrates; no wonder their religion is so little known. Even the name *Baul* originates in the Sanskrit as "mad and affected by the wind". These are sacred, crazy people who seek, not a God in Heaven, but *Adhar Manush*, the Essential Being, firmly on Earth. There is no need to create a Temple to God for the temple of this essential being is the body. The seeker must travel the road inward. And to find this essence the seeker must live completely in the here and now, responding only with total spontaneity.

If you want to reach to the essential man
Then the way is through the spontaneous man.

The Baul's spontaneity is such that no two of them are in any way alike. There can be no organization or rituals. Every moment is a surprise, unique; to be lived totally.

Blind One, how can you stumble,
On a straight spontaneous path?
Be spontaneous in your own self,
And find the way that you are born to.

The whole search is for the essential, natural core of being and the method they have chosen to find it is love. The path of the Baul is the path of love.

You must be single-minded,
To visit the court of my beloved.
If your mind is torn in two, you will swim in confusion,
And never reach the shore.

The Baul's central question is "Who am I?" Who is this essential core of being? Not the peripheral personality, or the dreaming ego with whom we indentify, but the central hub around which we spin.

Look!
Look for Him in the temple of your limbs;
He is there as the Lord of the world ~
Speaking, singing enchanting melodies.
He is an expert at hide-and-seek;
No one can see Him.
Do not try to catch Him, O my heart!
He can never be caught ~
You can only hope for Him in whole faith.

The Baul have tremendous faith in the potential of humankind. They do not look to a separate God who is somewhere else, in Heaven or the sky. They see Him within.

Commit yourself to the earth while on the earth,
My heart, if you wish to attain the unattainable man.
Place at his feet your flowers of feelings
and the prayer of tears flooding your eyes.

MEDITATION

*"Look lovingly at an object. Do not go to another object.
Here in the middle of the object ~ the blessing."*

Choose an object that you find beautiful. It can be
your beloved, a flower or some single treasured item.
Look at it and lose yourself completely – become
absent as you bring more love into your gaze. Allow
whatever you have chosen to become the centre of
your love. Suddenly you have forgotten yourself and
only the object remains and then the blessing happens.
The object disappears and only consciousness remains.
Because you are absorbed in the other, bliss arises and
the consciousness identified with the ego, your false
sense of self, begins to move away from you.

God lives in you wholly intermingled.
　　O my unseeing heart, your eyes are so unwise!
How then can you find the treasured man?
　　That unseen man dwelling in the brilliance of light
　　Hides his identity from those blinded by stupor.

All of us think of God in different ways,
　　Beyond senses and feelings.
And yet it is only in the essence of loving
　　That God is found.

He who has seen the beauty of the Beloved friend,
　　Can never forget it.
The form is for seeing, not for discourse,
　　As beauty has no comparison.
He who has seen that form flashing on the mirror,
　　The darkness of his heart is gone.
He lives with his eyes focused on the form,
　　Careless of the river between life and death.
His heart forever devoted to beauty,
　　Dares the Gods.

98

ARE YOU A PHILOSOPHER SAGE? *(thinking type)*

HERACLITUS IS KNOWN IN THE West as "Heraclitus the Obscure", "Heraclitus the Dark", or "Heraclitus the Riddling". He lived in ancient Greece at around the same time as two other enlightened men, Socrates and Pythagoras. Like them, he did not fit into the mind-dominated philosophic tradition. Part of the difficulty in understanding him comes from the fact that his major antagonist was Aristotle, who even now dominates the rational tradition of Western thought.

Heraclitus talks in mystical paradoxes in a way that is completely unfamiliar to us, whether in religion or philosophy. If the mystical words of Socrates, Pythagoras and Heraclitus had not been overridden by Aristotelian logic, the religious history of the West might have taken a very different path. If any of these three philosophers had lived in the East during the extraordinary spiritual renaissance of that time they would have been honoured as enlightened Buddhas. [61]

The Hidden Harmony is better than the obvious.
Opposition brings concord.
Out of discord comes the fairest harmony.
It is in changing that things find repose.
People do not understand how
That which is at variance with itself,
Agrees with itself.
There is a harmony in the bending back,
As in the case of the bow and lyre.
The name of the bow is life, but its work is death.

Such words could have been attributed to his contemporary, the Chinese founder of Tao, Lao Tzu. Two thousand five hundred years ago Lao Tzu said:

The visible world is born of the invisible;
The world of forms is born of the formless.
…The one called Tao is subtle, beyond vision
Yet latent in it is all forms.
It is dark and obscure,
Yet latent in it is the creative power of life.
From the ancient days until now
Its manifestation has source and is reabsorbed into that Infinite.
The world exists in and on that infinite Void;
How it comes into existence, is sustained
And once again dissolved is a mystery.
It is fathomless, like the sea.
Wondrously, the cycle of creation begins after every completion.
The Tao sustains all creation, yet is never exhausted.
…That which gives life to all creation yet which is
Itself never drawn upon ~ that is the Tao.

Lao Tzu then says something that Heraclitus would totally approve of:
My teaching is very easy to practise; yet no one understands it
And no one practises it; it is this
The sage wears a tattered coat and carries jade within his breast.

Heraclitus:
Although this truth is eternally valid
    Yet men are unable to understand it.
Not only before hearing it
    But even after they have heard it.

As far away as Tibet another great mystic, Atisha, was instructing his disciples, "Treat all phenomena as a dream", in order that they learn to awaken.

MEDITATION

"Whenever your mind is wandering, internally or externally, at this very place,…this."

This is a perfect meditation for the philosopher type in which the witness is revealed.

There are two ways of approaching thinking. You can either bring your attention to the thoughts themselves, as if they were clouds in the sky on a summer's day, or you can focus on the sky behind the clouds—on consciousness itself.

Whenever your mind wanders don't attempt to stop it. Allow the thoughts to come. Just be aware they are gathering, passing by, but change the focus to the consciousness that is witnessing the thoughts. You can do this at any time.

It is simple. No austerities, no breathing techniques are necessary. Whatever you are doing, just be aware of the mind itself, of the one who is thinking.

This is the basis for Zen Schools of Sudden Enlightenment. For the switch of attention from the thought to the witness, watching the thoughts pass is always sudden. It is not a gradual process. It is here, now and instant that the mind-set changes and with it the illumination, the glimpse of the reality of the situation. It is the THIS at the end of the description of the meditation. So be alert in doing anything. Move your focus from the thing to the mind itself, from the object to the subject and you will know who you really are.

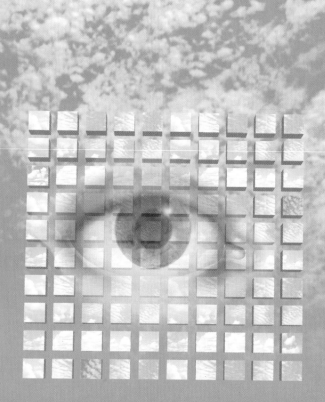

Thousands of miles away in Greece Heraclitus said:

Men are as forgetful and heedless in their waking moments
     Of what is going on around them as they are during their sleep.
Fools, although they hear, are like the deaf,
To them the adage applies that
Whenever they are present they are absent.
The waking have one world in common;
Sleepers have each a private world of his own.

You cannot step twice in the same river.
Everything flows and nothing abides.
Everything gives way and nothing stays fixed.

99

DARE YOU LOOK AT REALITY? *(thinking type)*

IKKYU WAS THE abbot of the Buddhist Daitokuji monastery in Kyoto in fifteenth-century Japan. Even by the fierce standards of Zen masters, Ikkyu stands out as being totally uncompromising. In his view we walk "the Leaky Road", where we lose energy on a road of illusions, desires and dreams. We have carefully constructed this virtual world and doggedly maintain it, but as its foundations are set in memories – or in futures that do not yet exist – where, asks Ikkyu, is its reality?

He jokingly points out in his verses that it is those ideal, sacred desires and conceptions we have, like "enlightenment", or "nirvana" and "liberation", that are the most illusory of all. All grasping for either sacred or secular ideals is futile, there is nothing to be grasped.

Since our true nature is already Buddha nature we do not need to *do* anything to make it so. On the contrary to seek Buddhahood outside oneself is the surest way to miss it.

Even birth and death are not part of the real world. Ikkyu insists that we should give no importance to such ideas. The duality of good and bad, happy or sad, are only part of the robotic, conceptual world of our brain whose inherent nature is to classify. The Real world is seamless, with no boundaries or dividing walls. It is One. It is Suchness.

So, says Ikkyu, what remains is to celebrate when it rains or even when it doesn't rain. Don't choose one above the other.

> *A rest on the way back from the Leaky Road*
> *To the Never-Leaky Road;*
> > *If it rain, let it rain;*
> *If it rain not, let it not rain;*
> > *But should it not rain,*
> *You must travel*
> *With wet sleeves.*

Even if it doesn't rain we all live, we all grow older and we all die – we all end up travelling with wet sleeves. It remains a dream. Wake up! he shouts and you will see it.

> *The mind:*
> > *Since there is really*
> *No such thing as mind,*
> *With what enlightenment*
> *Shall it be enlightened?"*
> *The mind:*
> > *Without end, without beginning,*
> *Though it is born, though it dies*
> *The essence of emptiness.*

> *To write something and leave it behind us,*
> > *It is but a dream.*
> *When we awake we know*
> > *There is not even anyone to read it.* [62]

Ikkyu's message is that there is nothing to say and nothing to teach. The truth is self-evident the moment you are natural, spontaneous and free of others' beliefs and ideas. What someone else knows is not your own unique understanding, and that includes the words of Ikkyu himself. To him, perfection is found in the ordinary, natural human being, and in not taking ourselves, or God, too seriously. His uncompromising viewpoint only suits a certain type of person. It takes courage to look at the reality of the situation and few of us are prepared to travel his road, whether it is non-leaky or not.

Ikkyu's name, left, means "take it easy", a rest between activities – a coffee break.

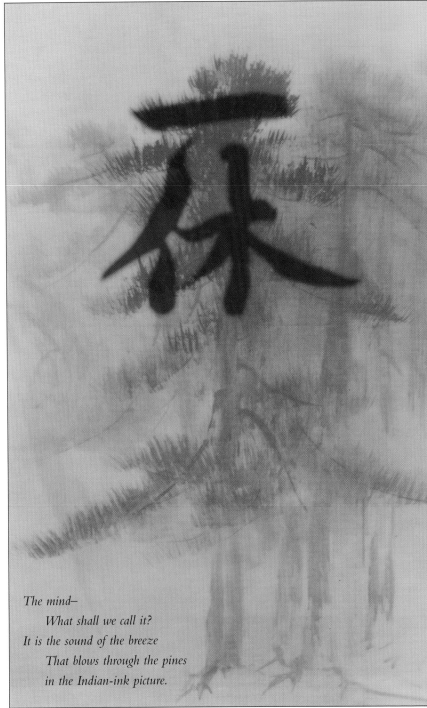

The mind—
What shall we call it?
It is the sound of the breeze
That blows through the pines
in the Indian-ink picture.

MEDITATION

"This so-called universe appears as a juggling, a picture show. To be happy, look upon it so."

The Tibetan mystic Atisha presented the same meditation in another form, which was *"Treat all phenomena as a dream"*. Choose whichever suits your nature best. The message behind each is to not take the world and its actions too seriously. The existential law is that the more serious you become, the more the world takes on substance and a heaviness. The more you are identified with the "Leaky Road" the more you feel as if you are wading through treacle. You become easily exhausted. Yet, things that seemed so important and serious one day are forgotten the next. Loves come and go, disputes happen and are resolved. Life is a continuing flux and nothing lasts. In the East this universe is even considered as nothing more than God's play.

View the world as if it were a dream – a mythic setting for dramas to unfold. Really imagine that you are dreaming all the events that surround you. Keep this attitude for a whole day and you will begin to feel lighter and more festive; you will find a distance arising between you and the events around you. You will become a witness on a hill, watching things happen as if they were part of a pageant. In the last part of the meditation, before going to sleep, imagine you will wake up in your dreams. This usually needs time and persistence, but there will come a moment when you wake up while still sleeping. The experience of a lucid dream – in which you awaken in a dream yet *know* you are still asleep in bed – will give you a taste of what the mystics are describing.

100

ARE YOU SPLIT OR WHOLE? *(thinking type)*

SENGSTAN, OR SOSAN, is known as the Third Zen Patriarch. His *Hsin Hsin Ming*, or *"Verses on a Faith Mind"*, [63] is one of the shortest, yet most beautiful, teachings of the East. These excerpts illustrate his central theme of nondualism and the attainment of no-mind. The paradox is that the focus on no-mind should come from the very thinking type that uses the mind so vigorously.

Sosan saw the core issue as being that our normal mind is "dis-eased", unhealthy and unwhole. Mind can never be whole simply because it is a bio-computer dedicated to our survival. It has to divide. It has to separate the foreground from the background, to distinguish between good and bad strategies; it needs to choose this or that. There is nothing wrong in this. It does a marvellous job in keeping us alive, but if our consciousness continues to identify with its workings we will never be able to realize the oneness of existence. The mind is simply not the right mechanism with which to approach the mysteries, but unfortunately most of us are hypnotized by its chattering spell. Sosan insists that while it is a great servant it is an appalling master.

> The Great Way is not difficult
> for those who have no preferences.
> When love and hate are both absent
> Everything becomes clear and undisguised.
> Make the smallest distinction, however,
> And heaven and earth are infinitely set apart.
> If you wish to see the truth
> Then hold no opinion ~ for or against.
> The struggle of what one likes and dislikes
> Is the disease of the mind.

> The Way is perfect like vast space
> Where nothing is lacking and nothing in excess.
> Indeed, it is due to choosing to accept or reject
> That we do not see the true nature of things.
> Live neither in the entanglements of outer things,
> Nor in inner feelings of emptiness.
> Be serene without striving activity in the Oneness of things
> And such erroneous views will disappear by themselves.
> When you try to stop activity to achieve passivity
> Your very effort fills you with activity.
> As long as you remain in one extreme or the other
> You will never know Oneness.

> Do not remain in the dualistic state; avoid such pursuits,
> If there is a trace of this and that, of right and wrong,
> The Mind-essence will be lost in confusion.
> Although all dualities come from the One,
> Do not be attached even to this One
> When the mind exists undisturbed in the Way.
> Nothing in the world can offend,
> And when a thing can no longer offend,
> It ceases to exist in the old way.

> To deny the reality of things
> is to miss their reality;
> to assert the emptiness of things
> is to miss their reality.
> The more you talk and think about it,
> the further astray you wander from the truth.
> Stop talking and thinking
> and there is nothing
> you will not be able to know.

To come directly into harmony
with this reality
Just simply say when doubts arise,
"Not two."
In this "not two"
nothing is separate,
nothing is excluded.
No matter when or where,
Enlightenment means
entering this truth.
And this truth is beyond
extension or diminution
In time and space;
In it a single thought
is ten thousand years.

MEDITATION

Techniques to quiet the mind and allow the silent witness to arise are those most suited to thinking types. This meditation is one that was favoured by Gautama the Buddha. It is a variant of the first four breathing methods of Shiva's hundred and twelve. It is said that more people have become enlightened through this device than any other. It can be done in three ways. Choose whichever feels most comfortable to you. You can do these meditations singly or combine 20 minutes of walking with 45 minutes of sitting and breathing.

1. Sitting quietly in a relaxed position watch your breathing. Feel how your belly rises and falls with the breath. Bring your total attention to the belly. Gradually you will find that the mind becomes more silent. Allow thoughts to come and go but don't identify with them – just watch the belly rising and falling.

2. Walk slowly, either outside or indoors, bringing your total attention to your feet. Keep your eyes on the ground and your moving feet. If anything catches your attention allow for it, give it your full awareness and move on whenever that awareness begins to falter. Return to focusing on your feet. Walk for 20-30 minutes.

3. Bring your entire attention to the incoming and outgoing breath through the nostrils – nothing else is needed. The mind stills and the silent witness arises.

101

YOU ARE THE GRAIL

YOU HAVE NOW LOOKED INTO ONE HUNDRED mirrors on your journey of self-discovery. Each mirror has reflected a partial portrait, but has it made you any the wiser about who the *real* you might be? The fragments you have seen in the mirror cannot, by their nature, reflect the real being. So what of that being?

The one legend in the West, [64] that transcends all others as a mirror of our essential nature, is that of the Holy Grail. Its central theme is that of a Fisher King who is wounded. As a consequence his realm has become a Wasteland (our condition). A young knight called Perceval (meaning "piercing through the middle"), who is on a quest for the Holy Grail, arrives at the King's castle. At his first attempt, he fails to heal the King because he acts as he has been instructed by both society and the Church, rather than being true to his spontaneous nature. In shame he wanders the Wasteland, renouncing God and Church until he rediscovers love through a woman. He returns in his heart to God, but this is not the God of the Church but the one he discovers at the core of his nature. In this natural state, he gains the Grail and asks the question that heals the King, and restores the land.

This legend is the core theme of all self-discovery. It is enacted far from the Tao and Ch'an mystics of China, yet their message is identical – just be natural, for you are already that which you seek, and the more you try to find your inner nature in the outer world, the further you will be from it. The Grail Knight on his quest for his true nature travels far in search of it. In reality it has never left his side.

This reveals the inbuilt absurdity of all our spiritual quests. Christ's instruction to "Seek and ye shall find", is only part of the journey. It can actually take you further away from yourself.

Gautama the Buddha left his wife, his child and his palace to seek the truth. Only when he gave up his spiritual goal, out of exhaustion from trying every meditation, austerity and technique, did he finally understand. He just had to stay where he was, *for that was where he was.*

There is another story from seventh-century China which runs parallel to those of both Buddha and the Grail.

A man once went to the Fifth Zen Patriarch in order to become a monk. The Patriarch asked him, "Do you want to *know about* truth or *be* truth?" The man replied, "To be truth." He was given a lowly job cleaning and pounding rice for the monastery, but with no spiritual guidance and no initiation. Slowly he relaxed into his natural state and just pounded rice.

The Patriarch was dying and needed a successor. He told his hundreds of monks to write a poem to show what they had learned while with him. Whosoever wrote the best verse would receive the robe as the Sixth Patriarch.

The chief disciple, Shenxiu, was the most knowledgeable monk and a most diligent, cross-legged meditator. He wrote:

The body is the Bodhi tree of perfect wisdom,
The mind like a bright mirror standing.
At all times diligently wipe it,
And allow no dust to cling.

The Patriarch declared it good, but far from perfect. Hui-neng, the rice cleaner, was illiterate so he had to ask someone else to write down his poem.

There never was a Bodhi tree.
Nor a bright mirror standing,
In essence, no-mind exists,
So where is the dust to gather?

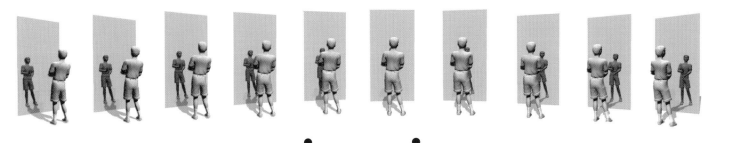

The Patriarch immediately recognized whose poem this was and conferred the robe on Hui-neng.

This story reveals two basic attitudes toward the spirit. One is that you can, through discipline, sitting cross-legged and attending to rituals and seeking knowledge, purify the body, mind and soul. Or, as a man like Hui-neng reveals, the whole idea of seeking, of trying to do something to purify the mind, is irrelevant and confusing. Our true nature is already pure and clear so any attempt to purify it would actually contaminate it. Any artificial discipline takes us further and further away from our natural state, or that which is called no-mind.

Both methods have their weaknesses. If you hear that nothing is needed and you already are a Buddha there is no incentive to awaken fully to this. You can be lazy, take someone's word for it, and resume your usual snoring. If, on the other hand, you strive to transform yourself, you move further away from who you already are, developing a more than average spiritual ego in the process.

The solution lies on a path between the two attitudes, like the "piercing through the middle" of Perceval, the Grail Knight. This middle way is an acceptance of who you are, perfect in your imperfections. There is nothing to strive for. You are neither worthy nor unworthy, saint nor sinner. Your natural essence is divine. And your real nature is already a Buddha. The quest for the Grail ends here.

Relax your gaze over the two dots below the small images. They will gradually change into three dots. Slowly bring your eyes up to the images and you will see the mirrors in three dimensions. It is this kind of change in our understanding of reality that the mystics assure us will happen if our thirst for truth is great enough. And it's a knack!

So, at the end of these one hundred and one ways of looking at yourself you arrive at the exit of the hall of mirrors, like one of those found in the old fairgrounds and amusement arcades of an earlier era. Each mirror's surface has been curved, rippled or twisted in some way so that your reflected image was completely distorted. Sometimes your head appeared normal yet sat on a monstrous body. In front of other mirrors your head was vast and, by contrast, your body miniscule. Through seeing so many reflections, however distorted, you have been able to assemble an inner picture of what you are really like. The assessments in this book are much like those distorting surfaces. None of the reflections is wholly accurate, but the more of them you have looked at, the more you will have been able to build up a good idea of what you might be like.

Usually our mirrors are other people and we strive to adjust our reflections to meet their approval, yet each change we make takes us further from our real selves. If you really want to know who you are then you must accept yourself as you are. Acceptance is the first, and last, step on the road to yourself.

NOTES

The following are those reference numbers found in each assessment. In some cases they are direct source material while in others they are useful reference books dealing with aspects found in the text.

PART I

[1,2,3] *The Varieties of Human Physique.* William Sheldon, Hafner Publishing, N.Y. ,1963.

[4] This is a typical BMI calculation based on tables from a number of Internet health clubs and weight guides. Use the Internet for further information by searching "Body Mass Index".

[5] *Journal of Abnormal Psychology.* April Fallon & Paul Rozin, University of Pennsylvania, 1984.

"Dislike of Own Body Found Common Among Women". *The New York Times*, March 19, 1984.

[6] *Physical Attractiveness, Individual Differences & Personality Stereotyping.* G. Luckner, University of Texas Dissertation Extracts 1976. (Also in the *Wall Street Journal*).

[7] *First impressions of female bust size.* C. Kleinke & R. Staneski, Journal of Social Psychology, 1980.

[8] "Measuring the Physical in Physical Attractiveness: Quasi-Experiments in the Sociobiology of Female Facial Beauty". M. Cunningham, *Journal of Personality and Social Psychology*, University of Louisville, 1980.

[9] Wilhelm Reich, 1897-1957. Books include *The Function of the Orgasm*.

[10] Alexander Lowen founded the Institute of Bio-energetic Analysis in 1956. Books include *The Betrayal of the Body*, Macmillan, N.Y., 1969 and *Bioenergetics*, Penguin, N.Y., 1975.

[11] *Between Heaven and Earth*. Harriet Benfield & Efrem Korngold Ballantine, N.Y., 1988.

[12] *Perfect Health: The Complete Mind/Body Guide.* Harmony Books, N.Y., 1990.

[13] *The Four Temperaments.* Rudolf Steiner, The Anthroposophic Press, 1968.

[14] Original material by George Ivanovitch Gurdjieff: *Views from the Real World,* Routledge & Kegan Paul, 1973. *Meetings with Remarkable Men,* Routledge & Kegan Paul, 1973. *Beelzebub's Tales to his Grandson,* Routledge & Kegan Paul, 1950. *Life is Real Only Then 'When I Am',* Triangle Editions, N.Y., 1975. *In Search of the Miraculous: Fragments of an Unknown Teaching,* Routledge & Kegan Paul, 1950.

[15] *Consciousness: Brain, States of Awareness, and Mysticism.* D. Goleman & R. Davidson, Harper & Row, N.Y., 1979.

[16] *Relating: An Astrological Guide to Living with Others on a Small Planet.* Liz Greene, Weiser, 1977.

[17] *Synchronicity: An Acausal Connecting Principle.* C.G. Jung Routledge & Kegan Paul, London, 1972.

[18] *The Handbook of Chinese Horoscopes.* T. Lau, Harper & Row, N.Y., 1979.

[19] *Psychological Types.* C.G. Jung, Harcourt, N.Y., 1923. *Man and his Symbols.* C.G. Jung, Doubleday, N.Y., 1964.

PART II

20   *Mapping the Mind*. Rita Carter, Weidenfeld & Nicolson, 1999.

21   *The Emotional Brain*. Joseph LeDoux, Simon & Schuster, 1996.

22   *Method in Madness*. A. Young & K. Leafhead, Psychology Press, 1996.

23   *The Woman's Encyclopedia of Myths and Secrets*. Barbara Walker, Harper & Row, San Francisco, 1983 (page 602).

24-26   *The Goddess Wheel*. Jennifer and Roger Woolger, Ballantine, N.Y., 1989.

27   *King, Warrior, Magician, Lover*. R. Moore & D. Gillette, Harper San Francisco, 1990.

28   Assessments 47, 48, 49 are loosely based on the work of Karen Horney who outlines her approach in *Our Inner Conflicts*. Karen Horney, Norton, N.Y., 1945.

29   *Oxford Psychologists Press. 1996.*

30   *Mapping the Mind*. Rita Carter, Weidenfeld & Nicolson, 1999 (page 93).

31   *Psychological Types*. Volume 6 from *Collected Works*. C.G. Jung, Princeton University Press, 1971.

32   *Fact and Fiction in Psychology*. Professor H.J. Eysenck, Penguin Books, 1965.

33   "Women and Stress on the Job and at Home". Nina Darnton, *The New York Times*, 9 May, 1985.

34   *New Introductory Lectures on Psychoanalysis*. Sigmund Freud, Norton, N.Y., 1949.

35   *The Art of Courtly Love. A.* Capellanus. Introduction, edited text, translation and notes by John Jay Parry, Edinburgh University Press, 1971.

36   *Mapping the Mind*. Rita Carter, Weidenfeld & Nicolson, 1999.

37   "Hemisphere Disconnection and Unity in Conscious Awareness". R.W. Sperry, *American Psychologist, 23,*1968.

PART III

38   *The Human Brain*. J. Nolte & J. B. Angevine, Mosby, St Louis, 1995.

39   *Nature's Mind: The Biological Roots of Thinking, Emotions, Sexuality, Language and Intelligence*. M.S. Gazzaniga, Penguin Books, 1992.

40   *Deliberate, Directive, Collaborative and Counseling: Interpersonal Styles* J. Corbett, International Learning Inc., 1986. The assessment is partly based on the principal concepts found in the book above. If interested, the reader should consult this material.

41   *The Gamesman*. M. Maccoby, Simon & Schuster, N.Y., 1976.

The Leader. A New Face for American Management. M. Maccoby, Ballantine, N.Y., 1983.

42   *The Gurdjieff Work*. K.R. Speeth, Tarcher, L. A., 1989.

Enneagram Studies. J.G. Bennett, Samuel Weiser, 1983.

Views from the Real World. Routledge & Kegan Paul, 1973.

Meetings with Remarkable Men. Routledge & Kegan Paul, 1973.

In Search of the Miraculous: Fragments of an Unknown Teaching. P.D. Ouspensky, Routledge & Kegan Paul, 1950.

43   *Enneatype Structures*. C. Naranjo, Gateways, 1990.

Personality Types. R. Riso, Houghton Mifflin, 1987.

The Secret of Enneagrams. K. Vollmar, Element, 1997.

44   *Frames of Mind*. Howard Gardner, Basic Books, 1983.

In Their Own Way. T. Armstrong, Tarcher, 1987.

45   *Know Your Own Personality*. H. J. Eysenck & G. Wilson, Maurice Temple Smith, 1976.

PART IV

[46] "Hemisphere Disconnection and Unity in Conscious Awareness". R.W. Sperry, *American Psychologist, 23,*1968.

[47] *Gurdjieff: TheAnatomy of a Myth.* James Moore, Element Books, 1991.

[48] *Philosophia Ultima: Discourses on the Madukya Upanishad.* Osho, Rebel Publishing, 1983.

[49] *The Perennial Philosophy*
Aldous Huxley, Chatto & Windus, London, 1946.

[50] *Up From Eden: A Transpersonal View of Human Evolution.*
Ken Wilber, Routledge & Kegan Paul, 1983.

[51/52] *In Search of the Miraculous: Chakras, Kundalini and the Seven Bodies.*
Osho, C.W. Daniel, Saffron Walden, 1996.

[53] *Why Men don't listen and Women can't read maps.*
Allan & Barbara Pease, Pease Training International, 1999.

[54] *Aphorisms of Yoga: Bhagwan Shree Patanjali.*
Translated by Shree Purohit Swami, Introduction W. B.Yeats,
Faber & Faber, London, 1938.

[55] *Tibet's Great Yogi Milarepa: A Biography from the Tibetan*
Edited by W.Y. Evans-Wentz, Oxford University Press, 1928.

[56] *Delicious Laughter.* Coleman Barks Translation, Maypop, 1989.

Open Secret, Threshold, 1984.

[57] From *Sun of Tabriz (XXI).* Translated by Sir Colin Garbett,
R. Berman, Cape Town, 1956.

[58] From *Poems of Kabir.* Translated by Rabindranath Tagore,
Macmillan, London, 1962.

[59] From *Fakhruddin Iraqi:Divine Flashes.* Translated by
W.C. Chittock & P. Wilson, Paulist Press, 1982.

[60] From *Songs of the Bards of Bengal.* Translated by D. Bettacharya,
Grove Press, 1976.

[61] *Heraclitus:The Cosmic Fragments.* G.S. Kirk, Cambridge University
Press, 1962

[62] *Zen and Zen Classics.*Volumes I-V.

[63] From *Hsin Hsin Ming − Verses on a Faith Mind of Sengstan, 3rd
Zen Patriarch.* Translated by Richard B.Clarke, Living Dharma
Centers.

[64] *The Holy Grail: Its Origins, Secrets & Meaning Revealed.*
Malcolm Godwin,Viking Studio Books, 1994.

SUGGESTED FURTHER READING

Arroyo, Stephen. *Astrology, Psychology and the Four Elements*. Davis, CA: CRCS Publications, 1975.

Bolen, J. S. *The Goddesses in Every Woman*. San Fransisco: Harper & Row, 1984.

Eysenck, H.J. *Know Your Own I.Q.* London: Penguin Books, 1962.
> This has been reprinted almost every year since it was first published in 1962. Along with its sequel, *Check Your Own I.Q.*, also published by Penguin, it rightly remains the most popular and accessible of all the books of this genre.

Goleman, Daniel & Richard Davidson. *Consciousness: Brain, States of Awareness and Mysticism*. New York: Harper & Row, 1979.

Kimura, D. "Sex Differences in the Brain," *Scientific American* 118:125, 1992.

Moore, Robert & Douglas Gillette. *The King Within*. San Francisco: HarperSanFrancisco, 1992.
—, *The Warrior Within*. San Francisco: HarperSanFrancisco, 1992.
—, *The Magician Within*. San Francisco: HarperSanFrancisco, 1993.
—, *The Lover Within*. San Francisco: HarperSanFrancisco,1995.
> This series is the original source material for assessment 46—Grail symbols of the male archetypes.

Morris, Desmond. *Bodywatching*. London: Jonathan Cape, 1988.

Oken, Alan. *The Horoscope, The Road and Its Travelers*. New York: Bantam Books, 1973.

Osho (Rajneesh). The author of over 150 books. The suggested titles for the three main types are all published by The Rebel Publishing House GmbH, Cologne, Germany. For other publications contact Osho Commune International, 17 Koregaon Park, Poona 411 001, Maharastra, India.

Body Orientation
Yoga: The Alpha and the Omega. The Yoga Sutras of Patanjali. Volumes 1-10.
Vigyan Bhairav Tantra: The Book of Secrets. Volumes 1-2.
The Orange Book. Meditation techniques.

Feeling Orientation
The Beloved: The Baul Mystics of Bengal. Volumes 1-2.
Ecstasy: The Forgotten Language. Kabir.
Unio Mystica: The Hadiqa of Hakim Sanai. Volumes 1-2.

Thinking Orientation
Tao: The Three Treasures. The Tao Te Ching of Lao Tzu. Volumes 1-4.
I Am That: The Isa Upanishad.
Take it Easy: The Poems of Ikkyu. Volumes 1-2.

Peters, Fritz. *Boyhood with Gurdjieff*. London: Gollancz, 1964.
—, *Gurdjieff Remembered*. London: Gollancz, 1965.

Watts, Alan.W. *The Way of Zen*. New York: Penguin, 1957.
> Remains the classic on the subject as well as beautiful insights on the Hui-Neng, the sixth Zen Patriarch of the earlier Ch'an Buddhism of southern China.

Frager, Robert (ed.). *Who am I? Personality Types for Self-Discovery*. New York: Tarcher/Putnam, 1994.
> This is an excellent all-round background to many of the assessments found in this book.

Wilbur, Ken. *Up from Eden, A Transpersonal View of Human Evolution*. London: Routledge & Kegan Paul, 1983.
> Wilbur once said that on spiritual paths there is "too much talk, talk and too little walk, walk". This book is talk, talk but nevertheless might galvanize the thinking type into walk, walk.

Wolf, Naomi. *The Beauty Myth*. London: Anchor, 1992.

ACKNOWLEDGEMENTS

The author is truly indebted to Tracy Timson, Carroll & Brown's very patient deputy art director, for her many design suggestions which made the book both more accessible and colourful. Very particular thanks go to my editor and old friend Geoffrey Chesler, who has carefully shepherded this book through all its stages and who was largely instrumental in its publication. I would like to acknowledge the pioneering work of those authors mentioned in the notes, whose work in the field has formed the basis for many of the assessments. I would specially like to thank Rita Carter for triggering my interest in how the brain functions.

There is no way to thank my wife and co-designer for the work she has put into the design and typesetting as well as supporting my body-emotions-thinking-spirit package, except by taking her on a very long vacation, far from any computers. And my debt to the Old Boy, Osho, who did his best to shake me awake even when I was having such great esoteric dreams, just cannot be measured.

PICTURES

The twelve Sun signs in assessment 31 are reproduced by kind permission of the Bodleian Library, University of Oxford, England:
MS. AUCT. D. ins 2. 11, folios 1-12.